CONTENTS

FIRST SERIES

SECOND SERIES

ESSAYS

FIRST SERIES

——◆——

HISTORY

There is no great and no small
To the Soul that maketh all:
And where it cometh, all things are
And it cometh everywhere.

I.

HISTORY.

————

THERE is one mind common to all individual men. Every man is an inlet to the same and to all of the same. He that is once admitted to the right of reason is made a freeman of the whole estate. What Plato has thought, he may think; what a saint has felt, he may feel; what at any time has befallen any man, he can understand. Who hath access to this universal mind is a party to all that is or can be done, for this is the only and sovereign agent.

Of the works of this mind history is the record. Its genius is illustrated by the entire series of days. Man is explicable by nothing less than all his history. Without hurry, without rest, the human spirit goes forth from the beginning to embody every faculty, every thought, every emotion which belongs to it, in appropriate events. But the thought is always prior to the fact; all the facts of history preëxist in the mind as laws. Each law in turn is made by circumstances predominant, and the limits

or nature give power to but one at a time. A man
is the whole encyclopædia of facts. The creation
of a thousand forests is in one acorn, and Egypt,
Greece, Rome, Gaul, Britain, America, lie folded
already in the first man. Epoch after epoch, camp,
kingdom, empire, republic, democracy, are merely
the application of his manifold spirit to the manifold world.

This human mind wrote history, and this must
read it. The Sphinx must solve her own riddle.
If the whole of history is in one man, it is all to be
explained from individual experience. There is a
relation between the hours of our life and the centuries of time. As the air I breathe is drawn
from the great repositories of nature, as the light
on my book is yielded by a star a hundred millions
of miles distant, as the poise of my body depends
on the equilibrium of centrifugal and centripetal
forces, so the hours should be instructed by the ages
and the ages explained by the hours. Of the universal mind each individual man is one more incarnation. All its properties consist in him. Each
new fact in his private experience flashes a light on
what great bodies of men have done, and the crises
of his life refer to national crises. Every revolution
was first a thought in one man's mind, and when
the same thought occurs to another man, it is the
key to that era. Every reform was once a private

opinion, and when it shall be a private opinion
again it will solve the problem of the age. The
fact narrated must correspond to something in me
to be credible or intelligible. We, as we read,
must become Greeks, Romans, Turks, priest and
king, martyr and executioner; must fasten these
images to some reality in our secret experience, or
we shall learn nothing rightly. What befell As-
drubal or Cæsar Borgia is as much an illustration
of the mind's powers and depravations as what has
befallen us. Each new law and political movement
has meaning for you. Stand before each of its tab-
lets and say, 'Under this mask did my Proteus nature hide itself.' This remedies the defect of our
too great nearness to ourselves. This throws our
actions into perspective; and as crabs, goats, scorpions, the balance and the waterpot lose their meanness when hung as signs in the zodiac, so I can see
my own vices without heat in the distant persons of
Solomon, Alcibiades, and Catiline.

It is the universal nature which gives worth to
particular men and things. Human life, as con-
taining this, is mysterious and inviolable, and we
hedge it round with penalties and laws. All laws
derive hence their ultimate reason; all express more
or less distinctly some command of this supreme, illimitable essence. Property also holds of the soul,
covers great spiritual facts, and instinctively we at

first hold to it with swords and laws and wide and complex combinations. The obscure consciousness of this fact is the light of all our day, the claim of claims; the plea for education, for justice, for charity; the foundation of friendship and love and of the heroism and grandeur which belong to acts of self-reliance. It is remarkable that involuntarily we always read as superior beings. Universal history, the poets, the romancers, do not in their stateliest pictures, — in the sacerdotal, the imperial palaces, in the triumphs of will or of genius, — anywhere lose our ear, anywhere make us feel that we intrude, that this is for better men; but rather is it true that in their grandest strokes we feel most at home. All that Shakspeare says of the king, yonder slip of a boy that reads in the corner feels to be true of himself. We sympathize in the great moments of history, in the great discoveries, the great resistances, the great prosperities of men; — because there law was enacted, the sea was searched, the land was found, or the blow was struck, *for us*, as we ourselves in that place would have done or applauded.

We have the same interest in condition and chai' acter. We honor the rich because they have exter nally the freedom, power, and grace which we feel to be proper to man, proper to us. So all that is said of the wise man by Stoic or Oriental or modern essayist, describes to each reader his own idea, describes his unattained but attainable self. All literature writes the character of the wise man. Books, monuments, pictures, conversation, are portraits in which he finds the lineaments he is forming. The silent and the eloquent praise him and accost him, and he is stimulated wherever he moves, as by personal allusions. A true aspirant therefore never needs look for allusions personal and laudatory in discourse. He hears the commendation, not of himself, but, more sweet, of that character he seeks, in every word that is said concerning character, yea further in every fact and circumstance, — in the running river and the rustling corn. Praise is looked, homage tendered, love flows, from mute nature, from the mountains and the lights of the firmament.

These hints, dropped as it were from sleep and night, let us use in broad day. The student is to read history actively and not passively; to esteem his own life the text, and books the commentary. Thus compelled, the Muse of history will utter oracles, as never to those who do not respect themselves. I have no expectation that any man will read history aright who thinks that what was done in a remote age, by men whose names have resounded far, has any deeper sense than what he is doing to-day.

The world exists for the education of each man. There is no age or state of society or mode of action in history to which there is not somewhat corresponding in his life. Every thing tends in a wonderful manner to abbreviate itself and yield its own virtue to him. He should see that he can live all history in his own person. He must sit solidly at home, and not suffer himself to be bullied by kings or empires, but know that he is greater than all the geography and all the government of the world; he must transfer the point of view from which history is commonly read, from Rome and Athens and London, to himself, and not deny his conviction that he is the court, and if England or Egypt have any thing to say to him he will try the case ; if not, let them forever be silent. He must attain and maintain that lofty sight where facts yield their secret sense, and poetry and annals are alike. The instinct of the mind, the purpose of nature, betrays itself in the use we make of the signal narrations of history. Time dissipates to shining ether the solid angularity of facts. No anchor, no cable, no fences avail to keep a fact a fact. Babylon, Troy, Tyre, Palestine, and even early Rome are passing already into fiction. The Garden of Eden, the sun standing still in Gibeon, is poetry thenceforward to all nations. Who cares what the fact was, when we have made a constellation of it to hang in heaven an immortal sign? London and Paris and New York must go the same way. "What is history," said Napoleon, "but a fable agreed upon?" This life of ours is stuck round with Egypt, Greece, Gaul, England, War, Colonization, Church, Court and Commerce, as with so many flowers and wild ornaments grave and gay. I will not make more account of them. I believe in Eternity. I can find Greece, Asia, Italy, Spain and the Islands, — the genius and creative principle of each and of all eras, in my own mind.

We are always coming up with the emphatic facts of history in our private experience and verifying them here. All history becomes subjective; in other words there is properly no history, only biography. Every mind must know the whole lesson for itself, — must go over the whole ground. What it does not see, what it does not live, it will not know. What the former age has epitomized into a formula or rule for manipular convenience, it will lose all the good of verifying for itself, by means of the wall of that rule. Somewhere, sometime, it will demand and find compensation for that loss, by doing the work itself. Ferguson discovered many things in astronomy which had long been known. The better for him.

History must be this or it is nothing. Every law which the state enacts indicates a fact in human nature; that is all. We must in ourselves see the necessary reason of every fact, — see how it could and must be. So stand before every public and private work; before an oration of Burke, before a victory of Napoleon, before a martyrdom of Sir Thomas More, of Sidney, of Marmaduke Robinson; before a French Reign of Terror, and a Salem hanging of witches; before a fanatic Revival and the Animal Magnetism in Paris, or in Providence. We assume that we under like influence should be alike affected, and should achieve the like; and we aim to master intellectually the steps and reach the same height or the same degradation that our fellow, our proxy has done.

All inquiry into antiquity, all curiosity respecting the Pyramids, the excavated cities, Stonehenge, the Ohio Circles, Mexico, Memphis, — is the desire to do away this wild, savage, and preposterous There or Then, and introduce in its place the Here and the Now. Belzoni digs and measures in the mummy-pits and pyramids of Thebes until he can see the end of the difference between the monstrous work and himself. When he has satisfied himself, in general and in detail, that it was made by such a person as he, so armed and so motived, and to ends to which he himself should also have worked, the problem is solved; his thought lives along the whole line of temples and sphinxes and catacombs,

passes through them all with satisfaction, and they
live again to the mind, or are *now*.

A Gothic cathedral affirms that it was done by
us and not done by us. Surely it was by man, but
we find it not in our man. But we apply ourselves
to the history of its production. We put ourselves
into the place and state of the builder. We remember the forest-dwellers, the first temples, the
adherence to the first type, and the decoration of it
as the wealth of the nation increased; the value
which is given to wood by carving led to the carving over the whole mountain of stone of a cathedral. When we have gone through this process,
and added thereto the Catholic Church, its cross,
its music, its processions, its Saints' days and image-
worship, we have as it were been the man that
made the minster; we have seen how it could and
must be. We have the sufficient reason.

The difference between men is in their principle
of association. Some men classify objects by color
and size and other accidents of appearance; others
by intrinsic likeness, or by the relation of cause
and effect. The progress of the intellect is to the
clearer vision of causes, which neglects surface differences. To the poet, to the philosopher, to the
saint, all things are friendly and sacred, all events
profitable, all days holy, all men divine. For the
eye is fastened on the life, and slights the circum-

stance.   Every chemical substance, every plant,
every animal in its growth, teaches the unity of
cause, the variety of appearance.

Upborne and surrounded as we are by this all-
creating nature, soft and fluid as a cloud or the air,
why should we be such hard pedants, and magnify a few forms?   Why should we make account
of time, or of magnitude, or of figure?   The soul
knows them not, and genius, obeying its law, knows
how to play with them as a young child plays with
graybeards and in churches.   Genius studies the
causal thought, and far back in the womb of things
sees the rays parting from one orb, that diverge,
ere they fall, by infinite diameters.   Genius watches
the monad through all his masks as he performs
the metempsychosis of nature.   Genius detects
through the fly, through the caterpillar, through
the grub, through the egg, the constant individual;
through countless individuals the fixed species;
through many species the genus; through all genera
the steadfast type; through all the kingdoms of organized life the eternal unity.   Nature is a muta-
ble cloud which is always and never the same.   She
casts the same thought into troops of forms, as a
poet makes twenty fables with one moral.   Through
the bruteness and toughness of matter, a subtle
spirit bends all things to its own will.   The adamant streams into soft but precise form before it.

and whilst I look at it its outline and texture are changed again. Nothing is so fleeting as form; yet never does it quite deny itself. In man we still trace the remains or hints of all that we esteem badges of servitude in the lower races; yet in him they enhance his nobleness and grace; as Io, in Æschylus, transformed to a cow, offends the imagination; but how changed when as Isis in Egypt she meets Osiris-Jove, a beautiful woman with nothing of the metamorphosis left but the lunar horns as the splendid ornament of her brows!

The identity of history is equally intrinsic, the diversity equally obvious. There is, at the surface, infinite variety of things; at the centre there is simplicity of cause. How many are the acts of one man in which we recognize the same character! Observe the sources of our information in respect to the Greek genius. We have the *civil history* of that people, as Herodotus, Thucydides, Xenophon, and Plutarch have given it; a very sufficient account of what manner of persons they were and what they did. We have the same national mind expressed for us again in their *literature*, in epic and lyric poems, drama, and philosophy; a very complete form. Then we have it once more in their *architecture*, a beauty as of temperance itself, limited to the straight line and the square, — a builded geometry. Then we have it once again in *sculpture*, the " tongue on the balance of expression," a multitude of forms in the utmost freedom of action and never transgressing the ideal serenity; like votaries performing some religious dance before the gods, and, though in convulsive pain or mortal combat, never daring to break the figure and decorum of their dance. Thus of the genius of one remarkable people we have a fourfold representation: and to the senses what more unlike than an ode of Pindar, a marble centaur, the peristyle of the Parthenon, and the last actions of Phocion?

Every one must have observed faces and forms which, without any resembling feature, make a like impression on the beholder. A particular picture or copy of verses, if it do not awaken the same train of images, will yet superinduce the same sentiment as some wild mountain walk, although the resemblance is nowise obvious to the senses, but is occult and out of the reach of the understanding. Nature is an endless combination and repetition of a very few laws. She hums the old well-known air through innumerable variations.

Nature is full of a sublime family likeness throughout her works, and delights in startling us with resemblances in the most unexpected quarters. I have seen the head of an old sachem of the forest which at once reminded the eye of a bald mountain summit, and the furrows of the brow suggested the strata of the rock. There are men whose manners have the same essential splendor as the simple and awful sculpture on the friezes of the Parthenon and the remains of the earliest Greek art. And there are compositions of the same strain to be found in the books of all ages. What is Guido's Rospigliosi Aurora but a morning thought, as the horses in it are only a morning cloud? If any one will but take pains to observe the variety of actions to which he is equally inclined in certain moods of mind, and those to which he is averse, he will see how deep is the chain of affinity.

A painter told me that nobody could draw a tree without in some sort becoming a tree; or draw a child by studying the outlines of its form merely, — but, by watching for a time his motions and plays, the painter enters into his nature and can then draw him at will in every attitude. So Roos "entered into the inmost nature of a sheep." 1 knew a draughtsman employed in a public survey who found that he could not sketch the rocks until their geological structure was first explained to him. In a certain state of thought is the common origin of very diverse works. It is the spirit and not the fact that is identical. By a deeper apprehension, and not primarily by a painful acquisition of many manual skills, the artist attains the power of awakening other souls to a given activity.

It has been said that " common souls pay with
what they do, nobler souls with that which they
are." And why ? Because a profound nature
awakens in us by its actions and words, by its very
looks and manners, the same power and beauty
that a gallery of sculpture or of pictures addresses.

Civil and natural history, the history of art and
of literature, must be explained from individual
history, or must remain words. There is nothing
but is related to us, nothing that does not interest
us, — kingdom, college, tree, horse, or iron shoe, —
the roots of all things are in man. Santa Croce
and the Dome of St. Peter's are lame copies after
a divine model. Strasburg Cathedral is a material
counterpart of the soul of Erwin of Steinbach.
The true poem is the poet's mind; the true ship is
the ship-builder. In the man, could we lay him
open, we should see the reason for the last flourish
and tendril of his work ; as every spine and tint in
the sea-shell preëxists in the secreting organs of the
fish. The whole of heraldry and of chivalry is in
courtesy. A man of fine manners shall pronounce
your name with all the ornament that titles of nobility could ever add.

The trivial experience of every day is always
verifying some old prediction to us and converting
into things the words and signs which we had heard
and seen without heed. A lady with whom I was

riding in the forest said to me that the woods always seemed to her *to wait*, as if the genii who inhabit them suspended their deeds until the way-
farer had passed onward; a thought which poetry
has celebrated in the dance of the fairies, which
breaks off on the approach of human feet. The
man who has seen the rising moon break out of the
clouds at midnight, has been present like an archangel at the creation of light and of the world. I
remember one summer day in the fields my companion pointed out to me a broad cloud, which
might extend a quarter of a mile parallel to the
horizon, quite accurately in the form of a cherub
as painted over churches, — a round block in the
centre, which it was easy to animate with eyes and
mouth, supported on either side by wide-stretched
symmetrical wings. What appears once in the atmosphere may appear often, and it was undoubtedly the archetype of that familiar ornament. I
have seen in the sky a chain of summer lightning
which at once showed to me that the Greeks drew
from nature when they painted the thunderbolt in
the hand of Jove. I have seen a snow-drift along
the sides of the stone wall which obviously gave
the idea of the common architectural scroll to abut
a tower.

By surrounding ourselves with the original circumstances we invent anew the orders and the or-

naments of architecture, as we see how each people merely decorated its primitive abodes.   The
Doric temple preserves the semblance of the wooden
cabin in which the Dorian dwelt.   The Chinese
pagoda is plainly a Tartar tent.   The Indian and
Egyptian temples still betray the mounds and subterranean houses of their forefathers.   " The custom of making houses and tombs in the living
rock," says Heeren in his Researches on the Ethio-
pians, " determined very naturally the principal
character of the Nubian Egyptian architecture to
the colossal form which it assumed.   In these cav-
erns, already prepared by nature, the eye was accustomed to dwell on huge shapes and masses, so
that when art came to the assistance of nature it
could not move on a small scale without degrading
itself.   What would statues of the usual size, or
neat porches and wings have been, associated with
those gigantic halls before which only Colossi could
sit as watchmen or lean on the pillars of the interior ? "

The Gothic church plainly originated in a rude
adaptation of the forest trees, with all their boughs,
to a festal or solemn arcade ; as the bands about
the cleft pillars still indicate the green withes that
tied them.   No one can walk in a road cut through
pine woods, without being struck with the architectural appearance of the grove, especially in winter,

when the barrenness of all other trees shows the low arch of the Saxons. In the woods in a winter afternoon one will see as readily the origin of the stained glass window, with which the Gothic cathedrals are adorned, in the colors of the western sky seen through the bare and crossing branches of the forest. Nor can any lover of nature enter the old piles of Oxford and the English cathedrals, without feeling that the forest overpowered the mind of the builder, and that his chisel, his saw and plane still reproduced its ferns, its spikes of flowers, its locust, elm, oak, pine, fir and spruce.

The Gothic cathedral is a blossoming in stone subdued by the insatiable demand of harmony in man. The mountain of granite blooms into an eternal flower, with the lightness and delicate finish as well as the aerial proportions and perspective of vegetable beauty.

In like manner all public facts are to be individualized, all private facts are to be generalized. Then at once History becomes fluid and true, and Biography deep and sublime. As the Persian imitated in the slender shafts and capitals of his architecture the stem and flower of the lotus and palm, so the Persian court in its magnificent era never gave over the nomadism of its barbarous tribes, but travelled from Ecbatana, where the spring was spent, to Susa in summer and to Babylon for the winter.

In the early history of Asia and Africa, Nomadism and Agriculture are the two antagonist facts.
The geography of Asia and of Africa necessitated
a nomadic life. But the nomads were the terror
of all those whom the soil or the advantages of a
market had induced to build towns. Agriculture
therefore was a religious injunction, because of the
perils of the state from nomadism. And in these
late and civil countries of England and America
these propensities still fight out the old battle, in
the nation and in the individual. The nomads of
Africa were constrained to wander, by the attacks
of the gad-fly, which drives the cattle mad, and so
compels the tribe to emigrate in the rainy season
and to drive off the cattle to the higher sandy regions. The nomads of Asia follow the pasturage
from month to month. In America and Europe
the nomadism is of trade and curiosity; a progress,
certainly, from the gad-fly of Astaboras to the An-
glo and Italo-mania of Boston Bay. Sacred cities,
to which a periodical religious pilgrimage was en-
joined, or stringent laws and customs tending to
invigorate the national bond, were the check on the
old rovers ; and the cumulative values of long residence are the restraints on the itinerancy of the
present day. The antagonism of the two tendencies is not less active in individuals, as the love of
adventure or the love of repose happens to predom-

inate. A man of rude health and flowing spirits
has the faculty of rapid domestication, lives in his
wagon and roams through all latitudes as easily as
a Calmuc. At sea, or in the forest, or in the snow,
he sleeps as warm, dines with as good appetite,
and associates as happily as beside his own chim-
neys. Or perhaps his facility is deeper seated, in
the increased range of his faculties of observation,
which yield him points of interest wherever fresh
objects meet his eyes. The pastoral nations were
needy and hungry to desperation ; and this intellectual nomadism, in its excess, bankrupts the mind
through the dissipation of power on a miscellany of
objects. The home-keeping wit, on the other hand,
is that continence or content which finds all the
elements of life in its own soil; and which has its
own perils of monotony and deterioration, if not
stimulated by foreign infusions.

Every thing the individual sees without him corresponds to his states of mind, and every thing is
in turn intelligible to him, as his onward thinking leads him into the truth to which that fact or
series belongs.

The primeval world, — the Fore-World, as the
Germans say, — I can dive to it in myself as well
as grope for it with researching fingers in catacombs, libraries, and the broken reliefs and torso
of ruined villas.

What is the foundation of that interest all men
feel in Greek history, letters, art and poetry, in all
its periods from the Heroic or Homeric age down
to the domestic life of the Athenians and Spartans,
four or five centuries later? What but this, that
every man passes personally through a Grecian period. The Grecian state is the era of the bodily
nature, the perfection of the senses, — of the spiritual nature unfolded in strict unity with the body.
In it existed those human forms which supplied the
sculptor with his models of Hercules, Phœbus, and
Jove; not like the forms abounding in the streets
of modern cities, wherein the face is a confused
blur of features, but composed of incorrupt, sharply
defined and symmetrical features, whose eye-sock-
ets are so formed that it would be impossible for
such eyes to squint and take furtive glances on
this side and on that, but they must turn the whole
head. The manners of that period are plain and
fierce. The reverence exhibited is for personal
qualities; courage, address, self-command, justice,
strength, swiftness, a loud voice, a broad chest.
Luxury and elegance are not known. A sparse
population and want make every man his own valet,
cook, butcher and soldier, and the habit of supply
ing his own needs educates the body to wonderful
performances. Such are the Agamemnon and
Diomed of Homer, and not far different is the pic

ture Xenophon gives of himself and his compatri-
ots in the Retreat of the Ten Thousand. "After
the army had crossed the river Teleboas in Arme-
nia, there fell much snow, and the troops lay miserably on the ground covered with it. But Xenophon arose naked, and taking an axe, began to split
wood ; whereupon others rose and did the like."
Throughout his army exists a boundless liberty of
speech. They quarrel for plunder, they wrangle
with the generals on each new order, and Xenophon
is as sharp-tongued as any and sharper-tongued
than most, and so gives as good as he gets. Who
does not see that this is a gang of great boys, with
such a code of honor and such lax discipline as
great boys have?

The costly charm of the ancient tragedy, and indeed of all the old literature, is that the persons
speak simply, — speak as persons who have great
good sense without knowing it, before yet the reflective habit has become the predominant habit of
the mind. Our admiration of the antique is not
admiration of the old, but of the natural. The
Greeks are not reflective, but perfect in their senses
and in their health, with the finest physical organization in the world. Adults acted with the simplicity and grace of children. They made vases,
tragedies and statues, such as healthy senses should,
— that is, in good taste. Such things have con-

tinued to be made in all ages, and are now, whei
ever a healthy physique exists ; but, as a class, from
their superior organization, they have surpassed all.
They combine the energy of manhood with the engaging unconsciousness of childhood. The attraction of these manners is that they belong to man,
and are known to every man in virtue of his being
once a child ; besides that there are always individuals who retain these characteristics. A person of
childlike genius and inborn energy is still a Greek,
and revives our love of the Muse of Hellas. I admire the love of nature in the Philoctetes. In reading those fine apostrophes to sleep, to the stars,
rocks, mountains and waves, I feel time passing
away as an ebbing sea. I feel the eternity of man,
the identity of his thought. The Greek had it
seems the same fellow-beings as I. The sun and
moon, water and fire, met his heart precisely as
they meet mine. Then the vaunted distinction between Greek and English, between Classic and Romantic schools, seems superficial and pedantic.
When a thought of Plato becomes a thought to me,
— when a truth that fired the soul of Pindar fires
mine, time is no more. When I feel that we two
meet in a perception, that our two souls are tinged
with the same hue, and do as it were run into one,
why should I measure degrees of latitude, why
should I count Egyptian years ?

The student interprets the age of chivalry by his own age of chivalry, and the days of maritime adventure and circumnavigation by quite parallel miniature experiences of his own. To the sacred history of the world he has the same key. When the voice of a prophet out of the deeps of antiquity merely echoes to him a sentiment of his infancy, a prayer of his youth, he then pierces to the truth through all the confusion of tradition and the caricature of institutions.

Rare, extravagant spirits come by us at intervals, who disclose to us new facts in nature. I see that men of God have from time to time walked among men and made their commission felt in the heart and soul of the commonest hearer. Hence evidently the tripod, the priest, the priestess inspired by the divine afflatus.

Jesus astonishes and overpowers sensual people. They cannot unite him to history, or reconcile him with themselves. As they come to revere their intuitions and aspire to live holily, their own piety explains every fact, every word.

How easily these old worships of Moses, of Zoroaster, of Menu, of Socrates, domesticate themselves in the mind. I cannot find any antiquity in them. They are mine as much as theirs.

I have seen the first monks and anchorets, without crossing seas or centuries. More than once some individual has appeared to me with such negligence of labor and such commanding contemplation, a haughty beneficiary begging in the name of God, as made good to the nineteenth century Simeon the Stylite, the Thebais, and the first Capuchins.

The priestcraft of the East and West, of the Magian, Brahmin, Druid, and Inca, is expounded in the individual's private life. The cramping influence of a hard formalist on a young child, in repressing his spirits and courage, paralyzing the understanding, and that without producing indignation, but only fear and obedience, and even much sympathy with the tyranny, — is a familiar fact, explained to the child when he becomes a man, only by seeing that the oppressor of his youth is himself a child tyrannized over by those names and words and forms of whose influence he was merely the organ to the youth. The fact teaches him how Belus was worshipped and how the Pyramids were built, better than the discovery by Champollion of the names of all the workmen and the cost of every tile. He finds Assyria and the Mounds of Cholula at his door, and himself has laid the courses.

Again, in that protest which each considerate person makes against the superstition of his times, he repeats step for step the part of old reformers, and in the search after truth finds, like them, new

perils to virtue. He learns again what moral vigor
is needed to supply the girdle of a superstition.
A great licentiousness treads on the heels of a reformation. How many times in the history of the
world has the Luther of the day had to lament the
decay of piety in his own household! "Doctor,"
said his wife to Martin Luther, one day, "how is
it that whilst subject to papacy we prayed so often
and with such fervor, whilst now we pray with the
utmost coldness and very seldom?"

The advancing man discovers how deep a property he has in literature, — in all fable as well as in
all history. He finds that the poet was no odd fellow who described strange and impossible situations,
but that universal man wrote by his pen a confession true for one and true for all. His own secret
biography he finds in lines wonderfully intelligible to him, dotted down before he was born. One
after another he comes up in his private adventures
with every fable of Æsop, of Homer, of Hafiz, of
Ariosto, of Chaucer, of Scott, and verifies them
with his own head and hands.

The beautiful fables of the Greeks, being proper
creations of the imagination and not of the fancy,
are universal verities. What a range of meanings
and what perpetual pertinence has the story of Prometheus! Beside its primary value as the first
chapter of the history of Europe, (the mythology

thinly veiling authentic facts, the invention of the
mechanic arts and the migration of colonies,) it gives
the history of religion, with some closeness to the
faith of later ages.   Prometheus is the Jesus of the
old mythology.   He is the friend of man; stands
between the unjust "justice" of the Eternal Father
and the race of mortals, and readily suffers all
things on their account.   But where it departs from
the Calvinistic Christianity and exhibits him as the
defier of Jove, it represents a state of mind which
readily appears wherever the doctrine of Theism is
taught in a crude, objective form, and which seems
the self-defence of man against this untruth, namely
a discontent with the believed fact that a God exists, and a feeling that the obligation of reverence
is onerous.   It would steal if it could the fire of the
Creator, and live apart from him and independent
of him.   The Prometheus Vinctus is the romance
of skepticism.   Not less true to all time are the
details of that stately apologue.   Apollo kept the
flocks of Admetus, said the poets.   When the gods
come among men, they are not known.   Jesus was
not; Socrates and Shakspeare were not.   Antæus
was suffocated by the gripe of Hercules, but every
time he touched his mother earth his strength was
renewed.   Man is the broken giant, and in all his
weakness both his body and his mind are invigorated by habits of conversation with nature.   The

power of music, the power of poetry, to unfix and
as it were clap wings to solid nature, interprets
the riddle of Orpheus.   The philosophical perception of identity through endless mutations of form
makes him know the Proteus.   What else am I
who laughed or wept yesterday, who slept last night
like a corpse, and this morning stood and ran?   And
what see I on any side but the transmigrations of
Proteus?   I can symbolize my thought by using
the name of any creature, of any fact, because every
creature is man agent or patient.   Tantalus is but
a name for you and me.   Tantalus means the impossibility of drinking the waters of thought which
are always gleaming and waving within sight of
the soul.   The transmigration of souls is no fable.
I would it were ; but men and women are only half
human.   Every animal of the barn-yard, the field
and the forest, of the earth and of the waters that
are under the earth, has contrived to get a footing
and to leave the print of its features and form in
some one or other of these upright, heaven-facing
speakers.   Ah! brother, stop the ebb of thy soul, —
ebbing downward into the forms into whose habits
thou hast now for many years slid.   As near and
proper to us is also that old fable of the Sphinx,
who was said to sit in the road-side and put riddles
to every passenger.   If the man could not answer,
she swallowed him alive   If he could solve the

riddle, the Sphinx was slain.   What is our life but
an endless flight of winged facts or events?   In
splendid variety these changes come, all putting
questions to the human spirit.   Those men who
cannot answer by a superior wisdom these facts or
questions of time, serve them.   Facts encumber
them, tyrannize over them, and make the men of
routine, the men of *sense*, in whom a literal obedience to facts has extinguished every spark of that
light by which man is truly man.   But if the man
is true to his better instincts or sentiments, and refuses the dominion of facts, as one that comes of a
higher race; remains fast by the soul and sees the
principle, then the facts fall aptly and supple into
their places ; they know their master, and the meanest of them glorifies him.

See in Goethe's Helena the same desire that
every word should be a thing.   These figures, he
would say, these Chirons, Griffins, Phorkyas, Helen
and Leda, are somewhat, and do exert a specific influence on the mind.   So far then are they eternal
entities, as real to-day as in the first Olympiad.
Much revolving them he writes out freely his
humor, and gives them body to his own imagination.
And although that poem be as vague and fantastic
as a dream, yet is it much more attractive than the
more regular dramatic pieces of the same author, for
the reason that it operates a wonderful relief to the

mind from the routine of customary images, — awakens the reader's invention and fancy by the wild freedom of the design, and by the unceasing succession of brisk shocks of surprise.

The universal nature, too strong for the petty nature of the bard, sits on his neck and writes through his hand ; so that when he seems to vent a mere caprice and wild romance, the issue is an exact allegory. Hence Plato said that " poets utter great and wise things which they do not themselves understand." All the fictions of the Middle Age explain themselves as a masked or frolic expression of that which in grave earnest the mind of that period toiled to achieve. Magic and all that is ascribed to it is a deep presentiment of the powers of science. The shoes of swiftness, the sword of sharpness, the power of subduing the elements, of using the secret virtues of minerals, of understanding the voices of birds, are the obscure efforts of the mind in a right direction. The preternatural prowess of the hero, the gift of perpetual youth, and the like, are alike the endeavor of the human spirit " to bend the shows of things to the desires of the mind."

In Perceforest and Amadis de Gaul a garland and a rose bloom on the head of her who is faithful, and fade on the brow of the inconstant. In the story of the Boy and the Mantle even a mature reader may be surprised with a glow of virtuous

pleasure at the triumph of the gentle Venelas; **and**
indeed all the postulates of elfin annals, — that the
fairies do not like to be named; that their gifts
are capricious and not to be trusted; that who
seeks a treasure must not speak; and the like, — I
find true in Concord, however they might be in
Cornwall or Bretagne.

Is it otherwise in the newest romance? I read
the Bride of Lammermoor. Sir William Ashton
is a mask for a vulgar temptation, Ravenswood
Castle a fine name for proud poverty, and the foreign mission of state only a Bunyan disguise for
honest industry. We may all shoot a wild bull
that would toss the good and beautiful, by fighting
down the unjust and sensual. Lucy Ashton is another name for fidelity, which is always beautiful
and always liable to calamity in this world.

But along with the civil and metaphysical history of man, another history goes daily forward, —
that of the external world, — in which he is not less
strictly implicated. He is the compend of time;
he is also the correlative of nature. His power
consists in the multitude of his affinities, in the
fact that his life is intertwined with the whole
chain of organic and inorganic being. In old Rome
the public roads beginning at the Forum proceeded
north, south, east, west, to the centre of every **prov-**

ince of the empire, making each market-town of
Persia, Spain and Britain pervious to the soldiers
of the capital: so out of the human heart go as it
were highways to the heart of every object in nature, to reduce it under the dominion of man.   A
man is a bundle of relations, a knot of roots, whose
flower and fruitage is the world.   His faculties refer to natures out of him and predict the world he
is to inhabit, as the fins of the fish foreshow that
water exists, or the wings of an eagle in the egg
presuppose air.   He cannot live without a world.
Put Napoleon in an island prison, let his faculties
find no men to act on, no Alps to climb, no stake
to play for, and he would beat the air, and appear
stupid.   Transport him to large countries, dense
population, complex interests and antagonist power,
and you shall see that the man Napoleon, bounded
that is by such a profile and outline, is not the virtual Napoleon.   This is but Talbot's shadow; —

> " His substance is not here.
> For what you see is but the smallest part
> And least proportion of humanity ;
> But were the whole frame here,
> It is of such a spacious, lofty pitch,
> Your roof were not sufficient to contain it."
>
> *Henry VI.*

Columbus needs a planet to shape his course
upon.   Newton and Laplace need myriads of age

and thick-strewn celestial areas. One may say a gravitating solar system is already prophesied in the nature of Newton's mind. Not less does the brain of Davy or of Gay-Lussac, from childhood exploring the affinities and repulsions of particles, anticipate the laws of organization. Does not the eye of the human embryo predict the light ? the ear of Handel predict the witchcraft of harmonic sound ? Do not the constructive fingers of Watt, Fulton, Whittemore, Arkwright, predict the fusible, hard, and temperable texture of metals, the properties of stone, water, and wood ? Do not the lovely attributes of the maiden child predict the refinements and decorations of civil society? Here also we are reminded of the action of man on man. A mind might ponder its thoughts for ages and not gain so much self-knowledge as the passion of love shall teach it in a day. Who knows himself before he has been thrilled with indignation at an outrage, or has heard an eloquent tongue, or has shared the throb of thousands in a national exultation or alarm ? No man can antedate his experience, or guess what faculty or feeling a new object shall unlock, any more than he can draw to-day the face of a person whom he shall see to-morrow for the first time.

I will not now go behind the general statement to explore the reason of this correspondency. Let it suffice that in the light of these two facts, namely, that the mind is One, and that nature is its correl- ative, history is to be read and written.

Thus in all ways does the soul concentrate and reproduce its treasures for each pupil. He too shall pass through the whole cycle of experience. He shall collect into a focus the rays of nature. History no longer shall be a dull book. It shall walk incarnate in every just and wise man. You shall not tell me by languages and titles a catalogue of the volumes you have read. You shall make me feel what periods you have lived. A man shall be the Temple of Fame. He shall walk, as the poets have described that goddess, in a robe painted all over with wonderful events and experiences ; — his own form and features by their exalted intelligence shall be that variegated vest. I shall find in him the Foreworld ; in his childhood the Age of Gold, the Apples of Knowledge, the Argonautic Expedi- tion, the calling of Abraham, the building of the Temple, the Advent of Christ, Dark Ages, the Re- vival of Letters, the Reformation, the discovery of new lands, the opening of new sciences and new regions in man. He shall be the priest of Pan. and bring with him into humble cottages the bless- ing of the morning stars, and all the recorded ben- efits of heaven and earth.

Is there somewhat overweening in this claim ?

Then I reject all I have written, for what is the use of pretending to know what we know not? But it is the fault of our rhetoric that we cannot strongly state one fact without seeming to belie some other. I hold our actual knowledge very cheap. Hear the rats in the wall, see the lizard on the fence, the fungus under foot, the lichen on the log. What do I know sympathetically, morally, of either of these worlds of life? As old as the Caucasian man, — perhaps older, — these creatures have kept their counsel beside him, and there is no record of any word or sign that has passed from one to the other. What connection do the books show between the fifty or sixty chemical elements and the historical eras? Nay, what does history yet record of the metaphysical annals of man? What light does it shed on those mysteries which we hide under the names Death and Immortality? Yet every history should be written in a wisdom which divined the range of our affinities and looked at facts as symbols. I am ashamed to see what a shallow village tale our so-called History is How many times we must say Rome, and Paris, and Constantinople! What does Rome know of rat and lizard? What are Olympiads and Consulates to these neighboring systems of being? Nay, what food or experience or succor have they for the Esquimaux seal-hunter, for the Kanàka in his canoe, for the fisherman, the stevedore, the porter?

Broader and deeper we must write our annals, — from an ethical reformation, from an influx of the ever new, ever sanative conscience, — if we would trulier express our central and wide-related nature, instead of this old chronology of selfishness and pride to which we have too long lent our eyes. Already that day exists for us, shines in on us at unawares, but the path of science and of letters is not the way into nature. The idiot, the Indian, the child and unschooled farmer's boy stand nearer to the light by which nature is to be read. than the dissector or the antiquary

SELF-RELIANCE.

" Ne te quæsiveris extra."

——◆——

MAN is his own star ; and the soul that can
Render an honest and a perfect man
Commands all light, all influence, all fate ;
Nothing to him falls early or too late.
Our acts our angels are, or good or ill,
Our fatal shadows that walk by us still."

Epilogue to Beaumont and Fletcher's Honest Man's Fortune

II.

SELF-RELIANCE.

————•————

I READ the other day some verses written by an eminent painter which were original and not conventional. The soul always hears an admonition in such lines, let the subject be what it may. The sentiment they instil is of more value than any thought they may contain. To believe your own thought, to believe that what is true for you in your private heart is true for all men, — that is genius. Speak your latent conviction, and it shall be the universal sense; for the inmost in due time becomes the outmost, and our first thought is rendered back to us by the trumpets of the Last Judgment. Familiar as the voice of the mind is to each, the highest merit we ascribe to Moses, Plato and Milton is that they set at naught books and traditions, and spoke not what men, but what *they* thought. A man should learn to detect and watch that gleam of light which flashes across his mind from within, more than the lustre of the firmament of bards and sages. Yet he dismisses without notice his thought, because it is his. In every work of genius we recognize our own rejected thoughts; they come back to us with a certain alienated majesty. Great works of art have no more affecting lesson for us than this. They teach us to abide by our spontaneous impression with good-humored inflexibility then most when the whole cry of voices is on the other side. Else to-morrow a stranger will say with masterly good sense precisely what we have thought and felt all the time, and we shall be forced to take with shame our own opinion from another.

There is a time in every man's education when he arrives at the conviction that envy is ignorance; that imitation is suicide; that he must take himself for better for worse as his portion; that though the wide universe is full of good, no kernel of nourishing corn can come to him but through his toil bestowed on that plot of ground which is given to him to till. The power which resides in him is new in nature, and none but he knows what that is which he can do, nor does he know until he has tried. Not for nothing one face, one character, one fact, makes much impression on him, and another none. This sculpture in the memory is not without preëstablished harmony. The eye was placed where one ray should fall, that it might testify of that particular ray. We but half express our selves, and are ashamed of that divine idea which each of us represents. It may be safely trusted as proportionate and of good issues, so it be faithfully imparted, but God will not have his work made manifest by cowards. A man is relieved and gay when he has put his heart into his work and done his best; but what he has said or done otherwise shall give him no peace. It is a deliverance which does not deliver. In the attempt his genius deserts him; no muse befriends; no invention, no hope.

Trust thyself: every heart vibrates to that iron string. Accept the place the divine providence has found for you, the society of your contemporaries, the connection of events. Great men have always done so, and confided themselves childlike to the genius of their age, betraying their perception that the absolutely trustworthy was seated at their heart, working through their hands, predominating in all their being. And we are now men, and must accept in the highest mind the same transcendent destiny; and not minors and invalids in a protected corner, not cowards fleeing before a revolution, but guides, redeemers and benefactors, obeying the Almighty effort and advancing on Chaos and the Dark.

What pretty oracles nature yields us on this text in the face and behavior of children, babes, and even brutes! That divided and rebel mind, that distrust of a sentiment because our arithmetic has computed the strength and means opposed to our purpose, these have not. Their mind being whole, their eye is as yet unconquered, and when we look in their faces we are disconcerted. Infancy conforms to nobody; all conform to it; so that one babe commonly makes four or five out of the adults who prattle and play to it. So God has armed youth and puberty and manhood no less with its own piquancy and charm, and made it enviable and gracious and its claims not to be put by, if it will stand by itself. Do not think the youth has no force, because he cannot speak to you and me. Hark! in the next room his voice is sufficiently clear and emphatic. It seems he knows how to speak to his contemporaries. Bashful or bold then, he will know how to make us seniors very unnecessary.

The nonchalance of boys who are sure of a dinner, and would disdain as much as a lord to do or say aught to conciliate one, is the healthy attitude of human nature. A boy is in the parlor what the pit is in the playhouse; independent, irresponsible, looking out from his corner on such people and facts as pass by, he tries and sentences them on their merits, in the swift, summary way of boys, as good, bad, interesting, silly, eloquent, troublesome.

He cumbers himself never about consequences, about interests; he gives an independent, genuine verdict. You must court him; he does not court you. But the man is as it were clapped into jail by his consciousness. As soon as he has once acted or spoken with *éclat* he is a committed person, watched by the sympathy or the hatred of hundreds, whose affections must now enter into his account. There is no Lethe for this. Ah, that he could pass again into his neutrality! Who can thus avoid all pledges and, having observed, observe again from the same unaffected, unbiased, unbribable, unaffrighted innocence, — must always be formidable. He would utter opinions on all passing affairs, which being seen to be not private but necessary, would sink like darts into the ear of men and put them in fear.

These are the voices which we hear in solitude, but they grow faint and inaudible as we enter into the world. Society everywhere is in conspiracy against the manhood of every one of its members. Society is a joint-stock company, in which the members agree, for the better securing of his bread to each shareholder, to surrender the liberty and culture of the eater. The virtue in most request is conformity. Self-reliance is its aversion. It loves not realities and creators, but names and customs.

Whoso would be a man, must be a nonconformist. He who would gather immortal palms must not be hindered by the name of goodness, but must explore if it be goodness. Nothing is at last sacred but the integrity of your own mind. Absolve you to yourself, and you shall have the suffrage of the world. I remember an answer which when quite young I was prompted to make to a valued adviser who was wont to importune me with the dear old doctrines of the church. On my saying, " What have I to do with the sacredness of traditions, if I live wholly from within?" my friend suggested, — " But these impulses may be from below, not from above." I replied, " They do not seem to me to be such; but if I am the Devil's child, I will live then from the Devil." No law can be sacred to me but that of my nature. Good and bad are but names very readily transferable to that or this; the only right is what is after my constitution; the only wrong what is against it. A man is to carry himself in the presence of all opposition as if every thing were titular and ephemeral but he. I am ashamed to think how easily we capitulate to badges and names, to large societies and dead institutions. Every decent and well-spoken individual affects and sways me more than is right. I ought to go upright and vital, and speak the rude truth in all ways. If malice and vanity wear the coat of philanthropy, shall that pass? If an angry bigot assumes this bountiful cause of Abolition, and comes to me with his last news from Barbadoes, why should I not say to him, ' Go love thy infant; love thy wood-chopper ; be good - natured and modest ; have that grace ; and never varnish your hard, un-charitable ambition with this incredible tenderness for black folk a thousand miles off. Thy love afar is spite at home.' Rough and graceless would be such greeting, but truth is handsomer than the af. fectation of love. Your goodness must have some edge to it, — else it is none. The doctrine of ha. tred must be preached, as the counteraction of the doctrine of love, when that pules and whines. I shun father and mother and wife and brother when my genius calls me. I would write on the lintels of the door - post, *Whim.* I hope it is somewhat better than whim at last, but we cannot spend the day in explanation. Expect me not to show cause why I seek or why I exclude company. Then again, do not tell me, as a good man did to-day, of my ob-ligation to put all poor men in good situations. Are they *my* poor ? I tell thee thou foolish philan-thropist that I grudge the dollar, the dime, the cent I give to such men as do not belong to me and to whom I do not belong. There is a class of persons to whom by all spiritual affinity I am bought and sold ; for them I will go to prison if need be ; but your miscellaneous popular charities

the education at college of fools ; the building of
meeting-houses to the vain end to which many now
stand ; alms to sots, and the thousand-fold Relief
Societies ; — though I confess with shame I sometimes succumb and give the dollar, it is a wicked
dollar, which by and by I shall have the manhood
to withhold.

Virtues are, in the popular estimate, rather the
exception than the rule.   There is the man *and* his
virtues.   Men do what is called a good action, as
some piece of courage or charity, much as they
would pay a fine in expiation of daily non-appear-
ance on parade.   Their works are done as an apology or extenuation of their living in the world, —
as invalids and the insane pay a high board.   Their
virtues are penances.   I do not wish to expiate,
but to live.   My life is for itself and not for a
spectacle.   I much prefer that it should be of a
lower strain, so it be genuine and equal, than that
it should be glittering and unsteady.   I wish it to
be sound and sweet, and not to need diet and bleed-
ing.   I ask primary evidence that you are a man,
and refuse this appeal from the man to his actions.
I know that for myself it makes no difference
whether I do or forbear those actions which are
reckoned excellent.   I cannot consent to pay for a
privilege where I have intrinsic right.   Few and
mean as my gifts may be, I actually am, and do

not need for my own assurance or the assurance of my fellows any secondary testimony.

What I must do is all that concerns me, not what the people think. This rule, equally arduous in actual and in intellectual life, may serve for the whole distinction between greatness and meanness. It is the harder because you will always find those who think they know what is your duty better than you know it. It is easy in the world to live after the world's opinion; it is easy in solitude to live after our own; but the great man is he who in the midst of the crowd keeps with perfect sweetness the independence of solitude.

The objection to conforming to usages that have become dead to you is that it scatters your force. It loses your time and blurs the impression of your character. If you maintain a dead church, contribute to a dead Bible-society, vote with a great party either for the government or against it, spread your table like base housekeepers, — under all these screens I have difficulty to detect the precise man you are: and of course so much force is withdrawn from your proper life. But do your work, and I shall know you. Do your work, and you shall reinforce yourself. A man must consider what a blindman's-buff is this game of conformity. If I know your sect I anticipate your argument. I hear a preacher announce for his text and topic the ex-

pediency of one of the institutions of his church.
Do I not know beforehand that not possibly can he
say a new and spontaneous word? Do I not know
that with all this ostentation of examining the
grounds of the institution he will do no such thing?
Do I not know that he is pledged to himself not to
look but at one side, the permitted side, not as a
man, but as a parish minister? He is a retained
attorney, and these airs of the bench are the empti-
est affectation. Well, most men have bound their
eyes with one or another handkerchief, and attached
themselves to some one of these communities of
opinion. This conformity makes them not false in
a few particulars, authors of a few lies, but false in
all particulars. Their every truth is not quite true.
Their two is not the real two, their four not the
real four; so that every word they say chagrins us
and we know not where to begin to set them right.
Meantime nature is not slow to equip us in the
prison-uniform of the party to which we adhere.
We come to wear one cut of face and figure, and
acquire by degrees the gentlest asinine expression.
There is a mortifying experience in particular,
which does not fail to wreak itself also in the general history; I mean " the foolish face of praise,"
the forced smile which we put on in company where
we do not feel at ease, in answer to conversation
which does not interest us. The muscles, not spon-

taneously moved but moved by a low usurping wil.
fulness, grow tight about the outline of the face,
with the most disagreeable sensation.

For nonconformity the world whips you with its
displeasure. And therefore a man must know how
to estimate a sour face. The by-standers look ask-
ance on him in the public street or in the friend's
parlor. If this aversation had its origin in contempt
and resistance like his own he might well go home
with a sad countenance; but the sour faces of the
multitude, like their sweet faces, have no deep
cause, but are put on and off as the wind blows and
a newspaper directs. Yet is the discontent of the
multitude more formidable than that of the senate
and the college. It is easy enough for a firm man
who knows the world to brook the rage of the cultivated classes. Their rage is decorous and prudent,
for they are timid, as being very vulnerable themselves. But when to their feminine rage the indignation of the people is added, when the ignorant
and the poor are aroused, when the unintelligent
brute force that lies at the bottom of society is
made to growl and mow, it needs the habit of magnanimity and religion to treat it godlike as a trifle
of no concernment.

The other terror that scares us from self-trust is
our consistency; a reverence for our past act or
word because the eyes of others have no other data

for computing our orbit than our past acts, and we are loath to disappoint them.

But why should you keep your head over your shoulder? Why drag about this corpse of your memory, lest you contradict somewhat you have stated in this or that public place? Suppose you should contradict yourself; what then? It seems to be a rule of wisdom never to rely on your memory alone, scarcely even in acts of pure memory, but to bring the past for judgment into the thousand-eyed present, and live ever in a new day. In your metaphysics you have denied personality to the Deity, yet when the devout motions of the soul come, yield to them heart and life, though they should clothe God with shape and color. Leave your theory, as Joseph his coat in the hand of the harlot, and flee.

A foolish consistency is the hobgoblin of little minds, adored by little statesmen and philosophers and divines. With consistency a great soul has simply nothing to do. He may as well concern himself with his shadow on the wall. Speak what you think now in hard words and to-morrow speak what to-morrow thinks in hard words again, though it contradict every thing you said to-day. — 'Ah, so you shall be sure to be misunderstood.' — Is it so bad then to be misunderstood? Pythagoras was misunderstood, and Socrates, and Jesus, and

Luther, and Copernicus, and Galileo, and Newton, and every pure and wise spirit that ever took flesh. To be great is to be misunderstood.

I suppose no man can violate his nature. All the sallies of his will are rounded in by the law of his being, as the inequalities of Andes and Himmaleh are insignificant in the curve of the sphere. Nor does it matter how you gauge and try him. A character is like an acrostic or Alexandrian stanza; — read it forward, backward, or across, it still spells the same thing. In this pleasing contrite wood-life which God allows me, let me record day by day my honest thought without prospect or retrospect, and, I cannot doubt, it will be found symmetrical, though I mean it not and see it not. My book should smell of pines and resound with the hum of insects. The swallow over my window should interweave that thread or straw he carries in his bill into my web also. We pass for what we are. Character teaches above our wills. Men imagine that they communicate their virtue or vice only by overt actions, and do not see that virtue or vice emit a breath every moment.

There will be an agreement in whatever variety of actions, so they be each honest and natural in their hour. For of one will, the actions will be harmonious, however unlike they seem. These varieties are lost sight of at a little distance, at a little

height of thought.   One tendency unites them all.
The voyage of the best ship is a zigzag line of a
hundred tacks.   See the line from a sufficient distance, and it straightens itself to the average tendency.   Your genuine action will explain itself and
will explain your other genuine actions.   Your con
formity explains nothing.   Act singly, and what
you have already done singly will justify you now.
Greatness appeals to the future.   If I can be firm
enough to-day to do right and scorn eyes, I must
have done so much right before as to defend me
now.   Be it how it will, do right now.   Always
scorn appearances and you always may.   The force
of character is cumulative.   All the foregone days
of virtue work their health into this.   What makes
the majesty of the heroes of the senate and the
field, which so fills the imagination?   The consciousness of a train of great days and victories
behind.   They shed an united light on the advancing actor.   He is attended as by a visible escort of
angels.   That is it which throws thunder into Chatham's voice, and dignity into Washington's port,
and America into Adams's eye.   Honor is venerable
to us because it is no ephemera.   It is always ancient virtue.   We worship it to-day because it is
not of to-day.   We love it and pay it homage because it is not a trap for our love and homage, but
is self-dependent, self-derived, and therefore of an

old immaculate pedigree, even if shown in a young person.

I hope in these days we have heard the last of conformity and consistency. Let the words be gazetted and ridiculous henceforward. Instead of the gong for dinner, let us hear a whistle from the Spartan fife. Let us never bow and apologize more. A great man is coming to eat at my house. I do not wish to please him; I wish that he should wish to please me. I will stand here for humanity, and though I would make it kind, I would make it true. Let us affront and reprimand the smooth mediocrity and squalid contentment of the times, and hurl in the face of custom and trade and office, the fact which is the upshot of all history, that there is a great responsible Thinker and Actor working wherever a man works; that a true man belongs to no other time or place, but is the centre of things. Where he is, there is nature. He measures you and all men and all events. Ordinarily, every body in society reminds us of somewhat else, or of some other person. Character, reality, reminds you of nothing else; it takes place of the whole creation. The man must be so much that he must make all circumstances indifferent. Every true man is a cause, a country, and an age; requires infinite spaces and numbers and time fully to accomplish his design; — and posterity seem to fol-

low his steps as a train of clients. A man Cæsar
is born, and for ages after we have a Roman Empire.   Christ is born, and millions of minds so grow
and cleave to his genius that he is confounded with
virtue and the possible of man.   An institution is
the lengthened shadow of one man ; as, Monachism,
of the Hermit Antony; the Reformation, of Luther;
Quakerism, of Fox; Methodism, of Wesley; Abolition, of Clarkson.   Scipio, Milton called "the
height of Rome;" and all history resolves itself
very easily into the biography of a few stout and
earnest persons.

Let a man then know his worth, and keep things
under his feet.   Let him not peep or steal, or skulk
up and down with the air of a charity-boy, a bas-
tard, or an interloper in the world which exists for
him.   But the man in the street, finding no worth
in himself which corresponds to the force which
built a tower or sculptured a marble god, feels poor
when he looks on these.   To him a palace, a statue,
or a costly book have an alien and forbidding air,
much like a gay equipage, and seem to say like that,
'Who are you, Sir?' Yet they all are his, suitors
for his notice, petitioners to his faculties that they
will come out and take possession.   The picture
waits for my verdict; it is not to command me,
but I am to settle its claims to praise.   That
popular fable of the sot who was picked up

dead-drunk in the street, carried to the duke's house, washed and dressed and laid in the duke's bed, and, on his waking, treated with all obsequious ceremony like the duke, and assured that he had been insane, owes its popularity to the fact that it symbolizes so well the state of man, who is in the world a sort of sot, but now and then wakes up, exercises his reason and finds himself a true prince.

Our reading is mendicant and sycophantic. In history our imagination plays us false. Kingdom and lordship, power and estate, are a gaudier vocabulary than private John and Edward in a small house and common day's work; but the things of life are the same to both; the sum total of both is the same. Why all this deference to Alfred and Scanderbeg and Gustavus? Suppose they were virtuous; did they wear out virtue? As great a stake depends on your private act to-day as followed their public and renowned steps. When private men shall act with original views, the lustre will be transferred from the actions of kings to those of gentlemen.

The world has been instructed by its kings, who have so magnetized the eyes of nations. It has been taught by this colossal symbol the mutual reverence that is due from man to man. The joyful loyalty with which men have everywhere suffered the king, the noble, or the great proprietor to walk among them by a law of his own, make his own scale of men and things and reverse theirs, pay for benefits not with money but with honor, and represent the law in his person, was the hieroglyphic by which they obscurely signified their consciousness of their own right and comeliness, the right of every man.

The magnetism which all original action exerts is explained when we inquire the reason of self-trust. Who is the Trustee? What is the aboriginal Self, on which a universal reliance may be grounded? What is the nature and power of that science-baffling star, without parallax, without calculable elements, which shoots a ray of beauty even into trivial and impure actions, if the least mark of independence appear? The inquiry leads us to that source, at once the essence of genius, of virtue, and of life, which we call Spontaneity or Instinct. We denote this primary wisdom as Intuition, whilst all later teachings are tuitions. In that deep force, the last fact behind which analysis cannot go, all things find their common origin. For the sense of being which in calm hours rises, we know not how, in the soul, is not diverse from things, from space, from light, from time, from man, but one with them and proceeds obviously from the same source whence their life and being also proceed. We first share the life by which things exist and afterwards see them as appearances in nature and forget that we have shared their cause. Here is the fountain of action and of thought. Here are the lungs of that inspiration which giveth man wisdom and which cannot be denied without impiety and atheism. We lie in the lap of immense intelligence, which makes us receivers of its truth and organs of its activity. When we discern justice, when we discern truth, we do nothing of ourselves, but allow a passage to its beams. If we ask whence this comes, if we seek to pry into the soul that causes, all philosophy is at fault. Its presence or its absence is all we can affirm. Every man discriminates between the voluntary acts of his mind and his involuntary perceptions, and knows that to his involuntary perceptions a perfect faith is due. He may err in the expression of them, but he knows that these things are so, like day and night, not to be disputed. My wilful actions and acquisitions are but roving; — the idlest reverie, the faintest native emotion, command my curiosity and respect. Thoughtless people contradict as readily the statement of perceptions as of opinions, or rather much more readily; for they do not distinguish between perception and notion. They fancy that I choose to see this or that thing. But perception is not whimsical, but fatal. If I see a trait, my children will see it after me, and in course of time all mankind,

—although it may chance that no one has seen it
before me. For my perception of it is as much
a fact as the sun.

The relations of the soul to the divine spirit are
so pure that it is profane to seek to interpose helps.
It must be that when God speaketh he should communicate, not one thing, but all things; should fill
the world with his voice; should scatter forth light,
nature, time, souls, from the centre of the present
thought; and new date and new create the whole.
Whenever a mind is simple and receives a divine
wisdom, old things pass away, — means, teachers,
texts, temples fall; it lives now, and absorbs past
and future into the present hour. All things are
made sacred by relation to it, — one as much as another. All things are dissolved to their centre by
their cause, and in the universal miracle petty and
particular miracles disappear. If therefore a man
claims to know and speak of God and carries you
backward to the phraseology of some old mould
ered nation in another country, in another world,
believe him not. Is the acorn better than the oak
which is its fulness and completion? Is the par
ent better than the child into whom he has cast his
ripened being? Whence then this worship of the
past? The centuries are conspirators against the
sanity and authority of the soul. Time and space
are but physiological colors which the eye makes,

but the soul is light : where it is, is day ; where it was, is night ; and history is an impertinence and an injury if it be any thing more than a cheerful apologue or parable of my being and becoming.

Man is timid and apologetic ; he is no longer upright ; he dares not say ' I think,' ' I am,' but quotes some saint or sage. He is ashamed before the blade of grass or the blowing rose. These roses under my window make no reference to former roses or to better ones ; they are for what they are ; they exist with God to-day. There is no time to them. There is simply the rose ; it is perfect in every moment of its existence. Before a leaf-bud has burst, its whole life acts ; in the full-blown flower there is no more ; in the leafless root there is no less. Its nature is satisfied and it satisfies nature in all moments alike. But man postpones or remembers ; he does not live in the present, but with reverted eye laments the past, or, heedless of the riches that surround him, stands on tiptoe to foresee the future. He cannot be happy and strong until he too lives with nature in the present, above time.

This should be plain enough. Yet see what strong intellects dare not yet hear God himself unless he speak the phraseology of I know not what David, or Jeremiah, or Paul. We shall not always set so great a price on a few texts, on a few lives. We are like children who repeat by rote

the sentences of grandames and tutors, and, as they
grow older, of the men of talents and character
they chance to see, — painfully recollecting the exact words they spoke ; afterwards, when they come
into the point of view which those had who uttered
these sayings, they understand them and are willing
to let the words go ; for at any time they can use
words as good when occasion comes. If we live
truly, we shall see truly. It is as easy for the
strong man to be strong, as it is for the weak to be
weak. When we have new perception, we shall
gladly disburden the memory of its hoarded treasures as old rubbish. When a man lives with God,
his voice shall be as sweet as the murmur of the
brook and the rustle of the corn.

And now at last the highest truth on this subject
remains unsaid ; probably cannot be said ; for all
that we say is the far-off remembering of the intuition. That thought by what I can now nearest approach to say it, is this. When good is near you,
when you have life in yourself, it is not by any
known or accustomed way; you shall not discern
the footprints of any other ; you shall not see the
face of man ; you shall not hear any name ; — the
way, the thought, the good, shall be wholly strange
and new. It shall exclude example and experience.
You take the way from man, not to man. All persons that ever existed are its forgotten ministers.

Fear and hope are alike beneath it. There is somewhat low even in hope. In the hour of vision there is nothing that can be called gratitude, nor properly joy. The soul raised over passion beholds identity and eternal causation, perceives the self-existence of Truth and Right, and calms itself with knowing that all things go well. Vast spaces of nature, the Atlantic Ocean, the South Sea ; long intervals of time, years, centuries, are of no account. This which I think and feel underlay every former state of life and circumstances, as it does underlie my present, and what is called life and what is called death.

Life only avails, not the having lived. Power ceases in the instant of repose ; it resides in the moment of transition from a past to a new state, in the shooting of the gulf, in the darting to an aim. This one fact the world hates ; that the soul *becomes ;* for that forever degrades the past, turns all *r*iches to poverty, all reputation to a shame, confounds the saint with the rogue, shoves Jesus and Judas equally aside. Why then do we prate of self-reliance ? Inasmuch as the soul is present there will be power not confident but agent. To talk of reliance is a poor external way of speaking. Speak rather of that which relies because it works and is. Who has more obedience than I masters me, though he should not raise his finger. Round him I must revolve by the gravitation of spirits. We fancy it rhetoric when we speak of eminent virtue. We do not yet see that virtue is Height, and that a man or a company of men, plastic and permeable to principles, by the law of nature must overpower and ride all cities, nations, kings, rich men, poets, who are not.

This is the ultimate fact which we so quickly reach on this, as on every topic, the resolution of all into the ever-blessed ONE. Self-existence is the attribute of the Supreme Cause, and it constitutes the measure of good by the degree in which it enters into all lower forms. All things real are so by so much virtue as they contain. Commerce, husbandry, hunting, whaling, war, eloquence, personal weight, are somewhat, and engage my respect as examples of its presence and impure action. I see the same law working in nature for conservation and growth. Power is, in nature, the essential measure of right. Nature suffers nothing to remain in her kingdoms which cannot help itself. The genesis and maturation of a planet, its poise and orbit, the bended tree recovering itself from the strong wind, the vital resources of every animal and vegetable, are demonstrations of the self-sufficing and therefore self-relying soul.

Thus all concentrates : let us not rove ; let us sit at home with the cause. Let us stun and astonish the intruding rabble of men and books and institutions by a simple declaration of the divine fact. Bid the invaders take the shoes from off their feet, for God is here within. Let our simplicity judge them, and our docility to our own law demonstrate the poverty of nature and fortune beside our native riches.

But now we are a mob. Man does not stand in awe of man, nor is his genius admonished to stay at home, to put itself in communication with the internal ocean, but it goes abroad to beg a cup of water of the urns of other men. We must go alone. I like the silent church before the service begins, better than any preaching. How far off, how cool, how chaste the persons look, begirt each one with a precinct or sanctuary! So let us always sit. Why should we assume the faults of our friend, or wife, or father, or child, because they sit around our hearth, or are said to have the same blood? All men have my blood and I have all men's. Not for that will I adopt their petulance or folly, even to the extent of being ashamed of it. But your isolation must not be mechanical, but spiritual, that is, must be elevation. At times the whole world seems to be in conspiracy to importune you with emphatic trifles. Friend, client, child, sickness, fear, want, charity, all knock at once at thy closet door and say, — 'Come out unto us.' But keep thy state;

come not into their confusion. The power men possess to annoy me I give them by a weak curiosity. No man can come near me but through my act. "What we love that we have, but by desire we bereave ourselves of the love."

If we cannot at once rise to the sanctities of obedience and faith, let us at least resist our temptations; let us enter into the state of war and wake Thor and Woden, courage and constancy, in our Saxon breasts. This is to be done in our smooth times by speaking the truth. Check this lying hospitality and lying affection. Live no longer to the expectation of these deceived and deceiving people with whom we converse. Say to them, 'O father, O mother, O wife, O brother, O friend, I have lived with you after appearances hitherto. Henceforward I am the truth's. Be it known unto you that henceforward I obey no law less than the eternal law. I will have no covenants but proximities. I shall endeavor to nourish my parents, to support my family, to be the chaste husband of one wife, — but these relations I must fill after a new and unprecedented way. I appeal from your customs. I must be myself. I cannot break myself any longer for you, or you. If you can love me for what I am, we shall be the happier. If you cannot, I will still seek to deserve that you should. I will not hide my tastes or aversions. I will so trust

that what is deep is holy, that I will do strongly
before the sun and moon whatever inly rejoices
me and the heart appoints. If you are noble, I
will love you: if you are not, I will not hurt you
and myself by hypocritical attentions. If you are
true, but not in the same truth with me, cleave to
your companions ; I will seek my own. I do this
not selfishly but humbly and truly. It is alike
your interest, and mine, and all men's, however
long we have dwelt in lies, to live in truth. Does
this sound harsh to-day? You will soon love what
is dictated by your nature as well as mine, and if
we follow the truth it will bring us out safe at
last.' — But so may you give these friends pain.
Yes, but I cannot sell my liberty and my power, to
save their sensibility. Besides, all persons have
their moments of reason, when they look out into
the region of absolute truth ; then will they justify
me and do the same thing.

The populace think that your rejection of popular standards is a rejection of all standard, and
mere antinomianism ; and the bold sensualist will
use the name of philosophy to gild his crimes. But
the law of consciousness abides. There are two
confessionals, in one or the other of which we must
be shriven. You may fulfil your round of duties
by clearing yourself in the *direct*, or in the *reflex*
way. Consider whether you have satisfied your re-

lations to father, mother, cousin, neighbor, town, cat and dog; whether any of these can upbraid you. But I may also neglect this reflex standard and absolve me to myself. I have my own stern claims and perfect circle. It denies the name of duty to many offices that are called duties. But if I can discharge its debts it enables me to dispense with the popular code. If any one imagines that this law is lax, let him keep its commandment one day.

And truly it demands something godlike in him who has cast off the common motives of humanity and has ventured to trust himself for a taskmaster. High be his heart, faithful his will, clear his sight, that he may in good earnest be doctrine, society, law, to himself, that a simple purpose may be to him as strong as iron necessity is to others!

If any man consider the present aspects of what is called by distinction *society*, he will see the need of these ethics. The sinew and heart of man seem to be drawn out, and we are become timorous, desponding whimperers. We are afraid of truth, afraid of fortune, afraid of death and afraid of each other. Our age yields no great and perfect persons. We want men and women who shall renovate life and our social state, but we see that most natures are insolvent, cannot satisfy their own wants, have an ambition out of all proportion to

their practical force and do lean and beg day and
night continually. Our housekeeping is mendicant,
our arts, our occupations, our marriages, our religion we have not chosen, but society has chosen for
us. We are parlor soldiers. We shun the rugged
battle of fate, where strength is born.

If our young men miscarry in their first enter-
prises they lose all heart. If the young merchant
fails, men say he is *ruined*. If the finest genius
studies at one of our colleges and is not installed in
an office within one year afterwards in the cities or
suburbs of Boston or New York, it seems to his
friends and to himself that he is right in being dis-
heartened and in complaining the rest of his life.
A sturdy lad from New Hampshire or Vermont,
who in turn tries all the professions, who *teams it,
farms it, peddles*, keeps a school, preaches, edits a
newspaper, goes to Congress, buys a township, and
so forth, in successive years, and always like a cat
falls on his feet, is worth a hundred of these city
dolls. He walks abreast with his days and feels no
shame in not 'studying a profession,' for he does
not postpone his life, but lives already. He has not
one chance, but a hundred chances. Let a Stoic
open the resources of man and tell men they are not
leaning willows, but can and must detach themselves; that with the exercise of self - trust, new
powers shall appear; that a man is the word made

flesh, born to shed healing to the nations; that he
should be ashamed of our compassion, and that the
moment he acts from himself, tossing the laws, the
books, idolatries and customs out of the window,
we pity him no more but thank and revere him;—
and that teacher shall restore the life of man to
splendor and make his name dear to all history.

It is easy to see that a greater self-reliance must
work a revolution in all the offices and relations of
men; in their religion; in their education; in their
pursuits ; their modes of living ; their association ;
in their property; in their speculative views.

1. In what prayers do men allow themselves !
That which they call a holy office is not so much as
brave and manly.   Prayer looks abroad and asks
for some foreign addition to come through some
foreign virtue, and loses itself in endless mazes of
natural and supernatural, and mediatorial and miraculous.   Prayer that craves a particular commodity, anything less than all good, is vicious.   Prayer
is the contemplation of the facts of life from the
highest point of view.   It is the soliloquy of a beholding and jubilant soul.   It is the spirit of God
pronouncing his works good.   But prayer as a
means to effect a private end is meanness and theft.
It supposes dualism and not unity in nature and
consciousness.   As soon as the man is at one with
God, he will not beg.   He will then see prayer in

ʌll action. The prayer of the farmer kneeling in
his field to weed it, the prayer of the rower kneeling with the stroke of his oar, are true prayers
heard throughout nature, though for cheap ends.
Caratach, in Fletcher's Bonduca, when admonished
to inquire the mind of the god Audate, replies, —

> " His hidden meaning lies in our endeavors ;
> Our valors are our best gods."

Another sort of false prayers are our regrets
Discontent is the want of self-reliance: it is infirm
ity of will. Regret calamities if you can thereby
help the sufferer; if not, attend your own work and
already the evil begins to be repaired. Our sympathy is just as base. We come to them who weep
foolishly and sit down and cry for company, instead of imparting to them truth and health in
rough electric shocks, putting them once more in
communication with their own reason. The secret
of fortune is joy in our hands. Welcome evermore
to gods and men is the self-helping man. For him
all doors are flung wide ; him all tongues greet, all
honors crown, all eyes follow with desire. Our
love goes out to him and embraces him because he
did not need it. We solicitously and apologetically
caress and celebrate him because he held on his
way and scorned our disapprobation. The gods
love him because men hated him. " To the perse-

vering mortal," said Zoroaster, "the blessed Im
mortals are swift."

As men's prayers are a disease of the will, so
are their creeds a disease of the intellect. They say
with those foolish Israelites, ' Let not God speak
to us, lest we die. Speak thou, speak any man
with us, and we will obey.' Everywhere I am hindered of meeting God in my brother, because he has
shut his own temple doors and recites fables merely of his brother's, or his brother's brother's God.
Every new mind is a new classification. If it prove
a mind of uncommon activity and power, a Locke,
a Lavoisier, a Hutton, a Bentham, a Fourier, it im-
poses its classification on other men, and lo ! a new
system. In proportion to the depth of the thought,
and so to the number of the objects it touches
and brings within reach of the pupil, is his complacency. But chiefly is this apparent in creeds and
churches, which are also classifications of some pow
erful mind acting on the elemental thought of duty
and man's relation to the Highest. Such is Cal
vinism, Quakerism, Swedenborgism. The pupil
takes the same delight in subordinating every thing
to the new terminology as a girl who has just
learned botany in seeing a new earth and new seasons thereby. It will happen for a time that the
pupil will find his intellectual power has grown by
the study of his master's mind. But in all unbal-

anced minds the classification is idolized, passes for
the end and not for a speedily exhaustible means
so that the walls of the system blend to their eye
in the remote horizon with the walls of the uni،
verse ; the luminaries of heaven seem to them hung
on the arch their master built. They cannot imag،
ine how you aliens have any right to see, — how
you can see: 'It must be somehow that you stole
the light from us.' They do not yet perceive that
fight, unsystematic, indomitable, will break into
any cabin, even into theirs. Let them chirp awhile
and call it their own. If they are honest and do
well, presently their neat new pinfold will be too
strait and low, will crack, will lean, will rot and
vanish, and the immortal light, all young and joyful, million-orbed, million-colored, will beam over
the universe as on the first morning.

2. It is for want of self-culture that the super
stition of Travelling, whose idols are Italy, England, Egypt, retains its fascination for all educated Americans. They who made England, Italy,
or Greece venerable in the imagination, did so by
sticking fast where they were, like an axis of the
earth. In manly hours we feel that duty is our
place. The soul is no traveller ; the wise man
stays at home, and when his necessities, his duties,
on any occasion call him from his house, or into foreign lands, he is at home still and shall make men

sensible by the expression of his countenance that
he goes, the missionary of wisdom and virtue, and
visits cities and men like a sovereign and not like
an interloper or a valet.

I have no churlish objection to the circumnavigation of the globe for the purposes of art, of study,
and benevolence, so that the man is first domesticated, or does not go abroad with the hope of finding
somewhat greater than he knows. He who travels
to be amused, or to get somewhat which he does
not carry, travels away from himself, and grows old
even in youth among old things. In Thebes, in
Palmyra, his will and mind have become old and
dilapidated as they. He carries ruins to ruins.

Travelling is a fool's paradise. Our first journeys discover to us the indifference of places. At
home I dream that at Naples, at Rome, I can be intoxicated with beauty and lose my sadness. I pack
my trunk, embrace my friends, embark on the sea
and at last wake up in Naples, and there beside me
is the stern fact, the sad self, unrelenting, identical, that I fled from. I seek the Vatican and the
palaces. I affect to be intoxicated with sights and
suggestions, but I am not intoxicated. My giant
goes with me wherever I go.

3. But the rage of travelling is a symptom of a
deeper unsoundness affecting the whole intellectual
action. The intellect is vagabond, and our system

of education fosters restlessness. Our minds travel when our bodies are forced to stay at home. We imitate ; and what is imitation but the travelling of the mind ? Our houses are built with foreign taste ; our shelves are garnished with foreign ornaments ; our opinions, our tastes, our faculties, lean, and follow the Past and the Distant. The soul created the arts wherever they have flourished. It was in his own mind that the artist sought his model. It was an application of his own thought to the thing to be done and the conditions to be observed. And why need we copy the Doric or the Gothic model ? Beauty, convenience, grandeur of thought and quaint expression are as near to us as to any, and if the American artist will study with hope and love the precise thing to be done by him, considering the climate, the soil, the length of the day, the wants of the people, the habit and form of the government, he will create a house in which all these will find themselves fitted, and taste and sentiment will be satisfied also.

Insist on yourself ; never imitate. Your own gift you can present every moment with the cumulative force of a whole life's cultivation ; but of the adopted talent of another you have only an extemporaneous half possession. That which each can do best, none but his Maker can teach him. No man yet knows what it is, nor can, till that person

has exhibited it.   Where is the master who could
have taught Shakspeare?   Where is the master
who could have instructed Franklin, or Washington, or Bacon, or Newton?   Every great man is
a unique.   The Scipionism of Scipio is precisely
that part he could not borrow.   Shakspeare will
never be made by the study of Shakspeare.   Do
that which is assigned you, and you cannot hope
too much or dare too much.   There is at this moment for you an utterance brave and grand as that
of the colossal chisel of Phidias, or trowel of the
Egyptians, or the pen of Moses or Dante, but different from all these.   Not possibly will the soul,
all rich, all eloquent, with thousand-cloven tongue,
deign to repeat itself; but if you can hear what
these patriarchs say, surely you can reply to them
in the same pitch of voice ; for the ear and the
tongue are two organs of one nature.   Abide in
the simple and noble regions of thy life, obey thy
heart and thou shalt reproduce the Foreworld
again.

4. As our Religion, our Education, our Art look
abroad, so does our spirit of society.   All men
plume themselves on the improvement of society,
and no man improves.

Society never advances.   It recedes as fast on
one side as it gains on the other.   It undergoes
continual changes ; it is barbarous, it is civilized, it

is christianized, it is rich, it is scientific ; but this change is not amelioration. For every thing that is given something is taken. Society acquires new arts and loses old instincts. What a contrast between the well - clad, reading, writing, thinking American, with a watch, a pencil and a bill of exchange in his pocket, and the naked New Zealander, whose property is a club, a spear, a mat and an undivided twentieth of a shed to sleep under ! But compare the health of the two men and you shall see that the white man has lost his aboriginal strength. If the traveller tell us truly, strike the savage with a broad axe and in a day or two the flesh shall unite and heal as if you struck the blow into soft pitch, and the same blow shall send the white to his grave.

The civilized man has built a coach, but has lost the use of his feet. He is supported on crutches, but lacks so much support of muscle. He has a fine Geneva watch, but he fails of the skill to tell the hour by the sun. A Greenwich nautical almanac he has, and so being sure of the information when he wants it, the man in the street does not know a star in the sky. The solstice he does not observe ; the equinox he knows as little ; and the whole bright calendar of the year is without a dial in his mind. His note-books impair his memory ; is libraries overload his wit ; the insurance-office increases the number of accidents; and it may be a question whether machinery does not encumber; whether we have not lost by refinement some energy, by a Christianity entrenched in establishments and forms some vigor of wild virtue. For every Stoic was a Stoic; but in Christendom where is the Christian?

There is no more deviation in the moral standard than in the standard of height or bulk. No greater men are now than ever were. A singular equality may be observed between the great men of the first and of the last ages; nor can all the science, art, religion, and philosophy of the nineteenth century avail to educate greater men than Plutarch's heroes, three or four and twenty centuries ago. Not in time is the race progressive. Phocion, Socrates, Anaxagoras, Diogenes, are great men, but they leave no class. He who is really of their class will not be called by their name, but will be his own man, and in his turn the founder of a sect. The arts and inventions of each period are only its costume and do not invigorate men. The harm of the improved machinery may compensate its good. Hudson and Behring accomplished so much in their fishing-boats as to astonish Parry and Franklin, whose equipment exhausted the resources of science and art. Galileo, with an opera-glass, discovered a more splendid series of celestial phenom-

ena than any one since. Columbus found the New
World in an undecked boat. It is curious to see
the periodical disuse and perishing of means and
machinery which were introduced with loud lauda-
tion a few years or centuries before. The great
genius returns to essential man. We reckoned the
improvements of the art of war among the tri
umphs of science, and yet Napoleon conquered
Europe by the bivouac, which consisted of falling
back on naked valor and disencumbering it of all
aids. The Emperor held it impossible to make a
perfect army, says Las Cases, " without abolishing
our arms, magazines, commissaries and carriages,
until, in imitation of the Roman custom, the soldier
should receive his supply of corn, grind it in his
hand-mill and bake his bread himself."

Society is a wave. The wave moves onward,
but the water of which it is composed does not.
The same particle does not rise from the valley to
the ridge. Its unity is only phenomenal. The
persons who make up a nation to-day, next yeai
die, and their experience dies with them.

And so the reliance on Property, including the
reliance on governments which protect it, is the
want of self-reliance. Men have looked away from
themselves and at things so long that they have
come to esteem the religious, learned and civil institutions as guards of property, and they depr

cate assaults on these, because they feel them to be
assaults on property. They measure their esteem of each other by what each has, and not by
what each is. But a cultivated man becomes
ashamed of his property, out of new respect for his
nature. Especially he hates what he has if he see
that it is accidental,— came to him by inheritance,
or gift, or crime ; then he feels that it is not having;
it does not belong to him, has no root in him and
merely lies there because no revolution or no robber
takes it away. But that which a man is, does always by necessity acquire ; and what the man acquires, is living property, which does not wait the
beck of rulers, or mobs, or revolutions, or fire, or
storm, or bankruptcies, but perpetually renews itself
wherever the man breathes. " Thy lot or portion
of life," said the Caliph Ali, " is seeking after thee ;
therefore be at rest from seeking after it." Our
dependence on these foreign goods leads us to our
slavish respect for numbers. The political parties
meet in numerous conventions ; the greater the con-
course and with each new uproar of announcement,
The delegation from Essex ! The Democrats from
New Hampshire ! The Whigs of Maine ! the young
patriot feels himself stronger than before by a new
thousand of eyes and arms. In like manner the reformers summon conventions and vote and resolve
in multitude. Not so O friends ! will the God

deign to enter and inhabit you, but by a method precisely the reverse. It is only as a man puts off all foreign support and stands alone that I see him to be strong and to prevail. He is weaker by every recruit to his banner. Is not a man better than a town? Ask nothing of men, and, in the endless mutation, thou only firm column must presently appear the upholder of all that surrounds thee. He who knows that power is inborn, that he is weak because he has looked for good out of him and elsewhere, and, so perceiving, throws himself unhesitatingly on his thought, instantly rights himself, stands in the erect position, commands his limbs, works miracles; just as a man who stands on his feet is stronger than a man who stands on his head.

So use all that is called Fortune. Most men gamble with her, and gain all, and lose all, as her wheel rolls. But do thou leave as unlawful these winnings, and deal with Cause and Effect, the chancellors of God. In the Will work and acquire, and thou hast chained the wheel of Chance, and shalt sit hereafter out of fear from her rotations. A political victory, a rise of rents, the recovery of your sick or the return of your absent friend, or some other favorable event raises your spirits, and you think good days are preparing for you. Do not believe it. Nothing can bring you peace but yourself. Nothing can bring you peace but the triumph of principles.

COMPENSATION.

—◆—

THE wings of Time are black and white,
Pied with morning and with night.
Mountain tall and ocean deep
Trembling balance duly keep.
In changing moon, in tidal wave,
Glows the feud of Want and Have.
Gauge of more and less through space
Electric star and pencil plays.
The lonely Earth amid the balls
That hurry through the eternal halls,
A makeweight flying to the void,
Supplemental asteroid,
Or compensatory spark,
Shoots across the neutral Dark.

Man's the elm, and Wealth the vine,
Stanch and strong the tendrils twine:
Though the frail ringlets thee deceive.
None from its stock that vine can reave
Fear not, then, thou child infirm,
There's no god dare wrong a worm.
Laurel crowns cleave to deserts
And power to him who power exerts;
Hast not thy share?   On winged feet,
Lo! it rushes thee to meet;
And all that Nature made thy own,
Floating in air or pent in stone,
Will rive the hills and swim the sea
And, like thy shadow, follow thee.

III.

COMPENSATION.

EVER since I was a boy I have wished to write a discourse on Compensation; for it seemed to me when very young that on this subject life was ahead of theology and the people knew more than the preachers taught. The documents too from which the doctrine is to be drawn, charmed my fancy by their endless variety, and lay always before me, even in sleep; for they are the tools in our hands, the bread in our basket, the transactions of the street, the farm and the dwelling-house ; greetings, relations, debts and credits, the influence of character, the nature and endowment of all men. It seemed to me also that in it might be shown men a ray of divinity, the present action of the soul of this world, clean from all vestige of tradition ; and so the heart of man might be bathed by an inundation of eternal love, conversing with that which he knows was always and always must be, because it really is now. It appeared moreover that if this doctrine could be stated in terms with any resemblance to those bright intuitions in which this truth is sometimes revealed to us, it would be a star in many dark hours and crooked passages in our journey, that would not suffer us to lose our way.

I was lately confirmed in these desires by hearing a sermon at church. The preacher, a man esteemed for his orthodoxy, unfolded in the ordinary manner the doctrine of the Last Judgment. He assumed that judgment is not executed in this world; that the wicked are successful; that the good are miserable; and then urged from reason and from Scripture a compensation to be made to both parties in the next life. No offence appeared to be taken by the congregation at this doctrine. As far as I could observe when the meeting broke up they separated without remark on the sermon.

Yet what was the import of this teaching? What did the preacher mean by saying that the good are miserable in the present life? Was it that houses and lands, offices, wine, horses, dress, luxury, are had by unprincipled men, whilst the saints are poor and despised; and that a compensation is to be made to these last hereafter, by giving them the like gratifications another day, — bank-stock and doubloons, venison and champagne? This must be the compensation intended; for what else? Is it that they are to have leave to pray and praise? to love and serve men? Why, that they can do now. The

legitimate inference the disciple would draw was, —
' We are to have *such* a good time as the sinners
have now ' ; — or, to push it to its extreme import,
— ' You sin now, we shall sin by and by ; we would
sin now, if we could ; not being successful we ex
pect our revenge to-morrow.'

The fallacy lay in the immense concession that
the bad are successful ; that justice is not done now.
The blindness of the preacher consisted in deferring to the base estimate of the market of what constitutes a manly success, instead of confronting and
convicting the world from the truth ; announcing
the presence of the soul ; the omnipotence of the
will ; and so establishing the standard of good and
ill, of success and falsehood.

I find a similar base tone in the popular religious
works of the day and the same doctrines assumed
by the literary men when occasionally they treat the
related topics. I think that our popular theology
has gained in decorum, and not in principle, over
the superstitions it has displaced. But men are
better than their theology. Their daily life gives
it the lie. Every ingenuous and aspiring soul leaves
the doctrine behind him in his own experience, and
all men feel sometimes the falsehood which they
cannot demonstrate. For men are wiser than they
know. That which they hear in schools and pulpits
without afterthought, if said in conversation would

probably be questioned in silence. If a man dog-
matize in a mixed company on Providence and the
divine laws, he is answered by a silence which conveys well enough to an observer the dissatisfaction
of the hearer, but his incapacity to make his own
statement.

I shall attempt in this and the following chapter
to record some facts that indicate the path of the
law of Compensation ; happy beyond my expectation if I shall truly draw the smallest arc of this
circle.

POLARITY, or action and reaction, we meet in
every part of nature ; in darkness and light ; in
heat and cold ; in the ebb and flow of waters ; in
male and female ; in the inspiration and expiration
of plants and animals ; in the equation of quantity
and quality in the fluids of the animal body ; in the
systole and diastole of the heart ; in the undulations
of fluids and of sound ; in the centrifugal and centripetal gravity ; in electricity, galvanism, and chemical affinity. Superinduce magnetism at one end
of a needle, the opposite magnetism takes place at
the other end. If the south attracts, the north repels. To empty here, you must condense there.
An inevitable dualism bisects nature, so that each
thing is a half, and suggests another thing to make
it whole ; as, spirit, matter ; man, woman ; odd,

even; subjective, objective; in, out; upper, under, motion, rest ; yea, nay.

Whilst the world is thus dual, so is every one of its parts. The entire system of things gets represented in every particle. There is somewhat that resembles the ebb and flow of the sea, day and night, man and woman, in a single needle of the pine, in a kernel of corn, in each individual of every animal tribe. The reaction, so grand in the elements, is repeated within these small boundaries. For example, in the animal kingdom the physiologist has observed that no creatures are favorites, but a certain compensation balances every gift and every defect. A surplusage given to one part is paid out of a reduction from another part of the same creature. If the head and neck are enlarged, the trunk and extremities are cut short.

The theory of the mechanic forces is another example. What we gain in power is lost in time, and the converse. The periodic or compensating errors of the planets is another instance. The influences of climate and soil in political history is another. The cold climate invigorates. The barren soil does not breed fevers, crocodiles, tigers or scorpions.

The same dualism underlies the nature and condition of man. Every excess causes a defect; every defect an excess. Every sweet hath its sour ; every evil its good. Every faculty which is a receiver of pleasure has an equal penalty put on its abuse. It is to answer for its moderation with its life. For every grain of wit there is a grain of folly. For every thing you have missed, you have gained something else; and for every thing you gain, you lose something. If riches increase, they are increased that use them. If the gatherer gathers too much, Nature takes out of the man what she puts into his chest; swells the estate, but kills the owner. Nature hates monopolies and exceptions. The waves of the sea do not more speedily seek a level from their loftiest tossing than the varieties of condition tend to equalize themselves. There is always some levelling circumstance that puts down the overbearing, the strong, the rich, the fortunate, substantially on the same ground with all others. Is a man too strong and fierce for society and by temper and position a bad citizen, — a morose ruffian, with a dash of the pirate in him? — Nature sends him a troop of pretty sons and daughters who are getting along in the dame's classes at the village school, and love and fear for them smooths his grim scowl to courtesy. Thus she contrives to intenerate the granite and felspar, takes the boar out and puts the lamb in and keeps her balance true.

The farmer imagines power and place are fine things. But the President has paid dear for his White House. It has commonly cost him all his peace, and the best of his manly attributes. To preserve for a short time so conspicuous an appearance before the world, he is content to eat dust before the real masters who stand erect behind the throne. Or do men desire the more substantial and permanent grandeur of genius? Neither has this an immunity. He who by force of will or of thought is great and overlooks thousands, has the charges of that eminence. With every influx of light comes new danger. Has he light? he must bear witness to the light, and always outrun that sympathy which gives him such keen satisfaction, by his fidelity to new revelations of the incessant soul. He must hate father and mother, wife and child. Has he all that the world loves and admires and covets? — he must cast behind him their admiration, and afflict them bv faithfulness to his truth, and become a byword and a hissing.

This law writes the laws of cities and nations. It is in vain to build or plot or combine against it.. Things refuse to be mismanaged long. *Res nolunt diu male administrari.* Though no checks to a new evil appear, the checks exist, and will appear. If the government is cruel, the governor's life is not safe. If you tax too high, the revenue will yield nothing. If you make the criminal code sanguinary, juries will not convict. If the law is too mild, private vengeance comes in. If the government is a terrific democracy, the pressure is resisted by an over-charge of energy in the citizen, and life glows with a fiercer flame. The true life and satisfactions of man seem to elude the utmost rigors or felicities of condition and to establish themselves with great indifferency under all varieties of circumstances. Under all governments the influence of character remains the same, — in Turkey and in New England about alike. Under the primeval despots of Egypt, history honestly confesses that man must have been as free as culture could make him.

These appearances indicate the fact that the universe is represented in every one of its particles. Every thing in nature contains all the powers of nature. Every thing is made of one hidden stuff; as the naturalist sees one type under every metamorphosis, and regards a horse as a running man, a fish as a swimming man, a bird as a flying man, a tree as a rooted man. Each new form repeats not only the main character of the type, but part for part all the details, all the aims, furtherances, hindrances, energies and whole system of every other. Every occupation, trade, art, transaction, is a compend of the world and a correlative of every other. Each one is an entire emblem of human life; of its good and ill, its trials, its enemies, its course and its end. And each one must somehow accommodate the whole man and recite all his destiny.

The world globes itself in a drop of dew. The microscope cannot find the animalcule which is less perfect for being little. Eyes, ears, taste, smell, motion, resistance, appetite, and organs of repro- duction that take hold on eternity, — all find room to consist in the small creature. So do we put our life into every act. The true doctrine of omnipres- ence is that God reappears with all his parts in every moss and cobweb. The value of the universe contrives to throw itself into every point. If the good is there, so is the evil; if the affinity, so the repulsion; if the force, so the limitation.

Thus is the universe alive. All things are moral. That soul which within us is a sentiment, outside of us is a law. We feel its inspiration; out there in history we can see its fatal strength. " It is in the world, and the world was made by it." Justice is not postponed. A perfect equity adjusts its bal- ance in all parts of life. Οἱ κύβοι Διὸς ἀεὶ εὐπίπτουσι, — The dice of God are always loaded. The world looks like a multiplication-table, or a mathematical equation, which, turn it how you will, balances itself. Take what figure you will, its exact value, nor more nor less, still returns to you. Every secret is told, every crime is punished, every virtue rewarded, every wrong redressed, in silence and certainty. What we call retribution is the universal necessity by which the whole appears wherever a part ap pears. If you see smoke, there must be fire. If you see a hand or a limb, you know that the trunk to which it belongs is there behind.

Every act rewards itself, or in other words integrates itself, in a twofold manner; first in the thing, or in real nature ; and secondly in the circumstance, or in apparent nature. Men call the circumstance the retribution. The causal retribution is in the thing and is seen by the soul. The retribution in the circumstance is seen by the understanding ; it is inseparable from the thing, but is often spread over a long time and so does not become distinct until after many years. The specific stripes may follow late after the offence, but they follow because they accompany it. Crime and punishment grow out of one stem. Punishment is a fruit that unsuspected ripens within the flower of the pleasure which concealed it. Cause and effect, means and ends, seed and fruit, cannot be severed ; for the effect already blooms in the cause, the end preëxists in the means, the fruit in the seed.

Whilst thus the world will be whole and refuses to be disparted, we seek to act partially, to sunder, to appropriate ; for example,— to gratify the senses we sever the pleasure of the senses from the needs of the character. The ingenuity of man has always been dedicated to the solution of one problem, — how to detach the sensual sweet, the sensual strong, the sensual bright, etc., from the moral sweet, the moral deep, the moral fair; that is, again, to contrive to cut clean off this upper surface so thin as to leave it bottomless; to get a *one end*, without an *other end*. The soul says, ' Eat ;' the body would feast. The soul says, ' The man and woman shall be one flesh and one soul ;' the body would join the flesh only. The soul says, ' Have dominion over all things to the ends of virtue;' the body would have the power over things to its own ends.

The soul strives amain to live and work through all things. It would be the only fact. All things shall be added unto it, — power, pleasure, knowledge, beauty. The particular man aims to be somebody; to set up for himself; to truck and higgle for a private good; and, in particulars, to ride that he may ride ; to dress that he may be dressed; to eat that he may eat; and to govern, that he may be seen. Men seek to be great; they would have offices, wealth, power and fame. They think that to be great is to possess one side of nature, — the sweet, without the other side, the bitter.

This dividing and detaching is steadily counteracted. Up to this day it must be owned no projector has had the smallest success. The parted water reunites behind our hand. Pleasure is taken out of pleasant things, profit out of profitable things, power out of strong things, as soon as we seek to separate them from the whole. We can no more halve things and get the sensual good, by itself, than we can get an inside that shall have no outside, or a light without a shadow. " Drive out Nature with a fork, she comes running back."

Life invests itself with inevitable conditions, which the unwise seek to dodge, which one and another brags that he does not know, that they do not touch him ; — but the brag is on his lips, the conditions are in his soul. If he escapes them in one part they attack him in another more vital part. If he has escaped them in form and in the appearance, it is because he has resisted his life and fled from himself, and the retribution is so much death. So signal is the failure of all attempts to make this separation of the good from the tax, that the experiment would not be tried, — since to try it is to be mad, — but for the circumstance that when the disease began in the will, of rebellion and separation, the intellect is at once infected, so that the man ceases to see God whole in each object, but is able to see the sensual allurement of an object and not see the sensual hurt, he sees the mermaid's head but not the dragon's tail, and thinks he can cut off that which he would have from that which he would not have. " How secret art thou who dwellest in the highest heavens in silence, O thou only great God, sprinkling with an unwearied providence cer tain penal blindnesses upon such as have unbridled desires ! " [1]

The human soul is true to these facts in the painting of fable, of history, of law, of proverbs, of conversation. It finds a tongue in literature unawares. Thus the Greeks called Jupiter, Supreme Mind ; but having traditionally ascribed to him many base actions, they involuntarily made amends to reason by tying up the hands of so bad a god. He is made as helpless as a king of England. Prometheus knows one secret which Jove must bargain for; Minerva, another. He cannot get his own thunders ; Minerva keeps the key of them : —

> " Of all the gods, I only know the keys
> That ope the solid doors within whose vaults
> His thunders sleep."

A plain confession of the in-working of the All and of its moral aim. The Indian mythology ends in the same ethics ; and it would seem impossible for any fable to be invented and get any currency which was not moral. Aurora forgot to ask youth for her lover, and though Tithonus is immortal, he is old. Achilles is not quite invulnerable ; the sacred waters did not wash the heel by which Thetis held him. Siegfried, in the Nibelungen, is not quite immortal, for a leaf fell on his back whilst he was bathing in the dragon's blood, and that spot which

[1] St. Augustine. Confessions. B. I.

it covered is mortal. And so it must be. There is a crack in every thing God has made. It would seem there is always this vindictive circumstance stealing in at unawares even into the wild poesy in which the human fancy attempted to make bold holiday and to shake itself free of the old laws, — this back-stroke, this kick of the gun, certifying that the law is fatal; that in nature nothing can be given, all things are sold.

This is that ancient doctrine of Nemesis, who keeps watch in the universe and lets no offence go unchastised. The Furies they said are attendants on justice, and if the sun in heaven should transgress his path they would punish him. The poets related that stone walls and iron swords and leathern thongs had an occult sympathy with the wrongs of their owners; that the belt which Ajax gave Hector dragged the Trojan hero over the field at the wheels of the car of Achilles, and the sword which Hector gave Ajax was that on whose point Ajax fell. They recorded that when the Thasians erected a statue to Theagenes, a victor in the games, one of his rivals went to it by night and endeavored to throw it down by repeated blows, until at last he moved it from its pedestal and was crushed to death beneath its fall.

This voice of fable has in it somewhat divine. It came from thought above the will of the writer

That is the best part of each writer which has nothing private in it ; that which he does not know ;
that which flowed out of his constitution and not
from his too active invention ; that which in the
study of a single artist you might not easily find,
but in the study of many you would abstract as the
spirit of them all. Phidias it is not, but the work
of man in that early Hellenic world that I would
know. The name and circumstance of Phidias,
however convenient for history, embarrass when we
come to the highest criticism. We are to see that
which man was tending to do in a given period, and
was hindered, or, if you will, modified in doing, by
the interfering volitions of Phidias, of Dante, of
Shakspeare, the organ whereby man at the moment
wrought.

Still more striking is the expression of this fact
in the proverbs of all nations, which are always the
literature of reason, or the statements of an absolute truth without qualification. Proverbs, like
the sacred books of each nation, are the sanctuary
of the intuitions. That which the droning world,
chained to appearances, will not allow the realist
to say in his own words, it will suffer him to say in
proverbs without contradiction. And this law of
laws, which the pulpit, the senate and the college
deny, is hourly preached in all markets and work-
shops by flights of proverbs, whose teaching is as
true and as omnipresent as that of birds and flies.

All things are double, one against another. —
Tit for tat; an eye for an eye; a tooth for a tooth;
blood for blood; measure for measure; love for
love. — Give, and it shall be given you. — He that
watereth shall be watered himself. — What will
you have? quoth God; pay for it and take it. —
Nothing venture, nothing have. — Thou shalt be
paid exactly for what thou hast done, no more, no
less. — Who doth not work shall not eat. — Harm
watch, harm catch. — Curses always recoil on the
head of him who imprecates them. — If you put a
chain around the neck of a slave, the other end fastens itself around your own. — Bad counsel confounds the adviser. — The Devil is an ass.

It is thus written, because it is thus in life. Our
action is overmastered and characterized above our
will by the law of nature. We aim at a petty end
quite aside from the public good, but our act arranges itself by irresistible magnetism in a line
with the poles of the world.

A man cannot speak but he judges himself.
With his will or against his will he draws his portrait to the eye of his companions by every word.
Every opinion reacts on him who utters it. It is a
thread-ball thrown at a mark, but the other end
remains in the thrower's bag. Or rather it is a
harpoon hurled at the whale, unwinding, as it flies,
a coil of cord in the boat, and, if the harpoon is

not good, or not well thrown, it will go nigh to cut the steersman in twain or to sink the boat.

You cannot do wrong without suffering wrong. "No man had ever a point of pride that was not injurious to him," said Burke. The exclusive in fashionable life does not see that he excludes him self from enjoyment, in the attempt to appropriate it. The exclusionist in religion does not see that he shuts the door of heaven on himself, in striving to shut out others. Treat men as pawns and nine-pins and you shall suffer as well as they. If you leave out their heart, you shall lose your own. The senses would make things of all persons; of women, of children, of the poor. The vulgar proverb, "1 will get it from his purse or get it from his skin," is sound philosophy.

All infractions of love and equity in our social relations are speedily punished. They are pun-ished by fear. Whilst I stand in simple relations to my fellow-man, I have no displeasure in meet-ing him. We meet as water meets water, or as two currents of air mix, with perfect diffusion and interpenetration of nature. But as soon as there is any departure from simplicity and attempt at halfness, or good for me that is not good for him, my neighbor feels the wrong; he shrinks from me as far as I have shrunk from him; his eyes no longer seek mine; there is war between us; there is hate in him and fear in me.

All the old abuses in society, universal and particular, all unjust accumulations of property and power, are avenged in the same manner. Fear is an instructor of great sagacity and the herald of all revolutions. One thing he teaches, that there is rottenness where he appears. He is a carrion crow, and though you see not well what he hovers for, there is death somewhere. Our property is timid, our laws are timid, our cultivated classes are timid. Fear for ages has boded and mowed and gibbered over government and property. That obscene bird is not there for nothing. He indicates great wrongs which must be revised.

Of the like nature is that expectation of change which instantly follows the suspension of our voluntary activity. The terror of cloudless noon, the emerald of Polycrates, the awe of prosperity, the instinct which leads every generous soul to impose on itself tasks of a noble asceticism and vicarious virtue, are the tremblings of the balance of justice through the heart and mind of man.

Experienced men of the world know very well that it is best to pay scot and lot as they go along, and that a man often pays dear for a small frugality. The borrower runs in his own debt. Has a man gained any thing who has received a hundred favors and rendered none? Has he gained by borrowing, through indolence or cunning, his neigh-

bor's wares, or horses, or money ? There arises on
the deed the instant acknowledgment of benefit on
the one part and of debt on the other ; that is, of superiority and inferiority. The transaction remains
in the memory of himself and his neighbor; and
every new transaction alters according to its nature
their relation to each other. He may soon come
to see that he had better have broken his own bones
than to have ridden in his neighbor's coach, and
that "the highest price he can pay for a thing is to
ask for it."

A wise man will extend this lesson to all parts of
life, and know that it is the part of prudence to
face every claimant and pay every just demand on
your time, your talents, or your heart. Always
pay; for first or last you must pay your entire debt.
Persons and events may stand for a time between
you and justice, but it is only a postponement. You
must pay at last your own debt. If you are wise
you will dread a prosperity which only loads you
with more. Benefit is the end of nature. But for
every benefit which you receive, a tax is levied.
He is great who confers the most benefits. He is
base, — and that is the one base thing in the universe, — to receive favors and render none. In the
order of nature we cannot render benefits to those
from whom we receive them, or only seldom. But
the benefit we receive must be rendered again, line

for line, deed for deed, cent for cent, to somebody.
Beware of too much good staying in your hand. It
will fast corrupt and worm worms. Pay it away
quickly in some sort.

Labor is watched over by the same pitiless laws.
Cheapest, say the prudent, is the dearest labor.
What we buy in a broom, a mat, a wagon, a knife,
is some application of good sense to a common
want. It is best to pay in your land a skilful gardener, or to buy good sense applied to gardening;
in your sailor, good sense applied to navigation; in
the house, good sense applied to cooking, sewing,
serving; in your agent, good sense applied to accounts and affairs. So do you multiply your presence, or spread yourself throughout your estate.
But because of the dual constitution of things, in
labor as in life there can be no cheating. The thief
steals from himself. The swindler swindles himself. For the real price of labor is knowledge and
virtue, whereof wealth and credit are signs. These
signs, like paper money, may be counterfeited or
stolen, but that which they represent, namely, knowledge and virtue, cannot be counterfeited or stolen.
These ends of labor cannot be answered but by real
exertions of the mind, and in obedience to pure motives. The cheat, the defaulter, the gambler, cannot extort the knowledge of material and moral nature which his honest care and pains yield to the

operative. The law of nature is, Do the thing, and you shall have the power; but they who do not the thing have not the power.

Human labor, through all its forms, from the sharpening of a stake to the construction of a city or an epic, is one immense illustration of the perfect compensation of the universe. The absolute balance of Give and Take, the doctrine that every thing has its price, — and if that price is not paid, not that thing but something else is obtained, and that it is impossible to get any thing without its price, — is not less sublime in the columns of a leger than in the budgets of states, in the laws of light and darkness, in all the action and reaction of nature. I cannot doubt that the high laws which each man sees implicated in those processes with which he is conversant, the stern ethics which sparkle on his chisel-edge, which are measured out by his plumb and foot-rule, which stand as manifest in the footing of the shop-bill as in the history of a state, — do recommend to him his trade, and though seldom named, exalt his business to his imagination.

The league between virtue and nature engages all things to assume a hostile front to vice. The beautiful laws and substances of the world persecute and whip the traitor. He finds that things are arranged for truth and benefit, but there is no den in the wide world to hide a rogue. Commit a crime, and the earth is made of glass. Commit a crime, and it seems as if a coat of snow fell on the ground, such as reveals in the woods the track of every partridge and fox and squirrel and mole. You cannot recall the spoken word, you cannot wipe out the foot-track, you cannot draw up the ladder, so as to leave no inlet or clew. Some damning circumstance always transpires. The laws and substances of nature, — water, snow, wind, gravitation, — become penalties to the thief.

On the other hand the law holds with equal sureness for all right action. Love, and you shall be loved. All love is mathematically just, as much as the two sides of an algebraic equation. The good man has absolute good, which like fire turns every thing to its own nature, so that you cannot do him any harm; but as the royal armies sent against Napoleon, when he approached cast down their colors and from enemies became friends, so disasters of all kinds, as sickness, offence, poverty, prove benefactors: —

> "Winds blow and waters roll
> Strength to the brave and power and deity,
> Yet in themselves are nothing."

The good are befriended even by weakness and defect. As no man had ever a point of pride that was not injurious to him, so no man had ever a defect that was not somewhere made useful to him. The stag in the fable admired his horns and blamed his feet, but when the hunter came, his feet saved him, and afterwards, caught in the thicket, his horns destroyed him. Every man in his lifetime needs to thank his faults. As no man thoroughly understands a truth until he has contended against it, so no man has a thorough acquaintance with the hindrances or talents of men until he has suffered from the one and seen the triumph of the other over his own want of the same. Has he a defect of temper that unfits him to live in society ? Thereby he is driven to entertain himself alone and acquire habits of self-help; and thus, like the wounded oyster, he mends his shell with pearl.

Our strength grows out of our weakness. The indignation which arms itself with secret forces does not awaken until we are pricked and stung and sorely assailed. A great man is always willing to be little. Whilst he sits on the cushion of advantages, he goes to sleep. When he is pushed, tormented, defeated, he has a chance to learn something; he has been put on his wits, on his manhood; he has gained facts; learns his ignorance; is cured of the insanity of conceit; has got moderation and real skill. The wise man throws himself on the side of his assailants. It is more his interest than it is theirs to find his weak point. The wound cicatrizes and falls off from him like a dead skin and when they would triumph, lo ! he has passed on invulnerable. Blame is safer than praise. I hate to be defended in a newspaper. As long as all that is said is said against me, I feel a certain assurance of success. But as soon as honeyed words of praise are spoken for me I feel as one that lies unprotected before his enemies. In general, every evil to which we do not succumb is a benefactor. As the Sandwich Islander believes that the strength and valor of the enemy he kills passes into himself, so we gain the strength of the temptation we resist.

The same guards which protect us from disaster, defect and enmity, defend us, if we will, from selfishness and fraud. Bolts and bars are not the best of our institutions, nor is shrewdness in trade a mark of wisdom. Men suffer all their life long under the foolish superstition that they can be cheated. But it is as impossible for a man to be cheated by any one but himself, as for a thing to be and not to be at the same time. There is a third silent party to all our bargains. The nature and soul of things takes on itself the guaranty of the fulfilment of every contract, so that honest service cannot come to loss. If you serve an ungrateful master, serve him the more. Put God in your debt. Every stroke shall be repaid. The longer the payment is withholden, the better for you; for compound interest on compound interest is the rate and usage of this exchequer.

The history of persecution is a history of endeavors to cheat nature, to make water run up hill, to twist a rope of sand. It makes no difference whether the actors be many or one, a tyrant or a mob. A mob is a society of bodies voluntarily bereaving themselves of reason and traversing its work. The mob is man voluntarily descending to the nature of the beast. Its fit hour of activity is night. Its actions are insane, like its whole constitution. It persecutes a principle; it would whip a right; it would tar and feather justice, by inflicting fire and outrage upon the houses and persons of those who have these. It resembles the prank of boys, who run with fire-engines to put out the ruddy aurora streaming to the stars. The inviolate spirit turns their spite against the wrongdoers. The martyr cannot be dishonored. Every lash inflicted is a tongue of fame; every prison a more illustrious abode; every burned book or house enlightens the world; every suppressed or expunged word reverberates through the earth from side to side. Hours of sanity and consideration are always arriving to communities, as to individuals, when the truth is seen and the martyrs are justified.

Thus do all things preach the indifferency of cir
cumstances. The man is all. Every thing has two
sides, a good and an evil. Every advantage has
its tax. I learn to be content. But the doctrine
of compensation is not the doctrine of indifferency.
The thoughtless say, on hearing these representa-
tions, — What boots it to do well? there is one
event to good and evil; if I gain any good I must
pay for it; if I lose any good I gain some other;
all actions are indifferent.

There is a deeper fact in the soul than compensation, to wit, its own nature. The soul is not a compensation, but a life. The soul *is*. Under all this
running sea of circumstance, whose waters ebb and
flow with perfect balance, lies the aboriginal abyss
of real Being. Essence, or God, is not a relation
or a part, but the whole. Being is the vast affirmative, excluding negation, self-balanced, and swal-
lowing up all relations, parts and times within
itself. Nature, truth, virtue, are the influx from
thence. Vice is the absence or departure of the
same. Nothing, Falsehood, may indeed stand as
the great Night or shade on which as a background
the living universe paints itself forth, but no fact
is begotten by it; it cannot work, for it is not.
It cannot work any good; it cannot work any
harm. It is harm inasmuch as it is worse not to
be than to be.

We feel defrauded of the retribution due to evil acts, because the criminal adheres to his vice and contumacy and does not come to a crisis or judgment anywhere in visible nature. There is no stunning confutation of his nonsense before men and angels. Has he therefore outwitted the law ? Inasmuch as he carries the malignity and the lie with him he so far deceases from nature. In some manner there will be a demonstration of the wrong to the understanding also; but, should we not see it, this deadly deduction makes square the eternal account.

Neither can it be said, on the other hand, that the gain of rectitude must be bought by any loss. There is no penalty to virtue ; no penalty to wisdom ; they are proper additions of being. In a virtuous action I properly *am ;* in a virtuous act I add to the world ; I plant into deserts conquered from Chaos and Nothing and see the darkness receding on the limits of the horizon. There can be no excess to love, none to knowledge, none to beauty, when these attributes are considered in the purest sense. The soul refuses limits, and always affirms an Optimism, never a Pessimism.

His life is a progress, and not a station. His instinct is trust. Our instinct uses "more" and "less" in application to man, of the *presence of the soul,* and not of its absence ; the brave man is greater than the coward ; the true, the benevolent, the wise, is more a man and not less, than the fool and knave.   There is no tax on the good of virtue, for that is the incoming of God himself, or absolute existence, without any comparative.   Material good has its tax, and if it came without desert or sweat, has no root in me, and the next wind will blow it away.   But all the good of nature is the soul's, and may be had if paid for in nature's lawful coin, that is, by labor which the heart and the head allow.   I no longer wish to meet a good I do not earn, for example to find a pot of buried gold, knowing that it brings with it new burdens.   I do not wish more external goods, — neither possessions, nor honors, nor powers, nor persons.   The gain is apparent ; the tax is certain.   But there is no tax on the knowledge that the compensation exists and that it is not desirable to dig up treasure. Herein I rejoice with a serene eternal peace.   I contract the boundaries of possible mischief.   I learn the wisdom of St. Bernard, — " Nothing can work me damage except myself ; the harm that I sustain I carry about with me, and never am a real sufferer but by my own fault."

In the nature of the soul is the compensation for the inequalities of condition.   The radical tragedy of nature seems to be the distinction of More and Less.   How can Less not feel the pain ; how not

feel indignation or malevolence towards More ?
Look at those who have less faculty, and one feels
sad and knows not well what to make of it. He
almost shuns their eye; he fears they will upbraid
God. What should they do? It seems a great in
justice. But see the facts nearly and these moun-
tainous inequalities vanish. Love reduces them as
the sun melts the iceberg in the sea. The heart
and soul of all men being one, this bitterness of
His and *Mine* ceases. His is mine. I am my
brother and my brother is me. If I feel overshad-
owed and outdone by great neighbors, I can yet
love; I can still receive; and he that loveth maketh
his own the grandeur he loves. Thereby I make
the discovery that my brother is my guardian, acting for me with the friendliest designs, and the
estate I so admired and envied is my own. It is
the nature of the soul to appropriate all things.
Jesus and Shakspeare are fragments of the soul,
and by love I conquer and incorporate them in my
own conscious domain. His virtue, — is not that
mine ? His wit, — if it cannot be made mine, it is
not wit.

Such also is the natural history of calamity.
The changes which break up at short intervals the
prosperity of men are advertisements of a nature
whose law is growth. Every soul is by this intrinsic necessity quitting its whole system of things, its

friends and home and laws and faith, as the shell-
fish crawls out of its beautiful but stony case, because it no longer admits of its growth, and slowly
forms a new house. In proportion to the vigor of
the individual these revolutions are frequent, until
in some happier mind they are incessant and all
worldly relations hang very loosely about him, becoming as it were a transparent fluid membrane
through which the living form is seen, and not, as
in most men, an indurated heterogeneous fabric of
many dates and of no settled character, in which
the man is imprisoned. Then there can be enlarge-
ment, and the man of to-day scarcely recognizes
the man of yesterday. And such should be the
outward biography of man in time, a putting off of
dead circumstances day by day, as he renews his
raiment day by day. But to us, in our lapsed estate, resting, not advancing, resisting, not coöperat-
ing with the divine expansion, this growth comes
by shocks.

We cannot part with our friends. We cannot
let our angels go. We do not see that they only
go out that archangels may come in. We are idol-
aters of the old. We do not believe in the riches
of the soul, in its proper eternity and omnipresence.
We do not believe there is any force in to-day to
rival or recreate that beautiful yesterday. We linger in the ruins of the old tent where once we had

bread and shelter and organs, nor believe that the
spirit can feed, cover, and nerve us again. We
cannot again find aught so dear, so sweet, so graceful. But we sit and weep in vain. The voice of
the Almighty saith, ' Up and onward for evermore! ' We cannot stay amid the ruins. Neither
will we rely on the new; and so we walk ever with
reverted eyes, like those monsters who look back-
wards.

And yet the compensations of calamity are made
apparent to the understanding also, after long intervals of time. A fever, a mutilation, a cruel disappointment, a loss of wealth, a loss of friends, seems
at the moment unpaid loss, and unpayable. But
the sure years reveal the deep remedial force that
underlies all facts. The death of a dear friend,
wife, brother, lover, which seemed nothing but pri-
vation, somewhat later assumes the aspect of a
guide or genius; for it commonly operates revolutions in our way of life, terminates an epoch of infancy or of youth which was waiting to be closed,
breaks up a wonted occupation, or a household, or
style of living, and allows the formation of new
ones more friendly to the growth of character. It
permits or constrains the formation of new acquaintances and the reception of new influences
that prove of the first importance to the next years;
and the man or woman who would have remained

a sunny garden-flower, with no room for its roots and too much sunshine for its head, by the falling of the walls and the neglect of the gardener is made the banian of the forest, yielding shade and fruit to wide neighborhoods of men

SPIRITUAL LAWS.

—◆—

THE living Heaven thy prayers respect,
House at once and architect,
Quarrying man's rejected hours,
Builds there with eternal towers;
Sole and self-commanded works,
Fears not undermining days,
Grows by decays,
And, by the famous might that lurks
In reaction and recoil,
Makes flame to freeze and ice to boil;
Forging, through swart arms of Offence
The silver seat of Innocence.

IV

SPIRITUAL LAWS.

———◆———

WHEN the act of reflection takes place in the mind, when we look at ourselves in the light of thought, we discover that our life is embosomed in beauty. Behind us, as we go, all things assume pleasing forms, as clouds do far off. Not only things familiar and stale, but even the tragic and terrible are comely as they take their place in the pictures of memory. The river-bank, the weed at the water-side, the old house, the foolish person, however neglected in the passing, have a grace in the past. Even the corpse that has lain in the chambers has added a solemn ornament to the house. The soul will not know either deformity or pain. If in the hours of clear reason we should speak the severest truth, we should say that we had never made a sacrifice. In these hours the mind seems so great that nothing can be taken from us that seems much. All loss, all pain, is particular; the universe remains to the heart unhurt. Neither

vexations nor calamities abate our trust. No man
ever stated his griefs as lightly as he might. Allow
for exaggeration in the most patient and sorely ridden hack that ever was driven. For it is only the
finite that has wrought and suffered ; the infinite
lies stretched in smiling repose.

The intellectual life may be kept clean and
healthful if man will live the life of nature and not
import into his mind difficulties which are none of
his. No man need be perplexed in his speculations.
Let him do and say what strictly belongs to him, and
though very ignorant of books, his nature shall not
yield him any intellectual obstructions and doubts.
Our young people are diseased with the theological
problems of original sin, origin of evil, predestina-
tion and the like. These never presented a practical difficulty to any man, — never darkened across
any man's road who did not go out of his way to
seek them. These are the soul's mumps and mea-
sles and whooping-coughs, and those who have not
caught them cannot describe their health or prescribe the cure. A simple mind will not know
these enemies. It is quite another thing that he
should be able to give account of his faith and ex-
pound to another the theory of his self-union and
freedom. This requires rare gifts. Yet without
this self-knowledge there may be a sylvan strength
and integrity in that which he is. "A few strong
instincts and a few plain rules" suffice us.

My will never gave the images in my mind the rank they now take. The regular course of studies, the years of academical and professional education have not yielded me better facts than some idle books under the bench at the Latin School. What we do not call education is more precious than that which we call so. We form no guess, at the time of receiving a thought, of its comparative value. And education often wastes its effort in attempts to thwart and balk this natural magnetism, which is sure to select what belongs to it.

In like manner our moral nature is vitiated by any interference of our will. People represent virtue as a struggle, and take to themselves great airs upon their attainments, and the question is everywhere vexed when a noble nature is commended, whether the man is not better who strives with temptation. But there is no merit in the matter. Either God is there or he is not there. We love characters in proportion as they are impulsive and spontaneous. The less a man thinks or knows about his virtues the better we like him. Timoleon's victories are the best victories, which ran and flowed like Homer's verses, Plutarch said. When we see a soul whose acts are all regal, graceful and pleasant as roses, we must thank God that such things can be and are, and not turn sourly on the angel and say 'Crump is a better man with his grunting resistance to all his native devils.'

Not less conspicuous is the preponderance of nature over will in all practical life. There is less intention in history than we ascribe to it. We impute
deep-laid far-sighted plans to Cæsar and Napoleon;
but the best of their power was in nature, not in
them. Men of an extraordinary success, in their
honest moments, have always sung 'Not unto us,
not unto us.' According to the faith of their times
they have built altars to Fortune, or to Destiny, or
to St. Julian. Their success lay in their parallelism
to the course of thought, which found in them an
unobstructed channel ; and the wonders of which
they were the visible conductors seemed to the eye
their deed. Did the wires generate the galvanism?
It is even true that there was less in them on which
they could reflect than in another; as the virtue of
a pipe is to be smooth and hollow. That which externally seemed will and immovableness was willingness and self-annihilation. Could Shakspeare give
a theory of Shakspeare? Could ever a man of
prodigious mathematical genius convey to others any
insight into his methods ? If he could communicate that secret it would instantly lose its exaggerated value, blending with the daylight and the vital
energy the power to stand and to go.

The lesson is forcibly taught by these observations that our life might be much easier and simpler
than we make it; that the world might be a happier

place than it is ; that there is no need of struggles,
convulsions, and despairs, of the wringing of the
hands and the gnashing of the teeth ; that we mis-
create our own evils. We interfere with the optimism of nature ; for whenever we get this vantage-
ground of the past, or of a wiser mind in the present,
we are able to discern that we are begirt with laws
which execute themselves.

The face of external nature teaches the same lesson. Nature will not have us fret and fume. She
does not like our benevolence or our learning much
better than she likes our frauds and wars. When
we come out of the caucus, or the bank, or the
Abolition-convention, or the Temperance-meeting,
or the Transcendental club into the fields and
woods, she says to us, ' So hot ? my little Sir.'

We are full of mechanical actions. We must
needs intermeddle and have things in our own way,
until the sacrifices and virtues of society are odious.
Love should make joy ; but our benevolence is unhappy. Our Sunday-schools and churches and
pauper-societies are yokes to the neck. We pain
ourselves to please nobody. There are natural
ways of arriving at the same ends at which these
aim, but do not arrive. Why should all virtue
work in one and the same way ? Why should all
give dollars ? It is very inconvenient to us country
folk, and we do not think any good will come of it.

We have not dollars, merchants have; let them
give them. Farmers will give corn; poets will
sing; women will sew; laborers will lend a hand;
the children will bring flowers. And why drag
this dead weight of a Sunday-school over the whole
Christendom? It is natural and beautiful that
childhood should inquire and maturity should
teach; but it is time enough to answer questions
when they are asked. Do not shut up the young
people against their will in a pew and force the
children to ask them questions for an hour against
their will.

If we look wider, things are all alike; laws and
letters and creeds and modes of living seem a trav-
esty of truth. Our society is encumbered by pon-
derous machinery, which resembles the endless
aqueducts which the Romans built over hill and
dale and which are superseded by the discovery of
the law that water rises to the level of its source.
It is a Chinese wall which any nimble Tartar can
leap over. It is a standing army, not so good as a
peace. It is a graduated, titled, richly appointed
empire, quite superfluous when town-meetings are
found to answer just as well.

Let us draw a lesson from nature, which always
works by short ways. When the fruit is ripe, it
falls. When the fruit is despatched, the leaf falls.
The circuit of the waters is mere falling. The

walking of man and all animals is a falling forward. All our manual labor and works of
strength, as prying, splitting, digging, rowing and
so forth, are done by dint of continual falling, and
the globe, earth, moon, comet, sun, star, fall for
ever and ever.

The simplicity of the universe is very different
from the simplicity of a machine. He who sees
moral nature out and out and thoroughly knows
how knowledge is acquired and character formed,
is a pedant. The simplicity of nature is not that
which may easily be read, but is inexhaustible.
The last analysis can no wise be made. We judge
of a man's wisdom by his hope, knowing that the
perception of the inexhaustibleness of nature is an
immortal youth. The wild fertility of nature is
felt in comparing our rigid names and reputations
with our fluid consciousness. We pass in the world
for sects and schools, for erudition and piety, and
we are all the time jejune babes. One sees very
well how Pyrrhonism grew up. Every man sees
that he is that middle point whereof every thing
may be affirmed and denied with equal reason. He
is old, he is young, he is very wise, he is altogether
ignorant. He hears and feels what you say of the
seraphim, and of the tin-peddler. There is no permanent wise man except in the figment of the
Stoics. We side with the hero, as we read or

paint, against the coward and the robber; but we
have been ourselves that coward and robber, and
shall be again, — not in the low circumstance, but
in comparison with the grandeurs possible to the
soul.

A little consideration of what takes place around
us every day would show us that a higher law than
that of our will regulates events; that our painful
labors are unnecessary and fruitless; that only in
our easy, simple, spontaneous action are we strong,
and by contenting ourselves with obedience we become divine. Belief and love, — a believing love
will relieve us of a vast load of care. O my broth-
ers, God exists. There is a soul at the centre of
nature and over the will of every man, so that
none of us can wrong the universe. It has so infused its strong enchantment into nature that we
prosper when we accept its advice, and when we
struggle to wound its creatures our hands are glued
to our sides, or they beat our own breasts. The
whole course of things goes to teach us faith. We
need only obey. There is guidance for each of
us, and by lowly listening we shall hear the right
word. Why need you choose so painfully your
place and occupation and associates and modes of
action and of entertainment? Certainly there is a
possible right for you that precludes the need of
balance and wilful election. For you there is a re-

ality, a fit place and congenial duties. Place your-self in the middle of the stream of power and wis-dom which animates all whom it floats, and you are without effort impelled to truth, to right and a per-fect contentment. Then you put all gainsayers in the wrong. Then you are the world, the meas-ure of right, of truth, of beauty. If we would not be mar-plots with our miserable interferences, the work, the society, letters, arts, science, religion of men would go on far better than now, and the heaven predicted from the beginning of the world, and still predicted from the bottom of the heart, would organize itself, as do now the rose and the air and the sun.

I say, *do not choose* ; but that is a figure of speech by which I would distinguish what is com-monly called *choice* among men, and which is a partial act, the choice of the hands, of the eyes, of the appetites, and not a whole act of the man. But that which I call right or goodness, is the choice of my constitution ; and that which I call heaven, and inwardly aspire after, is the state or circum-stance desirable to my constitution ; and the action which I in all my years tend to do, is the work for my faculties. We must hold a man amenable to reason for the choice of his daily craft or profes-sion. It is not an excuse any longer for his deeds that they are the custom of his trade. What busi-

ness has he with an evil trade ? Has he not a *call-*
ing in his character ?

Each man has his own vocation. The talent is
the call. There is one direction in which all space
is open to him. He has faculties silently inviting
him thither to endless exertion. He is like a ship
in a river ; he runs against obstructions on every
side but one, on that side all obstruction is taken
away and he sweeps serenely over a deepening
channel into an infinite sea. This talent and this
call depend on his organization, or the mode in
which the general soul incarnates itself in him.
He inclines to do something which is easy to him
and good when it is done, but which no other man
can do. He has no rival. For the more truly he
consults his own powers, the more difference will
his work exhibit from the work of any other. His
ambition is exactly proportioned to his powers.
The height of the pinnacle is determined by the
breadth of the base. Every man has this call of
the power to do somewhat unique, and no man has
any other call. The pretence that he has another
call, a summons by name and personal election and
outward " signs that mark him extraordinary and
not in the roll of common men," is fanaticism, and
betrays obtuseness to perceive that there is one
mind in all the individuals, and no respect of persons therein.

By doing his work he makes the need felt which
he can supply, and creates the taste by which he is
enjoyed. By doing his own work he unfolds himself. It is the vice of our public speaking that it
has not abandonment. Somewhere, not only every
orator but every man should let out all the length
of all the reins; should find or make a frank and
hearty expression of what force and meaning is in
him. The common experience is that the man fits
himself as well as he can to the customary details
of that work or trade he falls into, and tends it as
a dog turns a spit. Then is he a part of the machine he moves; the man is lost. Until he can
manage to communicate himself to others in his
full stature and proportion, he does not yet find his
vocation. He must find in that an outlet for his
character, so that he may justify his work to their
eyes. If the labor is mean, let him by his thinking and character make it liberal. Whatever he
knows and thinks, whatever in his apprehension is
worth doing, that let him communicate, or men
will never know and honor him aright. Foolish, whenever you take the meanness and formality
of that thing you do, instead of converting it into
the obedient spiracle of your character and aims.

We like only such actions as have already long
had the praise of men, and do not perceive that
any thing man can do may be divinely done. We

think greatness entailed or organized in some places
or duties, in certain offices or occasions, and do not
see that Paganini can extract rapture from a cat-
gut, and Eulenstein from a jews-harp, and a nimble-
fingered lad out of shreds of paper with his scissors,
and Landseer out of swine, and the hero out of the
pitiful habitation and company in which he was
hidden.   What we call obscure condition or vulgar
society is that condition and society whose poetry is
not yet written, but which you shall presently make
as enviable and renowned as any.   In our estimates
let us take a lesson from kings.   The parts of hospitality, the connection of families, the impressiveness
of death, and a thousand other things, royalty makes
its own estimate of, and a royal mind will.   To
make habitually a new estimate, — that is elevation.

What a man does, that he has.   What has he to
do with hope or fear?   In himself is his might.
Let him regard no good as solid but that which is
in his nature and which must grow out of him as
long as he exists.   The goods of fortune may come
and go like summer leaves ; let him scatter them
on every wind as the momentary signs of his infinite productiveness.

He may have his own.   A man's genius, the
quality that differences him from every other, the
susceptibility to one class of influences, the selection of what is fit for him, the rejection of what is

anfit, determines for him the character of the universe. A man is a method, a progressive arrange-
ment; a selecting principle, gathering his like to
him wherever he goes. He takes only his own out
of the multiplicity that sweeps and circles round
him. He is like one of those booms which are set
out from the shore on rivers to catch drift-wood, or
like the loadstone amongst splinters of steel. Those
facts, words, persons, which dwell in his memory
without his being able to say why, remain because
they have a relation to him not less real for being
as yet unapprehended. They are symbols of value
to him as they can interpret parts of his consciousness which he would vainly seek words for in the
conventional images of books and other minds.
What attracts my attention shall have it, as I will
go to the man who knocks at my door, whilst a
thousand persons as worthy go by it, to whom I
give no regard. It is enough that these particulars
speak to me. A few anecdotes, a few traits of
character, manners, face, a few incidents, have an
emphasis in your memory out of all proportion to
their apparent significance if you measure them by
the ordinary standards. They relate to your gift.
Let them have their weight, and do not reject
them and cast about for illustration and facts more
usual in literature. What your heart thinks great,
is great. The soul's emphasis is always right.

Over all things that are agreeable to his nature
and genius the man has the highest right.   Every·
where he may take what belongs to his spiritual estate, nor can he take anything else though all doors
were open, nor can all the force of men hinder
him from taking so much.   It is vain to attempt to
keep a secret from one who has a right to know it.
It will tell itself.   That mood into which a friend
can bring us is his dominion over us.   To the
thoughts of that state of mind he has a right.   All
the secrets of that state of mind he can compel.
This is a law which statesmen use in practice.   All
the terrors of the French Republic, which held
Austria in awe, were unable to command her di-
plomacy.   But Napoleon sent to Vienna M. de Narbonne, one of the old noblesse, with the morals,
manners and name of that interest, saying that it
was indispensable to send to the old aristocracy of
Europe men of the same connection, which in fact
constitutes a sort of free-masonry.   M. de Narbonne
in less than a fortnight penetrated all the secrets of
the imperial cabinet.

Nothing seems so easy as to speak and to be un
derstood.   Yet a man may come to find *that* the
strongest of defences and of ties, — that he has been
understood ; and he who has received an opinion
may come to find it the most inconvenient of
bonds.

If a teacher have any opinion which he wishes to conceal, his pupils will become as fully indoctrinated into that as into any which he publishes. If you pour water into a vessel twisted into coils and angles, it is vain to say, I will pour it only into this or that ; — it will find its level in all. Men feel and act the consequences of your doctrine without being able to show how they follow. Show us an arc of the curve, and a good mathematician will find out the whole figure. We are always reasoning from the seen to the unseen. Hence the perfect intelligence that subsists between wise men of remote ages. A man cannot bury his meanings so deep in his book but time and like-minded men will find them. Plato had a secret doctrine, had he? What secret can he conceal from the eyes of Bacon? of Montaigne? of Kant? Therefore Aristotle said of his works, " They are published and not published."

No man can learn what he has not preparation for learning, however near to his eyes is the object. A chemist may tell his most precious secrets to a carpenter, and he shall be never the wiser, — the secrets he would not utter to a chemist for an estate. God screens us evermore from premature ideas. Our eyes are holden that we cannot see things that stare us in the face, until the hour arrives when the mind is ripened ; then we behold them, and the time when we saw them not is like a dream.

Not in nature but in man is all the beauty and worth he sees. The world is very empty, and is indebted to this gilding, exalting soul for all its pride. " Earth fills her lap with splendors " *not* her own. The vale of Tempe, Tivoli and Rome are earth and water, rocks and sky. There are as good earth and water in a thousand places, yet how unaffecting !

People are not the better for the sun and moon, the horizon and the trees; as it is not observed that the keepers of Roman galleries or the valets of painters have any elevation of thought, or that librarians are wiser men than others. There are graces in the demeanor of a polished and noble person which are lost upon the eye of a churl. These are like the stars whose light has not yet reached us.

He may see what he maketh. Our dreams are the sequel of our waking knowledge. The visions of the night bear some proportion to the visions of the day. Hideous dreams are exaggerations of the sins of the day. We see our evil affections embodied in bad physiognomies. On the Alps the traveller sometimes beholds his own shadow magnified to a giant, so that every gesture of his hand is terrific. " My children," said an old man to his boys scared by a figure in the dark entry, "my children, you will never see anything worse than yourselves." As in dreams, so in the scarcely less fluid events of the world every man sees himself in colossal, without knowing that it is himself. The good, compared to the evil which he sees, is as his own good to his own evil. Every quality of his mind is magnified in some one acquaintance, and every emotion of his heart in some one. He is like a quincunx of trees, which counts five, — east, west, north, or south; or an initial, medial, and terminal acrostic. And why not? He cleaves to one person and avoids another, according to their likeness or unlikeness to himself, truly seeking himself in his associates and moreover in his trade and habits and gestures and meats and drinks, and comes at last to be faithfully represented by every view you take of his circumstances.

He may read what he writes. What can we see or acquire but what we are? You have observed a skilful man reading Virgil. Well, that author is a thousand books to a thousand persons. Take the book into your two hands and read your eyes out, you will never find what I find. If any ingenious reader would have a monopoly of the wisdom or delight he gets, he is as secure now the book is Englished, as if it were imprisoned in the Pelews' tongue. It is with a good book as it is with good

company. Introduce a base person among gentlemen, it is all to no purpose ; he is not their fellow.
Every society protects itself. The company is per-
fectly safe, and he is not one of them, though his
body is in the room.

What avails it to fight with the eternal laws of
mind, which adjust the relation of all persons to
each other by the mathematical measure of their
havings and beings? Gertrude is enamored of Guy;
how high, how aristocratic, how Roman his mien
and manners! to live with him were life indeed,
and no purchase is too great; and heaven and earth
are moved to that end. Well, Gertrude has Guy;
but what now avails how high, how aristocratic,
how Roman his mien and manners, if his heart and
aims are in the senate, in the theatre and in the
billiard-room, and she has no aims, no conversation
that can enchant her graceful lord ?

He shall have his own society. We can love
nothing but nature. The most wonderful talents,
the most meritorious exertions really avail very little with us ; but nearness or likeness of nature, —
how beautiful is the ease of its victory ! Persons
approach us, famous for their beauty, for their accomplishments, worthy of all wonder for their
charms and gifts ; they dedicate their whole skill to
the hour and the company, — with very imperfect
result. To be sure it would be ungrateful in us not

to praise them loudly. Then, when all is done, a
person of related mind, a brother or sister by nature, comes to us so softly and easily, so nearly and
intimately, as if it were the blood in our proper
veins, that we feel as if some one was gone, instead
of another having come; we are utterly relieved
and refreshed; it is a sort of joyful solitude. We
foolishly think in our days of sin that we must
court friends by compliance to the customs of society, to its dress, its breeding, and its estimates.
But only that soul can be my friend which I encounter on the line of my own march, that soul to
which I do not decline and which does not decline
to me, but, native of the same celestial latitude, repeats in its own all my experience. The scholar
forgets himself and apes the customs and costumes
of the man of the world to deserve the smile of
beauty, and follows some giddy girl, not yet taught
by religious passion to know the noble woman with
all that is serene, oracular and beautiful in her soul.
Let him be great, and love shall follow him. Nothing is more deeply punished than the neglect of the
affinities by which alone society should be formed,
and the insane levity of choosing associates by others' eyes.

He may set his own rate. It is a maxim worthy
of all acceptation that a man may have that allowance he takes. Take the place and attitude which

belong to you, and all men acquiesce. The world
must be just. It leaves every man, with profound
unconcern, to set his own rate. Hero or driveller,
it meddles not in the matter. It will certainly accept your own measure of your doing and being,
whether you sneak about and deny your own name,
or whether you see your work produced to the concave sphere of the heavens, one with the revolution
of the stars.

The same reality pervades all teaching. The
man may teach by doing, and not otherwise. If he
can communicate himself he can teach, but not by
words. He teaches who gives, and he learns who
receives. There is no teaching until the pupil is
brought into the same state or principle in which
you are; a transfusion takes place; he is you and
you are he; then is a teaching, and by no unfriendly
chance or bad company can he ever quite lose the
benefit. But your propositions run out of one ear
as they ran in at the other. We see it advertised
that Mr. Grand will deliver an oration on the Fourth
of July, and Mr. Hand before the Mechanics' Association, and we do not go thither, because we
know that these gentlemen will not communicate
their own character and experience to the company.
If we had reason to expect such a confidence we
should go through all inconvenience and opposition.
The sick would be carried in litters. But a public

oration is an escapade, a non-committal, an apology, a gag, and not a communication, not a speech, not a man.

A like Nemesis presides over all intellectual works. We have yet to learn that the thing uttered in words is not therefore affirmed. It must affirm itself, or no forms of logic or of oath can give it evidence. The sentence must also contain its own apology for being spoken.

The effect of any writing on the public mind is mathematically measurable by its depth of thought. How much water does it draw? If it awaken you to think, if it lift you from your feet with the great voice of eloquence, then the effect is to be wide, slow, permanent, over the minds of men; if the pages instruct you not, they will die like flies in the hour. The way to speak and write what shall not go out of fashion is to speak and write sincerely. The argument which has not power to reach my own practice, I may well doubt will fail to reach yours. But take Sidney's maxim: — "Look in thy heart, and write." He that writes to himself writes to an eternal public. That statement only is fit to be made public which you have come at in attempting to satisfy your own curiosity. The writer who takes his subject from his ear and not from his heart, should know that he has lost as much as he seems to have gained, and when the empty book

has gathered all its praise, and half the people say,
' What poetry ! what genius ! ' it still needs fuel to
make fire. That only profits which is profitable.
Life alone can impart life ; and though we should
burst we can only be valued as we make ourselves
valuable. There is no luck in literary reputation.
They who make up the final verdict upon every
book are not the partial and noisy readers of the
hour when it appears, but a court as of angels, a
public not to be bribed, not to be entreated and not
to be overawed, decides upon every man's title to
fame. Only those books come down which deserve
to last. Gilt edges, vellum and morocco, and pres-
entation-copies to all the libraries will not preserve
a book in circulation beyond its intrinsic date. It
must go with all Walpole's Noble and Royal Authors to its fate. Blackmore, Kotzebue, or Pollok
may endure for a night, but Moses and Homer
stand for ever. There are not in the world at any
one time more than a dozen persons who read and
understand Plato, — never enough to pay for an
edition of his works ; yet to every generation these
come duly down, for the sake of those few persons,
as if God brought them in his hand. " No book,"
said Bentley, " was ever written down by any but
itself." The permanence of all books is fixed by
no effort, friendly or hostile, but by their own specific gravity, or the intrinsic importance of their

contents to the constant mind of man. " Do not trouble yourself too much about the light on your statue," said Michael Angelo to the young sculptor; " the light of the public square will test its value."

In like manner the effect of every action is measured by the depth of the sentiment from which it proceeds. The great man knew not that he was great. It took a century or two for that fact to appear. What he did, he did because he must ; it was the most natural thing in the world, and grew out of the circumstances of the moment. But now, every thing he did, even to the lifting of his finger or the eating of bread, looks large, all-related, and is called an institution.

These are the demonstrations in a few particulars of the genius of nature ; they show the direction of the stream. But the stream is blood ; every drop is alive. Truth has not single victories ; all things are its organs, — not only dust and stones, but errors and lies. The laws of disease, physicians say, are as beautiful as the laws of health. Our philosophy is affirmative and readily accepts the testimony of negative facts, as every shadow points to the sun. By a divine necessity every fact in nature is constrained to offer its testimony.

Human character evermore publishes itself. The most fugitive deed and word, the mere air of doing a thing, the intimated purpose, expresses character.

If you act you show character; if you sit still, if
you sleep, you show it. You think because you
have spoken nothing when others spoke, and have
given no opinion on the times, on the church, on
slavery, on marriage, on socialism, on secret societies, on the college, on parties and persons, that
your verdict is still expected with curiosity as a reserved wisdom. Far otherwise; your silence answers very loud. You have no oracle to utter, and
your fellow-men have learned that you cannot help
them; for oracles speak. Doth not Wisdom cry
and Understanding put forth her voice?

Dreadful limits are set in nature to the powers
of dissimulation. Truth tyrannizes over the unwilling members of the body. Faces never lie, it is
said. No man need be deceived who will study the
changes of expression. When a man speaks the
truth in the spirit of truth, his eye is as clear
as the heavens. When he has base ends and
speaks falsely, the eye is muddy and sometimes
asquint.

I have heard an experienced counsellor say that
he never feared the effect upon a jury of a lawyer
who does not believe in his heart that his client
ought to have a verdict. If he does not believe
it his unbelief will appear to the jury, despite all
his protestations, and will become their unbelief.
This is that law whereby a work of art, of whatever

kind, sets us in the same state of mind wherein the
artist was when he made it. That which we do
not believe we cannot adequately say, though we
may repeat the words never so often. It was this
conviction which Swedenborg expressed when he
described a group of persons in the spiritual world
endeavoring in vain to articulate a proposition
which they did not believe; but they could not,
though they twisted and folded their lips even to
indignation.

A man passes for that he is worth. Very idle is
all curiosity concerning other people's estimate of
us, and all fear of remaining unknown is not less
so. If a man know that he can do any thing, —
that he can do it better than any one else, — he
has a pledge of the acknowledgment of that fact
by all persons. The world is full of judgment-
days, and into every assembly that a man enters,
in every action he attempts, he is gauged and
stamped. In every troop of boys that whoop and
run in each yard and square, a new-comer is as
well and accurately weighed in the course of a few
days and stamped with his right number, as if he
had undergone a formal trial of his strength, speed
and temper. A stranger comes from a distant
school, with better dress, with trinkets in his pock-
ets, with airs and pretensions; an older boy says
to himself. ' It 's of no use; we shall find him out

to-morrow.' 'What has he done?' is the divine question which searches men and transpierces every false reputation. A fop may sit in any chair of the world nor be distinguished for his hour from Homer and Washington; but there need never be any doubt concerning the respective ability of human beings. Pretension may sit still, but cannot act. Pretension never feigned an act of real greatness. Pretension never wrote an Iliad, nor drove back Xerxes, nor christianized the world, nor abolished slavery.

As much virtue as there is, so much appears; as much goodness as there is, so much reverence it commands. All the devils respect virtue. The high, the generous, the self-devoted sect will always instruct and command mankind. Never was a sincere word utterly lost. Never a magnanimity fell to the ground, but there is some heart to greet and accept it unexpectedly. A man passes for that he is worth. What he is engraves itself on his face, on his form, on his fortunes, in letters of light. Concealment avails him nothing, boasting nothing. There is confession in the glances of our eyes, in our smiles, in salutations, and the grasp of hands. His sin bedaubs him, mars all his good impression. Men know not why they do not trust him, but they do not trust him. His vice glasses his eye, cuts lines of mean expression in his cheek, pinches the nose, sets the mark of the beast on the back of the head, and writes O fool! fool! on the forehead of a king.

If you would not be known to do any thing, never do it. A man may play the fool in the drifts of a desert, but every grain of sand shall seem to see. He may be a solitary eater, but he cannot keep his foolish counsel. A broken complexion, a swinish look, ungenerous acts and the want of due knowledge, — all blab. Can a cook, a Chiffinch, an Iachimo be mistaken for Zeno or Paul? Confucius exclaimed, — " How can a man be concealed? How can a man be concealed?"

On the other hand, the hero fears not that if he withhold the avowal of a just and brave act it will go unwitnessed and unloved. One knows it, — himself, — and is pledged by it to sweetness of peace and to nobleness of aim which will prove in the end a better proclamation of it than the relating of the incident. Virtue is the adherence in action to the nature of things, and the nature of things makes it prevalent. It consists in a perpetual substitution of being for seeming, and with sublime propriety God is described as saying, I AM.

The lesson which these observations convey is, Be, and not seem. Let us acquiesce. Let us take our bloated nothingness out of the path of the divine circuits. Let us unlearn our wisdom of the world. Let us lie low in the Lord's power and learn that truth alone makes rich and great.

If you visit your friend, why need you apologize for not having visited him, and waste his time and deface your own act? Visit him now. Let him feel that the highest love has come to see him, in thee its lowest organ. Or why need you torment yourself and friend by secret self-reproaches that you have not assisted him or complimented him with gifts and salutations heretofore? Be a gift and a benediction. Shine with real light and not with the borrowed reflection of gifts. Common men are apologies for men; they bow the head, excuse themselves with prolix reasons, and accumulate appearances because the substance is not.

We are full of these superstitions of sense, the worship of magnitude. We call the poet inactive, because he is not a president, a merchant, or a porter. We adore an institution, and do not see that it is founded on a thought which we have. But real action is in silent moments. The epochs of our life are not in the visible facts of our choice of a calling, our marriage, our acquisition of an office, and the like, but in a silent thought by the wayside as we walk; in a thought which revises our entire manner of life and says, — 'Thus hast thou done, but it were better thus.' And all our after years, like menials, serve and wait on this, and according to their ability execute its will. This revisal or correction is a constant force, which, as a tendency, reaches through our lifetime. The object of the man, the aim of these moments, is to make daylight shine through him, to suffer the law to traverse his whole being without obstruction, so that on what point soever of his doing your eye falls it shall report truly of his character, whether it be his diet, his house, his religious forms, his society, his mirth, his vote, his opposition. Now he is not homogeneous, but heterogeneous, and the ray does not traverse ; there are no thorough lights, but the eye of the beholder is puzzled, detecting many unlike tendencies and a life not yet at one.

Why should we make it a point with our false modesty to disparage that man we are and that form of being assigned to us ? A good man is contented. I love and honor Epaminondas, but I do not wish to be Epaminondas. I hold it more just to love the world of this hour than the world of his hour. Nor can you, if I am true, excite me to the least uneasiness by saying, ' He acted and thou sittest still.' I see action to be good, when the need is, and sitting still to be also good. Epaminondas, if he was the man I take him for, would have sat still with joy and peace, if his lot had been mine. Heaven is large, and affords space for all modes of love and fortitude. Why should we be busybodies

and superserviceable? Action and inaction are
alike to the true. One piece of the tree is cut for a
weathercock and one for the sleeper of a bridge;
the virtue of the wood is apparent in both.

I desire not to disgrace the soul. The fact that
I am here certainly shows me that the soul had need
of an organ here. Shall I not assume the post?
Shall I skulk and dodge and duck with my unseasonable apologies and vain modesty and imagine
my being here impertinent? less pertinent than
Epaminondas or Homer being there? and that
the soul did not know its own needs? Besides,
without any reasoning on the matter, I have no
discontent. The good soul nourishes me and unlocks new magazines of power and enjoyment to
me every day. I will not meanly decline the immensity of good, because I have heard that it has
come to others in another shape.

Besides, why should we be cowed by the name of
Action? 'T is a trick of the senses, — no more.
We know that the ancestor of every action is a
thought. The poor mind does not seem to itself
to be any thing unless it have an outside badge, —
some Gentoo diet, or Quaker coat, or Calvinistic
prayer-meeting, or philanthropic society, or a great
donation, or a high office, or, any how, some wild
contrasting action to testify that it is somewhat.
The rich mind lies in the sun and sleeps, and is Nature. To think is to act.

Let us, if we must have great actions, make our own so. All action is of an infinite elasticity, and the least admits of being inflated with the celestial air until it eclipses the sun and moon. Let us seek *one* peace by fidelity. Let me heed my duties. Why need I go gadding into the scenes and philosophy of Greek and Italian history before I have justified myself to my benefactors? How dare I read Washington's campaigns when I have not answered the letters of my own correspondents? Is not that a just objection to much of our reading? It is a pusillanimous desertion of our work to gaze after our neighbors. It is peeping. Byron says of Jack Bunting, —

"He knew not what to say, and so he swore."

I may say it of our preposterous use of books, — He knew not what to do, and so *he read*. I can think of nothing to fill my time with, and I find the Life of Brant. It is a very extravagant compliment to pay to Brant, or to General Schuyler, or to General Washington. My time should be as good as their time, — my facts, my net of relations, as good as theirs, or either of theirs. Rather let me do my work so well that other idlers if they choose may compare my texture with the texture of these and find it identical with the best.

This over-estimate of the possibilities of Paul and

Pericles, this under-estimate of our own, comes from a neglect of the fact of an identical nature. Bonaparte knew but one merit, and rewarded in one and the same way the good soldier, the good astronomer, the good poet, the good player. The poet uses the names of Cæsar, of Tamerlane, of Bonduca, of Belisarius; the painter uses the conventional story of the Virgin Mary, of Paul, of Peter. He does not therefore defer to the nature of these accidental men, of these stock heroes. If the poet write a true drama, then he is Cæsar, and not the player of Cæsar; then the selfsame strain of thought, emotion as pure, wit as subtle, motions as swift, mounting, extravagant, and a heart as great, self-sufficing, dauntless, which on the waves of its love and hope can uplift all that is reckoned solid and precious in the world, — palaces, gardens, money, navies, kingdoms, — marking its own incomparable worth by the slight it casts on these gauds of men; — these all are his, and by the power of these he rouses the nations. Let a man believe in God, and not in names and places and persons. Let the great soul incarnated in some woman's form, poor and sad and single, in some Dolly or Joan, go out to service and sweep chambers and scour floors, and its effulgent daybeams cannot be muffled or hid, but to sweep and scour will instantly appear supreme and beautiful actions, the top and radiance of human life, and all people will get mops and brooms ; until, lo! suddenly the great soul has en- shrined itself in some other form and done some other deed, and that is now the flower and head of all living nature.

We are the photometers, we the irritable gold- leaf and tinfoil that measure the accumulations of the subtle element. We know the authentic effects of the true fire through every one of its million dis- guises.

LOVE.

———✦———

"I was as a gem concealed ;
Me my burning ray revealed."

Koran.

LOVE.

EVERY promise of the soul has innumerable ful-
filments; each of its joys ripens into a new want.
Nature, uncontainable, flowing, forelooking, in the
first sentiment of kindness anticipates already a
benevolence which shall lose all particular regards
in its general light.   The introduction to this felicity is in a private and tender relation of one to one,
which is the enchantment of human life; which,
like a certain divine rage and enthusiasm, seizes on
man at one period and works a revolution in his
mind and body; unites him to his race, pledges
him to the domestic and civic relations, carries him
with new sympathy into nature, enhances the power
of the senses, opens the imagination, adds to his
character heroic and sacred attributes, establishes
marriage and gives permanence to human society.

The natural association of the sentiment of love
with the heyday of the blood seems to require that
in order to portray it in vivid tints, which every
youth and maid should confess to be true to their

throbbing experience, one must not be too old. The
delicious fancies of youth reject the least savor of
a mature philosophy, as chilling with age and ped
antry their purple bloom. And therefore I know
I incur the imputation of unnecessary hardness and
stoicism from those who compose the Court and
Parliament of Love. But from these formidable
censors I shall appeal to my seniors. For it is to
be considered that this passion of which we speak,
though it begin with the young, yet forsakes not the
old, or rather suffers no one who is its servant to
grow old, but makes the aged participators of it not
less than the tender maiden, though in a different
and nobler sort. For it is a fire that kindling its
first embers ᵢᵣ the narrow nook of a private bosom,
caught from a wandering spark out of another private heart, glows and enlarges until it warms and
beams upon multitudes of men and women, upon
the universal heart of all, and so lights up the
whole world and all nature with its generous flames.
It matters not therefore whether we attempt to describe the passion at twenty, thirty, or at eighty
years. He who paints it at the first period will
lose some of its later, he who paints it at the last,
some of its earlier traits. Only it is to be hoped
that by patience and the Muses' aid we may attain
to that inward view of the law which shall describe
a truth ever young and beautiful, so central that it

shall commend itself to the eye at whatever angle beholden.

And the first condition is that we must leave a too close and lingering adherence to facts, and study the sentiment as it appeared in hope, and not in history. For each man sees his own life defaced and disfigured, as the life of man is not to his imagination. Each man sees over his own experience a certain stain of error, whilst that of other men looks fair and ideal. Let any man go back to those delicious relations which make the beauty of his life, which have given him sincerest instruction and nourishment, he will shrink and moan. Alas! I know not why, but infinite compunctions embitter in mature life the remembrances of budding joy, and cover every beloved name. Every thing is beautiful seen from the point of the intellect, or as truth. But all is sour if seen as experience. Details are melancholy; the plan is seemly and noble. In the actual world — the painful kingdom of time and place — dwell care and canker and fear. With thought, with the ideal, is immortal hilarity, the rose of joy. Round it all the Muses sing. But grief cleaves to names and persons and the partial interests of to-day and yesterday.

The strong bent of nature is seen in the proportion which this topic of personal relations usurps in the conversation of society. What do we wish to

know of any worthy person so much as how he has
sped in the history of this sentiment ? What books
in the circulating library circulate ?   How we glow
over these novels of passion, when the story is told
with any spark of truth and nature! And what
fastens attention, in the intercourse of life, like any
passage betraying affection between two parties ?
Perhaps we never saw them before and never shall
meet them again. But we see them exchange a
glance or betray a deep emotion, and we are no
longer strangers. We understand them and take
the warmest interest in the development of the romance. All mankind love a lover. The earliest
demonstrations of complacency and kindness are
nature's most winning pictures.   It is the dawn of
civility and grace in the coarse and rustic. The
rude village boy teases the girls about the school-
house door ; — but to-day he comes running into
the entry and meets one fair child disposing her
satchel ; he holds her books to help her, and instantly it seems to him as if she removed herself
from him infinitely, and was a sacred precinct.
Among the throng of girls he runs rudely enough,
but one alone distances him ; and these two little
neighbors, that were so close just now, have learned
to respect each other's personality. Or who can
avert his eyes from the engaging, half-artful, half
artless ways of school-girls who go into the country

shops to buy a skein of silk or a sheet of paper, and
talk half an hour about nothing with the broad-
faced, good-natured shop-boy. In the village they
are on a perfect equality, which love delights in,
and without any coquetry the happy, affectionate
nature of woman flows out in this pretty gossip.
The girls may have little beauty, yet plainly do
they establish between them and the good boy the
most agreeable, confiding relations; what with their
fun and their earnest, about Edgar and Jonas and
Almira, and who was invited to the party, and who
danced at the dancing-school, and when the singing-
school would begin, and other nothings concerning
which the parties cooed. By and by that boy wants
a wife, and very truly and heartily will he know
where to find a sincere and sweet mate, without any
risk such as Milton deplores as incident to scholars
and great men.

I have been told that in some public discourses
of mine my reverence for the intellect has made me
unjustly cold to the personal relations. But now I
almost shrink at the remembrance of such disparag-
ing words. For persons are love's world, and the
coldest philosopher cannot recount the debt of the
young soul wandering here in nature to the power
of love, without being tempted to unsay, as treason-
able to nature, aught derogatory to the social instincts. For though the celestial rapture falling

out of heaven seizes only upon those of tender age,
and although a beauty overpowering all analysis or
comparison and putting us quite beside ourselves
we can seldom see after thirty years, yet the remembrance of these visions outlasts all other remembrances, and is a wreath of flowers on the oldest
brows.   But here is a strange fact; it may seem to
many men, in revising their experience, that they
have no fairer page in their life's book than the delicious memory of some passages wherein affection
contrived to give a witchcraft, surpassing the deep
attraction of its own truth, to a parcel of accidental
and trivial circumstances.   In looking backward
they may find that several things which were not
the charm have more reality to this groping memory
than the charm itself which embalmed them.   But
be our experience in particulars what it may, no man
ever forgot the visitations of that power to his heart
and brain, which created all things anew; which was
the dawn in him of music, poetry and art; which
made the face of nature radiant with purple light,
the morning and the night varied enchantments;
when a single tone of one voice could make the
heart bound, and the most trivial circumstance associated with one form is put in the amber of memory; when he became all eye when one was present,
and all memory when one was gone; when the
youth becomes a watcher of windows and studious

of a glove, a veil, a ribbon, or the wheels of a carriage; when no place is too solitary and none too silent for him who has richer company and sweeter conversation in his new thoughts than any old friends, though best and purest, can give him; for the figures, the motions, the words of the beloved object are not, like other images, written in water, but, as Plutarch said, "enamelled in fire," and make the study of midnight : —

> "Thou art not gone being gone, where'er thou art,
>   Thou leav'st in him thy watchful eyes, in him thy loving heart."

In the noon and the afternoon of life we still throb at the recollection of days when happiness was not happy enough, but must be drugged with the relish of pain and fear; for he touched the secret of the matter who said of love, —

> "All other pleasures are not worth its pains:"

and when the day was not long enough, but the night too must be consumed in keen recollections; when the head boiled all night on the pillow with the generous deed it resolved on ; when the moonlight was a pleasing fever and the stars were letters and the flowers ciphers and the air was coined into song ; when all business seemed an impertinence, and all the men and women running to and fro in the streets, mere pictures.

The passion rebuilds the world for the youth. It makes all things alive and significant. Nature grows conscious. Every bird on the boughs of the tree sings now to his heart and soul. The notes are almost articulate. The clouds have faces as he looks on them. The trees of the forest, the waving grass and the peeping flowers have grown intelligent; and he almost fears to trust them with the secret which they seem to invite. Yet nature soothes and sympathizes. In the green solitude he finds a dearer home than with men : —

> " Fountain-heads and pathless groves,
> Places which pale passion loves,
> Moonlight walks, when all the fowls
> Are safely housed, save bats and owls,
> A midnight bell, a passing groan, —
> These are the sounds we feed upon."

Behold there in the wood the fine madman! He is a palace of sweet sounds and sights ; he dilates; he is twice a man ; he walks with arms akimbo ; he soliloquizes ; he accosts the grass and the trees ; he feels the blood of the violet, the clover and the lily in his veins ; and he talks with the brook that wets his foot.

The heats that have opened his perceptions of natural beauty have made him love music and verse. It is a fact often observed, that men have written good verses under the inspiration of passion, who cannot write well under any other circumstances.

The like force has the passion over all his nature. It expands the sentiment; it makes the clown gentle and gives the coward heart. Into the most pitiful and abject it will infuse a heart and courage to defy the world, so only it have the countenance of the beloved object. In giving him to another it still more gives him to himself. He is a new man, with new perceptions, new and keener purposes, and a religious solemnity of character and aims. He does not longer appertain to his family and society; *he* is somewhat; *he* is a person; *he* is a soul.

And here let us examine a little nearer the nature of that influence which is thus potent over the human youth. Beauty, whose revelation to man we now celebrate, welcome as the sun wherever it pleases to shine, which pleases everybody with it and with themselves, seems sufficient to itself. The lover cannot paint his maiden to his fancy poor and solitary. Like a tree in flower, so much soft, budding, informing loveliness is society for itself; and she teaches his eye why Beauty was pictured with Loves and Graces attending her steps. Her existence makes the world rich. Though she extrudes all other persons from his attention as cheap and unworthy, she indemnifies him by carrying out her own being into somewhat impersonal, large, mundane, so that the maiden stands to him for a representative of all select things and virtues. For that reason the lover never sees personal resemblances in his mistress to her kindred or to others. His friends find in her a likeness to her mother, or her sisters, or to persons not of her blood. The lover sees no resemblance except to summer evenings and diamond mornings, to rainbows and the song of birds.

The ancients called beauty the flowering of virtue. Who can analyze the nameless charm which glances from one and another face and form? We are touched with emotions of tenderness and complacency, but we cannot find whereat this dainty emotion, this wandering gleam, points. It is destroyed for the imagination by any attempt to refer it to organization. Nor does it point to any relations of friendship or love known and described in society, but, as it seems to me, to a quite other and unattainable sphere, to relations of transcendent delicacy and sweetness, to what roses and violets hint and foreshow. We cannot approach beauty. Its nature is like opaline doves'-neck lustres, hovering and evanescent. Herein it resembles the most excellent things, which all have this rainbow character, defying all attempts at appropriation and use. What else did Jean Paul Richter signify, when he said to music, " Away! away! thou speakest to me of things which in all my endless life I have not

found and shall not find." The same fluency may
be observed in every work of the plastic arts. The
statue is then beautiful when it begins to be incom-
prehensible, when it is passing out of criticism and
can no longer be defined by compass and measur-
ing-wand, but demands an active imagination to go
with it and to say what it is in the act of doing.
The god or hero of the sculptor is always represented in a transition *from* that which is represent-
able to the senses, *to* that which is not. Then first
it ceases to be a stone. The same remark holds of
painting. And of poetry the success is not attained when it lulls and satisfies, but when it astonishes and fires us with new endeavors after the
unattainable. Concerning it Landor inquires
"whether it is not to be referred to some purer
state of sensation and existence."

In like manner, personal beauty is then first
charming and itself when it dissatisfies us with any
end; when it becomes a story without an end;
when it suggests gleams and visions and not earthly
satisfactions; when it makes the beholder feel his
unworthiness; when he cannot feel his right to it,
though he were Cæsar; he cannot feel more right
to it than to the firmament and the splendors of a
sunset.

Hence arose the saying, "If I love you, what is
that to you?" We say so because we feel that

what we love is not in your will, but above it. It is not you, but your radiance.   It is that which you know not in yourself and can never know.

This agrees well with that high philosophy of Beauty which the ancient writers delighted in ; for they said that the soul of man, embodied here on earth, went roaming up and down in quest of that other world of its own out of which it came into this, but was soon stupefied by the light of the natural sun, and unable to see any other objects than those of this world, which are but shadows of real things.   Therefore the Deity sends the glory of youth before the soul, that it may avail itself of beautiful bodies as aids to its recollection of the celestial good and fair ; and the man beholding such a person in the female sex runs to her and finds the highest joy in contemplating the form, movement and intelligence of this person, because it suggests to him the presence of that which indeed is within the beauty, and the cause of the beauty.

If however, from too much conversing with material objects, the soul was gross, and misplaced its satisfaction in the body, it reaped nothing but sorrow ; body being unable to fulfil the promise which beauty holds out ; but if, accepting the hint of these visions and suggestions which beauty makes to his mind, the soul passes through the body and

falls to admire strokes of character, and the lovers
contemplate one another in their discourses and
their actions, then they pass to the true palace of
beauty, more and more inflame their love of it, and
by this love extinguishing the base affection, as the
sun puts out fire by shining on the hearth, they become pure and hallowed. By conversation with
that which is in itself excellent, magnanimous,
lowly, and just, the lover comes to a warmer love
of these nobilities, and a quicker apprehension of
them. Then he passes from loving them in one to
loving them in all, and so is the one beautiful soul
only the door through which he enters to the society of all true and pure souls. In the particular
society of his mate he attains a clearer sight of any
spot, any taint which her beauty has contracted
from this world, and is able to point it out, and
this with mutual joy that they are now able, without offence, to indicate blemishes and hindrances
in each other, and give to each all help and comfort in curing the same. And beholding in many
souls the traits of the divine beauty, and separating
in each soul that which is divine from the taint
which it has contracted in the world, the lover ascends to the highest beauty, to the love and knowledge of the Divinity, by steps on this ladder of
created souls.

Somewhat like this have the truly wise told us of

love in all ages.   The doctrine is not old, nor is it
new.   If Plato, Plutarch and Apuleius taught it,
so have Petrarch, Angelo and Milton.   It awaits a
truer unfolding in opposition and rebuke to that
subterranean prudence which presides at marriages
with words that take hold of the upper world, whilst
one eye is prowling in the cellar; so that its gravest
discourse has a savor of hams and powdering-tubs.
Worst, when this sensualism intrudes into the education of young women, and withers the hope and
affection of human nature by teaching that marriage signifies nothing but a housewife's thrift, and
that woman's life has no other aim.

   But this dream of love, though beautiful, is only
one scene in our play.   In the procession of the
soul from within outward, it enlarges its circles
ever, like the pebble thrown into the pond, or the
light proceeding from an orb.   The rays of the soul
alight first on things nearest, on every utensil and
toy, on nurses and domestics, on the house and yard
and passengers, on the circle of household acquaintance, on politics and geography and history.   But
things are ever grouping themselves according to
higher or more interior laws.   Neighborhood, size,
numbers, habits, persons, lose by degrees their
power over us.   Cause and effect, real affinities, the
longing for harmony between the soul and the circumstance, the progressive, idealizing instinct, pre-

dominate later, and the step backward from the higher to the lower relations is impossible. Thus even love, which is the deification of persons, must become more impersonal every day. Of this at first it gives no hint. Little think the youth and maiden who are glancing at each other across crowded rooms with eyes so full of mutual intelligence, of the precious fruit long hereafter to proceed from this new, quite external stimulus. The work of vegetation begins first in the irritability of the bark and leaf-buds. From exchanging glances, they advance to acts of courtesy, of gallantry, then to fiery passion, to plighting troth and marriage. Passion beholds its object as a perfect unit. The soul is wholly embodied, and the body is wholly ensouled : —

> " Her pure and eloquent blood
> Spoke in her cheeks, and so distinctly wrought,
> That one might almost say her body thought."

Romeo, if dead, should be cut up into little stars to make the heavens fine. Life, with this pair, has no other aim, asks no more, than Juliet, — than Romeo. Night, day, studies, talents, kingdoms, religion, are all contained in this form full of soul, in this soul which is all form. The lovers delight in endearments, in avowals of love, in comparisons of their regards. When alone, they solace themselves with the remembered image of the other. Does that other see the same star, the same melting cloud, read the same book, feel the same emotion, that now delights me? They try and weigh their affection, and adding up costly advantages, friends, opportunities, properties, exult in discovering that willingly, joyfully, they would give all as a ransom for the beautiful, the beloved head, not one hair of which shall be harmed. But the lot of humanity is on these children. Danger, sorrow and pain arrive to them as to all. Love prays. It makes covenants with Eternal Power in behalf of this dear mate. The union which is thus effected and which adds a new value to every atom in nature — for it transmutes every thread throughout the whole web of relation into a golden ray, and bathes the soul in a new and sweeter element — is yet a temporary state. Not always can flowers, pearls, poetry, protestations, nor even home in another heart, content the awful soul that dwells in clay. It arouses itself at last from these endearments, as toys, and puts on the harness and aspires to vast and universal aims. The soul which is in the soul of each, craving a perfect beatitude, detects incongruities, defects and disproportion in the behavior of the other. Hence arise surprise, expostulation and pain. Yet that which drew them to each other was signs of loveliness, signs of virtue; and these virtues are there, however eclipsed. They appear and reappear and continue to attract; but the regard changes, quits the sign and attaches to the substance. This repairs the wounded affection. Meantime, as life wears on, it proves a game of permutation and combination of all possible positions of the parties, to employ all the resources of each and acquaint each with the strength and weakness of the other. For it is the nature and end of this relation, that they should represent the human race to each other. All that is in the world, which is or ought to be known, is cunningly wrought into the texture of man, of woman : —

"The person love does to us fit,
Like manna, has the taste of all in it."

The world rolls; the circumstances vary every hour. The angels that inhabit this temple of the body appear at the windows, and the gnomes and vices also. By all the virtues they are united. If there be virtue, all the vices are known as such; they confess and flee. Their once flaming regard is sobered by time in either breast, and losing in violence what it gains in extent, it becomes a thorough good understanding. They resign each other without complaint to the good offices which man and woman are severally appointed to discharge in time, and exchange the passion which once could not lose sight of its object, for a cheerful disengaged furtherance, whether present or absent, of each

other's designs. At last they discover that all which
at first drew them together, — those once sacred
features, that magical play of charms, — was decid-
uous, had a prospective end, like the scaffolding by
which the house was built; and the purification of
the intellect and the heart from year to year is the
real marriage, foreseen and prepared from the first,
and wholly above their consciousness. Looking at
these aims with which two persons, a man and a
woman, so variously and correlatively gifted, are
shut up in one house to spend in the nuptial society
forty or fifty years, I do not wonder at the emphasis
with which the heart prophesies this crisis from
early infancy, at the profuse beauty with which
the instincts deck the nuptial bower, and nature and
intellect and art emulate each other in the gifts and
the melody they bring to the epithalamium.

Thus are we put in training for a love which
knows not sex, nor person, nor partiality, but which
seeks virtue and wisdom everywhere, to the end of
increasing virtue and wisdom. We are by nature
observers, and thereby learners. That is our permanent state. But we are often made to feel that
our affections are but tents of a night. Though
slowly and with pain, the objects of the affections
change, as the objects of thought do. There are
moments when the affections rule and absorb the
man and make his happiness dependent on a per-

son or persons. But in health the mind is presently seen again, — its overarching vault, bright with galaxies of immutable lights, and the warm loves and fears that swept over us as clouds must lose their finite character and blend with God, to attain their own perfection. But we need not fear that we can lose any thing by the progress of the soul. The soul may be trusted to the end. That which is so beautiful and attractive as these relations, must be succeeded and supplanted only by what is more beautiful, and so on for ever.

FRIENDSHIP.

A RUDDY drop of manly blood
The surging sea outweighs;
The world uncertain comes and goes,
The lover rooted stays.
I fancied he was fled,
And, after many a year,
Glowed unexhausted kindliness
Like daily sunrise there.
My careful heart was free again, —
O friend, my bosom said,
Through thee alone the sky is arched,
Through thee the rose is red,
All things through thee take nobler form
And look beyond the earth,
The mill-round of our fate appears
A sun-path in thy worth.
Me too thy nobleness has taught
To master my despair;
The fountains of my hidden life
Are through thy friendship fair.

VI.

FRIENDSHIP.

WE have a great deal more kindness than is ever spoken. Maugre all the selfishness that chills like east winds the world, the whole human family is bathed with an element of love like a fine ether. How many persons we meet in houses, whom we scarcely speak to, whom yet we honor, and who honor us! How many we see in the street, or sit with in church, whom, though silently, we warmly rejoice to be with! Read the language of these wandering eye-beams. The heart knoweth.

The effect of the indulgence of this human affection is a certain cordial exhilaration. In poetry and in common speech the emotions of benevolence and complacency which are felt towards others are likened to the material effects of fire; so swift, or much more swift, more active, more cheering, are these fine inward irradiations. From the highest degree of passionate love to the lowest degree of good-will, they make the sweetness of life.

Our intellectual and active powers increase with our affection. The scholar sits down to write, and all his years of meditation do not furnish him with one good thought or happy expression; but it is necessary to write a letter to a friend, — and forthwith troops of gentle thoughts invest themselves, on every hand, with chosen words. See, in any house where virtue and self-respect abide, the palpitation which the approach of a stranger causes. A commended stranger is expected and announced, and an uneasiness betwixt pleasure and pain invades all the hearts of a household. His arrival almost brings fear to the good hearts that would welcome him. The house is dusted, all things fly into their places, the old coat is exchanged for the new, and they must get up a dinner if they can. Of a commended stranger, only the good report is told by others, only the good and new is heard by us. He stands to us for humanity. He is what we wish. Having imagined and invested him, we ask how we should stand related in conversation and action with such a man, and are uneasy with fear. The same idea exalts conversation with him. We talk better than we are wont. We have the nimblest fancy, a richer memory, and our dumb devil has taken leave for the time. For long hours we can continue a series of sincere, graceful, rich communications, drawn from the oldest, secretest experience, so that they who sit by, of our own kinsfolk and acquaintance, shall feel a lively surprise at our unusual powers. But as soon as the stranger begins to intrude his partialities, his definitions, his defects into the conversation, it is all over. He has heard the first, the last and best he will ever hear from us. He is no stranger now. Vulgarity, ignorance, misapprehension are old acquaintances. Now, when he comes, he may get the order, the dress and the dinner, — but the throbbing of the heart and the communications of the soul, no more.

What is so pleasant as these jets of affection which make a young world for me again? What so delicious as a just and firm encounter of two, in a thought, in a feeling? How beautiful, on their approach to this beating heart, the steps and forms of the gifted and the true! The moment we indulge our affections, the earth is metamorphosed; there is no winter and no night; all tragedies, all ennuis vanish, — all duties even; nothing fills the proceeding eternity but the forms all radiant of beloved persons. Let the soul be assured that somewhere in the universe it should rejoin its friend, and it would be content and cheerful alone for a thousand years.

I awoke this morning with devout thanksgiving for my friends, the old and the new. Shall I not call God the Beautiful, who daily showeth himself

so to me in his gifts? I chide society, I embrace
solitude, and yet I am not so ungrateful as not to
see the wise, the lovely and the noble-minded, as
from time to time they pass my gate. Who hears
me, who understands me, becomes mine, — a possession for all time. Nor is Nature so poor but she
gives me this joy several times, and thus we weave
social threads of our own, a new web of relations;
and, as many thoughts in succession substantiate
themselves, we shall by and by stand in a new world
of our own creation, and no longer strangers and
pilgrims in a traditionary globe. My friends have
come to me unsought. The great God gave them
to me. By oldest right, by the divine affinity of
virtue with itself, I find them, or rather not I but
the Deity in me and in them derides and cancels
the thick walls of individual character, relation, age,
sex, circumstance, at which he usually connives, and
now makes many one. High thanks I owe you, excellent lovers, who carry out the world for me to
new and noble depths, and enlarge the meaning of
all my thoughts. These are new poetry of the first
Bard, — poetry without stop, — hymn, ode and epic,
poetry still flowing, Apollo and the Muses chanting
still. Will these too separate themselves from me
again, or some of them? I know not, but I fear
it not; for my relation to them is so pure that we
hold by simple affinity, and the Genius of my life

being thus social, the same affinity will exert its energy on whomsoever is as noble as these men and women, wherever I may be.

I confess to an extreme tenderness of nature on this point. It is almost dangerous to me to "crush the sweet poison of misused wine" of the affections. A new person is to me a great event and hinders me from sleep. I have often had fine fancies about persons which have given me delicious hours; but the joy ends in the day; it yields no fruit. Thought is not born of it; my action is very little modified. I must feel pride in my friend's accomplishments as if they were mine, and a property in his virtues. I feel as warmly when he is praised, as the lover when he hears applause of his engaged maiden. We over-estimate the conscience of our friend. His goodness seems better than our goodness, his nature finer, his temptations less. Every thing that is his, — his name, his form, his dress, books and instruments, — fancy enhances. Our own thought sounds new and larger from his mouth.

Yet the systole and diastole of the heart are not without their analogy in the ebb and flow of love. Friendship, like the immortality of the soul, is too good to be believed. The lover, beholding his maiden, half knows that she is not verily that which he worships; and in the golden hour of

friendship we are surprised with shades of suspicion and unbelief. We doubt that we bestow on
our hero the virtues in which he shines, and afterwards worship the form to which we have ascribed
this divine inhabitation. In strictness, the soul does
not respect men as it respects itself. In strict science all persons underlie the same condition of an
infinite remoteness. Shall we fear to cool our love
by mining for the metaphysical foundation of this
Elysian temple? Shall I not be as real as the
things I see? If I am, I shall not fear to know
them for what they are. Their essence is not less
beautiful than their appearance, though it needs
finer organs for its apprehension. The root of the
plant is not unsightly to science, though for chaplets and festoons we cut the stem short. And I
must hazard the production of the bald fact amidst
these pleasing reveries, though it should prove an
Egyptian skull at our banquet. A man who stands
united with his thought conceives magnificently of
himself. He is conscious of a universal success,
even though bought by uniform particular failures.
No advantages, no powers, no gold or force, can be
any match for him. I cannot choose but rely on my
own poverty more than on your wealth. I cannot
make your consciousness tantamount to mine. Only
the star dazzles ; the planet has a faint, moon-like
ray. I hear what you say of the admirable parts

and tried temper of the party you praise, but I see
well that, for all his purple cloaks, I shall not like
him, unless he is at last a poor Greek like me. I
cannot deny it, O friend, that the vast shadow of
the Phenomenal includes thee also in its pied and
painted immensity, — thee also, compared with
whom all else is shadow. Thou art not Being, as
Truth is, as Justice is, — thou art not my soul, but
a picture and effigy of that. Thou hast come to
me lately, and already thou art seizing thy hat and
cloak. Is it not that the soul puts forth friends as
the tree puts forth leaves, and presently, by the
germination of new buds, extrudes the old leaf?
The law of nature is alternation for evermore.
Each electrical state superinduces the opposite.
The soul environs itself with friends that it may enter into a grander self-acquaintance or solitude;
and it goes alone for a season that it may exalt its
conversation or society. This method betrays itself
along the whole history of our personal relations.
The instinct of affection revives the hope of union
with our mates, and the returning sense of insulation recalls us from the chase. Thus every man
passes his life in the search after friendship, and if
he should record his true sentiment, he might write
a letter like this to each new candidate for his
love: —

Dear Friend,

If I was sure of thee, sure of thy capacity, sure
to match my mood with thine, I should never think
again of trifles in relation to thy comings and go-
ings.   I am not very wise; my moods are quite at
tainable, and I respect thy genius; it is to me as
yet unfathomed; yet dare I not presume in thee a
perfect intelligence of me, and so thou art to me a
delicious torment.   Thine ever, or never.

Yet these uneasy pleasures and fine pains are for
curiosity and not for life.   They are not to be indulged.   This is to weave cobweb, and not cloth.
Our friendships hurry to short and poor conclusions, because we have made them a texture of wine
and dreams, instead of the tough fibre of the human heart.   The laws of friendship are austere and
eternal, of one web with the laws of nature and of
morals.   But we have aimed at a swift and petty
benefit, to suck a sudden sweetness.   We snatch at
the slowest fruit in the whole garden of God, which
many summers and many winters must ripen.   We
seek our friend not sacredly, but with an adulterate
passion which would appropriate him to ourselves.
In vain.   We are armed all over with subtle an
tagonisms, which, as soon as we meet, begin to play,
and translate all poetry into stale prose.   Almost
all people descend to meet.   All association must

be a compromise, and, what is worst, the very
flower and aroma of the flower of each of the beau·
tiful natures disappears as they approach each other.
What a perpetual disappointment is actual society,
even of the virtuous and gifted ! After interviews
have been compassed with long foresight we must
be tormented presently by baffled blows, by sudden,
unseasonable apathies, by epilepsies of wit and of
animal spirits, in the heyday of friendship and
thought. Our faculties do not play us true, and
both parties are relieved by solitude.

I ought to be equal to every relation. It makes
no difference how many friends I have and what
content I can find in conversing with each, if there
be one to whom I am not equal. If I have shrunk
unequal from one contest, the joy I find in all the
rest becomes mean and cowardly. I should hate
myself, if then I made my other friends my asy·
lum : —

"The valiant warrior famoused for fight,
   After a hundred victories, once foiled,
   Is from the book of honor razed quite
   And all the rest forgot for which he toiled."

Our impatience is thus sharply rebuked. Bash-
fulness and apathy are a tough husk in which a delicate organization is protected from premature
ripening. It would be lost if it knew itself before
any of the best souls were yet ripe enough to know

and own it.   Respect the *naturlangsamkeit* which
hardens the ruby in a million years, and works in
duration in which Alps and Andes come and go as
rainbows.   The good spirit of our life has no heaven
which is the price of rashness.   Love, which is the
essence of God, is not for levity, but for the total
worth of man.   Let us not have this childish luxury in our regards, but the austerest worth ; let us
approach our friend with an audacious trust in the
truth of his heart, in the breadth, impossible to be
overturned, of his foundations.

The attractions of this subject are not to be resisted, and I leave, for the time, all account of subordinate social benefit, to speak of that select and
sacred relation which is a kind of absolute, and
which even leaves the language of love suspicious
and common, so much is this purer, and nothing is
so much divine.

I do not wish to treat friendships daintily, but
with roughest courage.   When they are real, they
are not glass threads or frostwork, but the solidest
thing we know.   For now, after so many ages of experience, what do we know of nature or of ourselves ?   Not one step has man taken toward the
solution of the problem of his destiny.   In one condemnation of folly stand the whole universe of men.
But the sweet sincerity of joy and peace which I
draw from this alliance with my brother's soul is

the nut itself whereof all nature and all thought is but the husk and shell. Happy is the house that shelters a friend! It might well be built, like a festal bower or arch, to entertain him a single day. Happier, if he know the solemnity of that relation and honor its law! He who offers himself a candidate for that covenant comes up, like an Olympian, to the great games where the first-born of the world are the competitors. He proposes himself for contests where Time, Want, Danger, are in the lists, and he alone is victor who has truth enough in his constitution to preserve the delicacy of his beauty from the wear and tear of all these. The gifts of fortune may be present or absent, but all the speed in that contest depends on intrinsic nobleness and the contempt of trifles. There are two elements that go to the composition of friendship, each so sovereign that I can detect no superiority in either, no reason why either should be first named. One is truth. A friend is a person with whom I may be sincere. Before him I may think aloud. I am arrived at last in the presence of a man so real and equal that I may drop even those undermost garments of dissimulation, courtesy, and second thought, which men never put off, and may deal with him with the simplicity and wholeness with which one chemical atom meets another. Sincerity is the luxury allowed, like diadems and au-

thority, only to the highest rank; *that* being permitted to speak truth, as having none above it to
court or conform unto. Every man alone is sincere.
At the entrance of a second person, hypocrisy begins. We parry and fend the approach of our fellow-man by compliments, by gossip, by amusements,
by affairs. We cover up our thought from him
under a hundred folds. I knew a man who under
a certain religious frenzy cast off this drapery, and
omitting all compliment and commonplace, spoke
to the conscience of every person he encountered,
and that with great insight and beauty. At first
he was resisted, and all men agreed he was mad.
But persisting — as indeed he could not help doing
— for some time in this course, he attained to the
advantage of bringing every man of his acquaintance into true relations with him. No man would
think of speaking falsely with him, or of putting
him off with any chat of markets or reading-rooms.
But every man was constrained by so much sincerity to the like plaindealing, and what love of nature,
what poetry, what symbol of truth he had, he did
certainly show him. But to most of us society
shows not its face and eye, but its side and its back.
To stand in true relations with men in a false age
is worth a fit of insanity, is it not? We can seldom
go erect. Almost every man we meet requires
some civility, — requires to be humored; he has

some fame, some talent, some whim of religion or philanthropy in his head that is not to be questioned, and which spoils all conversation with him. But a friend is a sane man who exercises not my ingenuity, but me. My friend gives me entertainment without requiring any stipulation on my part. A friend therefore is a sort of paradox in nature. I who alone am, I who see nothing in nature whose existence I can affirm with equal evidence to my own, behold now the semblance of my being, in all its height, variety and curiosity, reiterated in a foreign form ; so that a friend may well be reckoned the masterpiece of nature.

The other element of friendship is tenderness. We are holden to men by every sort of tie, by blood, by pride, by fear, by hope, by lucre, by lust, by hate, by admiration, by every circumstance and badge and trifle, — but we can scarce believe that so much character can subsist in another as to draw us by love. Can another be so blessed and we so pure that we can offer him tenderness? When a man becomes dear to me I have touched the goal of fortune. I find very little written directly to the heart of this matter in books. And yet I have one text which I cannot choose but remember. My author says, — " I offer myself faintly and bluntly to those whose I effectually am, and tender myself least to him to whom I am the

most devoted." I wish that friendship should have
feet, as well as eyes and eloquence. It must plant
itself on the ground, before it vaults over the
moon. I wish it to be a little of a citizen, before
it is quite a cherub. We chide the citizen because
he makes love a commodity. It is an exchange of
gifts, of useful loans ; it is good neighborhood; it
watches with the sick; it holds the pall at the funeral ; and quite loses sight of the delicacies and
nobility of the relation. But though we cannot
find the god under this disguise of a sutler, yet on
the other hand we cannot forgive the poet if he
spins his thread too fine and does not substantiate
his romance by the municipal virtues of justice,
punctuality, fidelity and pity. I hate the prostitu-
tion of the name of friendship to signify modish
and worldly alliances. I much prefer the company
of ploughboys and tin-peddlers to the silken and
perfumed amity which celebrates its days of encounter by a frivolous display, by rides in a curri-
cle and dinners at the best taverns. The end of
friendship is a commerce the most strict and
homely that can be joined ; more strict than any of
which we have experience. It is for aid and comfort through all the relations and passages of life
and death. It is fit for serene days and graceful
gifts and country rambles, but also for rough
roads and hard fare, shipwreck, poverty and perse

*ε*ution. It keeps company with the sallies of the
wit and the trances of religion. We are to dignify
to each other the daily needs and offices of man's
life, and embellish it by courage, wisdom and unity.
It should never fall into something usual and settled, but should be alert and inventive and add
rhyme and reason to what was drudgery.

Friendship may be said to require natures so
rare and costly, each so well tempered and so happily adapted, and withal so circumstanced (for
even in that particular, a poet says, love demands
that the parties be altogether paired), that its satisfaction can very seldom be assured. It cannot
subsist in its perfection, say some of those who are
learned in this warm lore of the heart, betwixt
more than two. I am not quite so strict in my
terms, perhaps because I have never known so high
a fellowship as others. I please my imagination
more with a circle of godlike men and women variously related to each other and between whom subsists a lofty intelligence. But I find this law of
one to one peremptory for conversation, which is
the practice and consummation of friendship. Do
not mix waters too much. The best mix as ill as
good and bad. You shall have very useful and
cheering discourse at several times with two several
men, but let all three of you come together and you
shall not have one new and hearty word. **Two**

may talk and one may hear, but three cannot take part in a conversation of the most sincere and searching sort. In good company there is never such discourse between two, across the table, as takes place when you leave them alone. In good company the individuals merge their egotism into a social soul exactly co-extensive with the several consciousnesses there present. No partialities of friend to friend, no fondnesses of brother to sister, of wife to husband, are there pertinent, but quite otherwise. Only he may then speak who can sail on the common thought of the party, and not poorly limited to his own. Now this convention, which good sense demands, destroys the high freedom of great conversation, which requires an absolute running of two souls into one.

No two men but being left alone with each other enter into simpler relations. Yet it is affinity that determines *which* two shall converse. Unrelated men give little joy to each other, will never suspect the latent powers of each. We talk sometimes of a great talent for conversation, as if it were a permanent property in some individuals. Conversation is an evanescent relation, — no more. A man is reputed to have thought and eloquence; he cannot, for all that, say a word to his cousin or his uncle. They accuse his silence with as much reason as they would blame the insignificance of a dial if

the shade. In the sun it will mark the hour.
Among those who enjoy his thought he will regain
his tongue.

Friendship requires that rare mean betwixt likeness and unlikeness that piques each with the pres
ence of power and of consent in the other party.
Let me be alone to the end of the world, rather
than that my friend should overstep, by a word or a
look, his real sympathy. I am equally balked by
antagonism and by compliance. Let him not cease
an instant to be himself. The only joy I have in
his being mine, is that the *not mine* is *mine*. I
hate, where I looked for a manly furtherance or at
least a manly resistance, to find a mush of concession. Better be a nettle in the side of your friend
than his echo. The condition which high friendship demands is ability to do without it. That
high office requires great and sublime parts.
There must be very two, before there can be very
one. Let it be an alliance of two large, formidable
natures, mutually beheld, mutually feared, before
yet they recognize the deep identity which, beneath these disparities, unites them.

He only is fit for this society who is magnanimous ; who is sure that greatness and goodness
are always economy ; who is not swift to intermeddle with his fortunes. Let him not intermeddle
with this. Leave to the diamond its ages to grow,

nor expect to accelerate the births of the eternal
Friendship demands a religious treatment. We
talk of choosing our friends, but friends are self-
elected. Reverence is a great part of it. Treat
your friend as a spectacle. Of course he has merits
that are not yours, and that you cannot honor if
you must needs hold him close to your person.
Stand aside; give those merits room; let them
mount and expand. Are you the friend of your
friend's buttons, or of his thought? To a great
heart he will still be a stranger in a thousand particulars, that he may come near in the holiest
ground. Leave it to girls and boys to regard a
friend as property, and to suck a short and all-con-
founding pleasure, instead of the noblest benefit.

Let us buy our entrance to this guild by a long
probation. Why should we desecrate noble and
beautiful souls by intruding on them? Why insist
on rash personal relations with your friend? Why
go to his house, or know his mother and brother
and sisters? Why be visited by him at your own?
Are these things material to our covenant? Leave
this touching and clawing. Let him be to me a
spirit. A message, a thought, a sincerity, a glance
from him, I want, but not news, nor pottage. I can
get politics and chat and neighborly conveniences
from cheaper companions. Should not the society
of my friend be to me poetic, pure, universal and

great as nature itself? Ought I to feel that our tie is profane in comparison with yonder bar of cloud that sleeps on the horizon, or that clump of waving grass that divides the brook? Let us not vilify, but raise it to that standard. That great defying eye, that scornful beauty of his mien and action, do not pique yourself on reducing, but rather fortify and enhance. Worship his superiorities; wish him not less by a thought, but hoard and tell them all. Guard him as thy counterpart. Let him be to thee for ever a sort of beautiful enemy, untamable, devoutly revered, and not a trivial conveniency to be soon outgrown and cast aside. The hues of the opal, the light of the diamond, are not to be seen if the eye is too near. To my friend I write a letter and from him I receive a letter. That seems to you a little. It suffices me. It is a spiritual gift, worthy of him to give and of me to receive. It profanes nobody. In these warm lines the heart will trust itself, as it will not to the tongue, and pour out the prophecy of a godlier existence than all the annals of heroism have yet made good.

Respect so far the holy laws of this fellowship as not to prejudice its perfect flower by your impatience for its opening. We must be our own before we can be another's. There is at least this satisfaction in crime, according to the Latin proverb; — you can speak to your accomplice on even terms. *Crimen quos inquinat, æquat.* To those whom we admire and love, at first we cannot. Yet the least defect of self-possession vitiates, in my judgment, the entire relation. There can never be deep peace between two spirits, never mutual respect, until in their dialogue each stands for the whole world.

What is so great as friendship, let us carry with what grandeur of spirit we can. Let us be silent,— so we may hear the whisper of the gods. Let us not interfere. Who set you to cast about what you should say to the select souls, or how to say any thing to such? No matter how ingenious, no matter how graceful and bland. There are innumerable degrees of folly and wisdom, and for you to say aught is to be frivolous. Wait, and thy heart shall speak. Wait until the necessary and everlasting overpowers you, until day and night avail themselves of your lips. The only reward of virtue is virtue; the only way to have a friend is to be one. You shall not come nearer a man by getting into his house. If unlike, his soul only flees the faster from you, and you shall never catch a true glance of his eye. We see the noble afar off and they repel us ; why should we intrude ? Late, — very late, — we perceive that no arrangements, no introductions, no consuetudes or habits of society would be of any avail to establish us in such relations with them as we desire, — but solely the uprise of nature in us to the same degree it is in them; then shall we meet as water with water; and if we should not meet them then, we shall not want them, for we are already they. In the last analysis, love is only the reflection of a man's own worthiness from other men. Men have sometimes exchanged names with their friends, as if they would signify that in their friend each loved his own soul.

The higher the style we demand of friendship, of course the less easy to establish it with flesh and blood. We walk alone in the world. Friends such as we desire are dreams and fables. But a sublime hope cheers ever the faithful heart, that elsewhere, in other regions of the universal power, souls are now acting, enduring and daring, which can love us and which we can love. We may congratulate ourselves that the period of nonage, of follies, of blunders and of shame, is passed in solitude, and when we are finished men we shall grasp heroic hands in heroic hands. Only be admonished by what you already see, not to strike leagues of friendship with cheap persons, where no friendship can be. Our impatience betrays us into rash and foolish alliances which no god attends. By persisting in your path, though you forfeit the little you gain the great. You demonstrate yourself, so as to put yourself out of the reach of false relations, and you draw to you the first-born of the world, — those rare pilgrims whereof only one or two wander in nature at once, and before whom the vulgar great show as spectres and shadows merely.

It is foolish to be afraid of making our ties too spiritual, as if so we could lose any genuine love. Whatever correction of our popular views we make from insight, nature will be sure to bear us out in, and though it seem to rob us of some joy, will repay us with a greater. Let us feel if we will the absolute insulation of man. We are sure that we have all in us. We go to Europe, or we pursue persons, or we read books, in the instinctive faith that these will call it out and reveal us to ourselves. Beggars all. The persons are such as we; the Europe, an old faded garment of dead persons; the books, their ghosts. Let us drop this idolatry. Let us give over this mendicancy. Let us even bid our dearest friends farewell, and defy them, saying ' Who are you? Unhand me : I will be dependent no more.' Ah! seest thou not, O brother, that thus we part only to meet again on a higher platform, and only be more each other's because we are more our own? A friend is Janus-faced; he looks to the past and the future. He is the child of all my foregoing hours, the prophet of those to come, and the harbinger of a greater friend.

I do then with my friends as I do with my books

I would have them where I can find them, but I seldom use them. We must have society on our own terms, and admit or exclude it on the slightest cause. I cannot afford to speak much with my friend. If he is great he makes me so great that I cannot descend to converse. In the great days, presentiments hover before me in the firmament. I ought then to dedicate myself to them. I go in that I may seize them, I go out that I may seize them. I fear only that I may lose them receding into the sky in which now they are only a patch of brighter light. Then, though I prize my friends, I cannot afford to talk with them and study their visions, lest I lose my own. It would indeed give me a certain household joy to quit this lofty seeking, this spiritual astronomy or search of stars, and come down to warm sympathies with you; but then I know well I shall mourn always the vanishing of my mighty gods. It is true, next week I shall have languid moods, when I can well afford to occupy myself with foreign objects; then I shall regret the lost literature of your mind, and wish you were by my side again. But if you come, perhaps you will fill my mind only with new visions; not with yourself but with your lustres, and I shall not be able any more than now to converse with you. So I will owe to my friends this evanescent intercourse. I will receive from them not what they

have but what they are.   They shall give me that
which properly they cannot give, but which emanates from them.   But they shall not hold me by
any relations less subtile and pure.   We will meet
as though we met not, and part as though we parted
not.

It has seemed to me lately more possible than 1
knew, to carry a friendship greatly, on one side, without due correspondence on the other.   Why should
I cumber myself with regrets that the receiver is
not capacious?   It never troubles the sun that some
of his rays fall wide and vain into ungrateful space,
and only a small part on the reflecting planet.   Let
your greatness educate the crude and cold companion.   If he is unequal he will presently pass away;
but thou art enlarged by thy own shining, and no
longer a mate for frogs and worms, dost soar and
burn with the gods of the empyrean.   It is thought
a disgrace to love unrequited.   But the great will
see that true love cannot be unrequited.   True love
transcends the unworthy object and dwells and
broods on the eternal, and when the poor interposed
mask crumbles, it is not sad, but feels rid of so
much earth and feels its independency the surer.
Yet these things may hardly be said without a sort
of treachery to the relation.   The essence of friendship is entireness, a total magnanimity and trust
It must not surmise or provide for infirmity.   It
treats its object as a god, that it may deify both.

PRUDENCE.

———◆———

THEME no poet gladly sung,
Fair to old and foul to young;
Scorn not thou the love of parts,
And the articles of arts.
Grandeur of the perfect sphere
Thanks the atoms that cohere.

VII.

PRUDENCE.

———•———

WHAT right have I to write on Prudence, where of I have little, and that of the negative sort? My prudence consists in avoiding and going without, not in the inventing of means and methods, not in adroit steering, not in gentle repairing. I have no skill to make money spend well, no genius in my economy, and whoever sees my garden discovers that I must have some other garden. Yet I love facts, and hate lubricity and people without perception. Then I have the same title to write on prudence that I have to write on poetry or holiness. We write from aspiration and antagonism, as well as from experience. We paint those qualities which we do not possess. The poet admires the man of energy and tactics; the merchant breeds his son for the church or the bar; and where a man is not vain and egotistic you shall find what he has not by his praise. Moreover it would be hardly honest in me not to balance these fine lyric words of Love and

Friendship with words of coarser sound, and whilst
my debt to my senses is real and constant, not to
own it in passing.

Prudence is the virtue of the senses. It is the
science of appearances. It is the outmost action of
the inward life. It is God taking thought for oxen.
It moves matter after the laws of matter. It is
content to seek health of body by complying with
physical conditions, and health of mind by the laws
of the intellect.

The world of the senses is a world of shows; it
does not exist for itself, but has a symbolic character; and a true prudence or law of shows recog
nizes the co-presence of other laws and knows that
its own office is subaltern; knows that it is surface
and not centre where it works. Prudence is false
when detached. It is legitimate when it is the Natural History of the soul incarnate, when it unfolds
the beauty of laws within the narrow scope of the
senses.

There are all degrees of proficiency in knowledge
of the world. It is sufficient to our present purpose
to indicate three. One class live to the utility of
the symbol, esteeming health and wealth a final
good. Another class live above this mark to the
beauty of the symbol, as the poet and artist and
the naturalist and man of science. A third class
live above the beauty of the symbol to the beauty

of the thing signified; these are wise men. The
first class have common sense; the second, taste;
and the third, spiritual perception. Once in a long
time, a man traverses the whole scale, and sees and
enjoys the symbol solidly, then also has a clear eye
for its beauty, and lastly, whilst he pitches his tent
on this sacred volcanic isle of nature, does not offer
to build houses and barns thereon, — reverencing
the splendor of the God which he sees bursting
through each chink and cranny.

The world is filled with the proverbs and acts
and winkings of a base prudence, which is a devotion to matter, as if we possessed no other faculties
than the palate, the nose, the touch, the eye and
ear; a prudence which adores the Rule of Three,
which never subscribes, which never gives, which
seldom lends, and asks but one question of any project, — Will it bake bread? This is a disease like
a thickening of the skin until the vital organs are
destroyed. But culture, revealing the high origin
of the apparent world and aiming at the perfection
of the man as the end, degrades every thing else,
as health and bodily life, into means. It sees prudence not to be a several faculty, but a name for
wisdom and virtue conversing with the body and
its wants. Cultivated men always feel and speak
so, as if a great fortune, the achievement of a civil
or social measure, great personal influence, a grace-

ful and commanding address, had their value as proofs of the energy of the spirit. If a man lose his balance and immerse himself in any trades or pleasures for their own sake, he may be a good wheel or pin, but he is not a cultivated man.

The spurious prudence, making the senses final, is the god of sots and cowards, and is the subject of all comedy. It is nature's joke, and therefore literature's. The true prudence limits this sensualism by admitting the knowledge of an internal and real world. This recognition once made, the order of the world and the distribution of affairs and times, being studied with the co-perception of their subordinate place, will reward any degree of attention. For our existence, thus apparently attached in nature to the sun and the returning moon and the periods which they mark, — so susceptible to climate and to country, so alive to social good and evil, so fond of splendor and so tender to hunger and cold and debt, — reads all its primary lessons out of these books.

Prudence does not go behind nature and ask whence it is. It takes the laws of the world whereby man's being is conditioned, as they are, and keeps these laws that it may enjoy their proper good. It respects space and time, climate, want, sleep, the law of polarity, growth and death. There revolve, to give bound and period to his being on all sides, the sun and moon, the great formalists in the sky: here lies stubborn matter, and will not swerve from its chemical routine. Here is a planted globe, pierced and belted with natural laws and fenced and distributed externally with civil partitions and properties which impose new restraints on the young inhabitant.

We eat of the bread which grows in the field. We live by the air which blows around us and we are poisoned by the air that is too cold or too hot, too dry or too wet. Time, which shows so vacant, indivisible and divine in its coming, is slit and peddled into trifles and tatters. A door is to be painted, a lock to be repaired. I want wood or oil, or meal or salt; the house smokes, or I have a headache; then the tax, and an affair to be transacted with a man without heart or brains, and the stinging recollection of an injurious or very awkward word, — these eat up the hours. Do what we can, summer will have its flies; if we walk in the woods we must feed mosquitos; if we go a-fishing we must expect a wet coat. Then climate is a great impediment to idle persons; we often resolve to give up the care of the weather, but still we regard the clouds and the rain.

We are instructed by these petty experiences which usurp the hours and years. The hard soil and four months of snow make the inhabitant of

the northern temperate zone wiser and abler than
his fellow who enjoys the fixed smile of the tropics.
The islander may ramble all day at will.   At
night he may sleep on a mat under the moon, and
wherever a wild date-tree grows, nature has, without a prayer even, spread a table for his morning
meal.   The northerner is perforce a householder.
He must brew, bake, salt and preserve his food,
and pile wood and coal.   But as it happens that
not one stroke can labor lay to without some new
acquaintance with nature, and as nature is inex-
haustibly significant, the inhabitants of these cli
mates have always excelled the southerner in force.
Such is the value of these matters that a man who
knows other things can never know too much of
these.   Let him have accurate perceptions.   Let
him, if he have hands, handle; if eyes, measure and
discriminate; let him accept and hive every fact of
chemistry, natural history and economics; the more
he has, the less is he willing to spare any one.
Time is always bringing the occasions that disclose
their value.   Some wisdom comes out of every natural and innocent action.   The domestic man, who
loves no music so well as his kitchen clock and the
airs which the logs sing to him as they burn on the
hearth, has solaces which others never dream of.
The application of means to ends insures victory
and the songs of victory not less in a farm or a

shop than in the tactics of party or of war. The
good husband finds method as efficient in the pack-
ing of fire-wood in a shed or in the harvesting of
fruits in the cellar, as in Peninsular campaigns or
the files of the Department of State. In the rainy
day he builds a work-bench, or gets his tool-box
set in the corner of the barn-chamber, and stored
with nails, gimlet, pincers, screwdriver and chisel.
Herein he tastes an old joy of youth and childhood,
the cat-like love of garrets, presses and corn-cham-
bers, and of the conveniences of long housekeeping.
His garden or his poultry-yard tells him many
pleasant anecdotes. One might find argument for
optimism in the abundant flow of this saccharine
element of pleasure in every suburb and extremity
of the good world. Let a man keep the law, —
any law, — and his way will be strown with satisfactions. There is more difference in the quality
of our pleasures than in the amount.

On the other hand, nature punishes any neglect
of prudence. If you think the senses final, obey
their law. If you believe in the soul, do not clutch
at sensual sweetness before it is ripe on the slow tree
of cause and effect. It is vinegar to the eyes to
deal with men of loose and imperfect perception.
Dr. Johnson is reported to have said, — "If the
child says he looked out of this window, when he
looked out of that, — whip him." Our American

character is marked by a more than average delight in accurate perception, which is shown by the currency of the byword, " No mistake." But the discomfort of unpunctuality, of confusion of thought about facts, inattention to the wants of to-morrow, is of no nation. The beautiful laws of time and space, once dislocated by our inaptitude, are holes and dens. If the hive be disturbed by rash and stupid hands, instead of honey it will yield us bees. Our words and actions to be fair must be timely. A gay and pleasant sound is the whetting of the scythe in the mornings of June, yet what is more lonesome and sad than the sound of a whetstone or mower's rifle when it is too late in the season to make hay? Scatter-brained and " afternoon " men spoil much more than their own affair in spoiling the temper of those who deal with them. I have seen a criticism on some paintings, of which I am reminded when I see the shiftless and unhappy men who are not true to their senses. The last Grand Duke of Weimar, a man of superior understanding, said, — " I have sometimes remarked in the presence of great works of art, and just now especially in Dresden, how much a certain property contributes to the effect which gives life to the figures, and to the life an irresistible truth. This property is the hitting, in all the figures we draw, the right centre of gravity. I mean the placing the figures firm

upon their feet, making the hands grasp, and fasten-
ing the eyes on the spot where they should look.
Even lifeless figures, as vessels and stools — let
them be drawn ever so correctly — lose all effect so
soon as they lack the resting upon their centre of
gravity, and have a certain swimming and oscillat-
ing appearance. The Raphael in the Dresden gallery (the only great affecting picture which I have
seen) is the quietest and most passionless piece you
can imagine; a couple of saints who worship the
Virgin and Child. Nevertheless it awakens a deeper
impression than the contortions of ten crucified
martyrs. For beside all the resistless beauty of
form, it possesses in the highest degree the property
of the perpendicularity of all the figures." This
perpendicularity we demand of all the figures in
this picture of life. Let them stand on their feet,
and not float and swing. Let us know where to find
them. Let them discriminate between what they
remember and what they dreamed, call a spade a
spade, give us facts, and honor their own senses
with trust.

But what man shall dare task another with im-
prudence? Who is prudent? The men we call
greatest are least in this kingdom. There is a certain fatal dislocation in our relation to nature, dis-
torting our modes of living and making every law
our enemy, which seems at last to have aroused all

the wit and virtue in the world to ponder the question of Reform. We must call the highest prudence to counsel, and ask why health and beauty and genius should now be the exception rather than the rule of human nature? We do not know the properties of plants and animals and the laws of nature, through our sympathy with the same; but this remains the dream of poets. Poetry and prudence should be coincident. Poets should be lawgivers; that is, the boldest lyric inspiration should not chide and insult, but should announce and lead the civil code and the day's work. But now the two things seem irreconcilably parted. We have violated law upon law until we stand amidst ruins, and when by chance we espy a coincidence between reason and the phenomena, we are surprised. Beauty should be the dowry of every man and woman, as invariably as sensation; but it is rare. Health or sound organization should be universal. Genius should be the child of genius and every child should be inspired; but now it is not to be predicted of any child, and nowhere is it pure. We call partial half-lights, by courtesy, genius; talent which converts itself to money; talent which glitters to-day that it may dine and sleep well to-morrow; and society is officered by *men of parts*, as they are properly called, and not by divine men. These use their gift to refine luxury, not to abolish it. Genius is always ascetic, and piety, and love. Appetite shows to the finer souls as a disease, and they find beauty in rites and bounds that resist it.

We have found out fine names to cover our sensuality withal, but no gifts can raise intemperance. The man of talent affects to call his transgressions of the laws of the senses trivial and to count them nothing considered with his devotion to his art. His art never taught him lewdness, nor the love of wine, nor the wish to reap where he had not sowed. His art is less for every deduction from his holiness, and less for every defect of common sense. On him who scorned the world as he said, the scorned world wreaks its revenge. He that despiseth small things will perish by little and little. Goethe's Tasso is very likely to be a pretty fair historical portrait, and that is true tragedy. It does not seem to me so genuine grief when some tyrannous Richard the Third oppresses and slays a score of innocent persons, as when Antonio and Tasso, both apparently right, wrong each other. One living after the maxims of this world and consistent and true to them, the other fired with all divine sentiments, yet grasping also at the pleasures of sense, without submitting to their law. That is a grief we all feel, a knot we cannot untie. Tasso's is no unfrequent case in modern biography. A man of genius. of an ardent temperament, reckless

of physical laws, self-indulgent, becomes presently
unfortunate, querulous, a " discomfortable cousin,'
a thorn to himself and to others.

The scholar shames us by his bifold life. Whilst
something higher than prudence is active, he is admirable ; when common sense is wanted, he is an
encumbrance. Yesterday, Cæsar was not so great ;
to-day, the felon at the gallows' foot is not more
miserable. Yesterday, radiant with the light of an
ideal world in which he lives, the first of men ; and
now oppressed by wants and by sickness, for which
he must thank himself. He resembles the pitiful
drivellers whom travellers describe as frequenting
the bazaars of Constantinople, who skulk about all
day, yellow, emaciated, ragged, sneaking ; and at
evening, when the bazaars are open, slink to the
opium-shop, swallow their morsel and become tranquil and glorified seers. And who has not seen
the tragedy of imprudent genius struggling for
years with paltry pecuniary difficulties, at last sink-
ing, chilled, exhausted and fruitless, like a giant
slaughtered by pins ?

Is it not better that a man should accept the first
pains and mortifications of this sort, which nature
is not slack in sending him, as hints that he must
expect no other good than the just fruit of his own
labor and self-denial ? Health, bread, climate, social position, have their importance, and he will

give them their due. Let him esteem Nature a
perpetual counsellor, and her perfections the exact
measure of our deviations. Let him make the
night night, and the day day. Let him control
the habit of expense. Let him see that as much
wisdom may be expended on a private economy as
on an empire, and as much wisdom may be drawn
from it. The laws of the world are written out for
him on every piece of money in his hand. There
is nothing he will not be the better for knowing,
were it only the wisdom of Poor Richard, or the
State-Street prudence of buying by the acre to sell
by the foot; or the thrift of the agriculturist, to
stick a tree between whiles, because it will grow
whilst he sleeps ; or the prudence which consists in
husbanding little strokes of the tool, little portions
of time, particles of stock and small gains. The
eye of prudence may never shut. Iron, if kept at
the ironmonger's, will rust; beer, if not brewed in
the right state of the atmosphere, will sour; timber
of ships will rot at sea, or if laid up high and dry,
will strain, warp and dry-rot; money, if kept by us,
yields no rent and is liable to loss; if invested, is
liable to depreciation of the particular kind of
stock. Strike, says the smith, the iron is white ;
keep the rake, says the haymaker, as nigh the
scythe as you can, and the cart as nigh the rake.
Our Yankee trade is reputed to be very much on

the extreme of this prudence. It takes bank-notes, good, bad, clean, ragged, and saves itself by the speed with which it passes them off. Iron cannot rust, nor beer sour, nor timber rot, nor calicoes go out of fashion, nor money stocks depreciate, in the few swift moments in which the Yankee suffers any one of them to remain in his possession. In skating over thin ice our safety is in our speed.

Let him learn a prudence of a higher strain. Let him learn that every thing in nature, even motes and feathers, go by law and not by luck, and that what he sows he reaps. By diligence and self-command let him put the bread he eats at his own disposal, that he may not stand in bitter and false relations to other men; for the best good of wealth is freedom. Let him practise the minor virtues. How much of human life is lost in waiting! let him not make his fellow-creatures wait. How many words and promises are promises of conversation! Let his be words of fate. When he sees a folded and sealed scrap of paper float round the globe in a pine ship and come safe to the eye for which it was written, amidst a swarming population, let him likewise feel the admonition to integrate his being across all these distracting forces, and keep a slender human word among the storms, distances and accidents that drive us hither and thither, and, by persistency, make the paltry force of one man reappear to redeem its pledge after months and years in the most distant climates.

We must not try to write the laws of any one virtue, looking at that only. Human nature loves no contradictions, but is symmetrical. The prudence which secures an outward well-being is not to be studied by one set of men, whilst heroism and holiness are studied by another, but they are reconcilable. Prudence concerns the present time, persons, property and existing forms. But as every fact hath its roots in the soul, and if the soul were changed would cease to be, or would become some other thing, — the proper administration of outward things will always rest on a just apprehension of their cause and origin ; that is, the good man will be the wise man, and the single-hearted the politic man. Every violation of truth is not only a sort of suicide in the liar, but is a stab at the health of human society. On the most profitable lie the course of events presently lays a destructive tax ; whilst frankness invites frankness, puts the parties on a convenient footing and makes their business a friendship. Trust men and they will be true to you ; treat them greatly and they will show themselves great, though they make an exception in your favor to all their rules of trade.

So, in regard to disagreeable and formidable things, prudence does not consist in evasion or in

flight, but in courage. He who wishes to walk in
the most peaceful parts of life with any serenity
must screw himself up to resolution. Let him front
the object of his worst apprehension, and his stoutness will commonly make his fear groundless. The
Latin proverb says, "In battles the eye is first over-
come." Entire self-possession may make a battle
very little more dangerous to life than a match at
foils or at football. Examples are cited by soldiers
of men who have seen the cannon pointed and the
fire given to it, and who have stepped aside from
the path of the ball. The terrors of the storm are
chiefly confined to the parlor and the cabin. The
drover, the sailor, buffets it all day, and his health
renews itself at as vigorous a pulse under the sleet
as under the sun of June.

In the occurrence of unpleasant things among
neighbors, fear comes readily to heart and magni-
fies the consequence of the other party ; but it is a
bad counsellor Every man is actually weak and
apparently strong. To himself he seems weak ; to
others, formidable. You are afraid of Grim ; but
Grim also is afraid of you. You are solicitous of
the good-will of the meanest person, uneasy at his
ill-will. But the sturdiest offender of your peace
and of the neighborhood, if you rip up *his* claims,
is as thin and timid as any, and the peace of society
is often kept, because, as children say, one is afraid

and the other dares not. Far off, men swell, bully and threaten ; bring them hand to hand, and they are a feeble folk.

It is a proverb that ' courtesy costs nothing ' ; but calculation might come to value love for its profit. Love is fabled to be blind, but kindness is necessary to perception ; love is not a hood, but an eye-water. If you meet a sectary or a hostile partisan, never recognize the dividing lines, but meet on what common ground remains, — if only that the sun shines and the rain rains for both; the area will widen very fast, and ere you know it, the boundary mountains on which the eye had fastened have melted into air. If they set out to contend, Saint Paul will lie and Saint John will hate. What low, poor, paltry, hypocritical people an argument on religion will make of the pure and chosen souls ! They will shuffle and crow, crook and hide, feign to confess here, only that they may brag and conquer there, and not a thought has enriched either party, and not an emotion of bravery, modesty, or hope. So neither should you put yourself in a false position with your contemporaries by indulging a vein of hostility and bitterness. Though your views are in straight antagonism to theirs, assume an identity of sentiment, assume that you are saying precisely that which all think, and in the flow of wit and love roll out your paradoxes in solid column, with not the infirmity of a doubt. So at least shall you get an adequate deliverance. The natural motions of the soul are so much better than the voluntary ones that you will never do yourself justice in dispute. The thought is not then taken hold of by the right handle, does not show itself proportioned and in its true bearings, but bears extorted, hoarse, and half witness. But assume a consent and it shall presently be granted, since really and underneath their external diversities, all men are of one heart and mind.

Wisdom will never let us stand with any man or men on an unfriendly footing. We refuse sympathy and intimacy with people, as if we waited for some better sympathy and intimacy to come. But whence and when? To-morrow will be like to-day. Life wastes itself whilst we are preparing to live. Our friends and fellow-workers die off from us. Scarcely can we say we see new men, new women, approaching us. We are too old to regard fashion, too old to expect patronage of any greater or more powerful. Let us suck the sweetness of those affections and consuetudes that grow near us. These old shoes are easy to the feet. Undoubtedly we can easily pick faults in our company, can easily whisper names prouder, and that tickle the fancy more. Every man's imagination hath its friends; and life would be dearer with such companions.

But if you cannot have them on good mutual terms, you cannot have them. If not the Deity but our ambition hews and shapes the new relations, their virtue escapes, as strawberries lose their flavor in garden-beds.

Thus truth, frankness, courage, love, humility and all the virtues range themselves on the side of prudence, or the art of securing a present well-being. I do not know if all matter will be found to be made of one element, as oxygen or hydrogen, at last, but the world of manners and actions is wrought of one stuff, and begin where we will we are pretty sure in a short space to be mumbling our ten commandments.

HEROISM.

———◆———

"Paradise is under the shadow of swords."

———◆———

RUBY wine is drunk by knaves,
Sugar spends to fatten slaves,
Rose and vine-leaf deck buffoons ;
Thunderclouds are Jove's festoons,
Drooping oft in wreaths of dread
Lightning-knotted round his head ;
The hero is not fed on sweets,
Daily his own heart he eats ;
Chambers of the great are jails,
And head-winds right for royal sails.

VIII.

HEROISM.

In the elder English dramatists, and mainly in the plays of Beaumont and Fletcher, there is a constant recognition of gentility, as if a noble behavior were as easily marked in the society of their age as color is in our American population. When any Rodrigo, Pedro or Valerio enters, though he be a stranger, the duke or governor exclaims, 'This is a gentleman,' — and proffers civilities without end ; but all the rest are slag and refuse. In harmony with this delight in personal advantages there is in their plays a certain heroic cast of character and dialogue, — as in Bonduca, Sophocles, the Mad Lover, the Double Marriage, — wherein the speaker is so earnest and cordial and on such deep grounds of character, that the dialogue, on the slightest additional incident in the plot, rises naturally into poetry. Among many texts take the following. The Roman Martius has conquered Athens, — all but the invincible spirits of Sophocles, the duke of Athens, and Dorigen, his wife. The beauty of the latter inflames Martius, and he seeks to save her husband; but Sophocles will not ask his life, although assured that a word will save him, and the execution of both proceeds: —

Valerius. Bid thy wife farewell.

Soph. No, I will take no leave. My Dorigen,
Yonder, above, 'bout Ariadne's crown,
My spirit shall hover for thee. Prithee, haste.

Dor. Stay, Sophocles, — with this tie up my sight;
Let not soft nature so transformed be,
And lose her gentler sexed humanity,
To make me see my lord bleed. So, 't is well;
Never one object underneath the sun
Will I behold before my Sophocles:
Farewell; now teach the Romans how to die.

Mar. Dost know what 't is to die?

Soph. Thou dost not, Martius,
And, therefore, not what 't is to live; to die
Is to begin to live. It is to end
An old, stale, weary work and to commence
A newer and a better. 'T is to leave
Deceitful knaves for the society
Of gods and goodness. Thou thyself must part
At last from all thy garlands, pleasures, triumphs,
And prove thy fortitude what then 't will do.

Val. But art not grieved nor vexed to leave thy life thus?

Soph. Why should I grieve or vex for being sent
To them I ever loved best? Now I 'll kneel,
But with my back toward thee: 't is the last duty
This trunk can do the gods.

Mar. Strike, strike, Valerius,
Or Martius' heart will leap out at his mouth.

This is a man, a woman. Kiss thy lord,
And live with all the freedom you were wont.
O love! thou doubly hast afflicted me
With virtue and with beauty. Treacherous heart,
My hand shall cast thee quick into my urn,
Ere thou transgress this knot of piety.

 Val. What ails my brother ?

 Soph. Martius, O Martius,
Thou now hast found a way to conquer me.

 Dor. O star of Rome! what gratitude can speak
Fit words to follow such a deed as this ?

 Mar. This admirable duke, Valerius,
With his disdain of fortune and of death,
Captived himself, has captivated me,
And though my arm hath ta'en his body here,
His soul hath subjugated Martius' soul.
By Romulus, he is all soul, I think;
He hath no flesh, and spirit cannot be gyved,
Then we have vanquished nothing; he is free,
And Martius walks now in captivity."

I do not readily remember any poem, play, sermon, novel or oration that our press vents in the last few years, which goes to the same tune. We have a great many flutes and flageolets, but not often the sound of any fife. Yet Wordsworth's "Laodamia," and the ode of "Dion," and some sonnets, have a certain noble music ; and Scott will sometimes draw a stroke like the portrait of Lord Evandale given by Balfour of Burley. Thomas Carlyle, with his natural taste for what is manly and daring in character, has suffered no heroic trait in his favorites to drop from his biographical and historical pictures. Earlier, Robert Burns has given us a song or two. In the Harleian Miscellanies there is an account of the battle of Lutzen which deserves to be read. And Simon Ockley's History of the Saracens recounts the prodigies of individual valor, with admiration all the more evident on the part of the narrator that he seems to think that his place in Christian Oxford requires of him some proper protestations of abhorrence. But if we explore the literature of Heroism we shall quickly come to Plutarch, who is its Doctor and historian. To him we owe the Brasidas, the Dion, the Epaminondas, the Scipio of old, and I must think we are more deeply indebted to him than to all the ancient writers. Each of his "Lives" is a refutation to the despondency and cowardice of our religious and political theorists. A wild courage, a Stoicism not of the schools but of the blood, shines in every anecdote, and has given that book its immense fame.

We need books of this tart cathartic virtue more than books of political science or of private economy. Life is a festival only to the wise. Seen from the nook and chimney-side of prudence, it wears a ragged and dangerous front. The violations of the laws of nature by our predecessors and our contemporaries are punished in us also. The disease and deformity around us certify the infraction of natural, intellectual and moral laws, and often violation on violation to breed such compound misery. A lock-jaw that bends a man's head back to his heels; hydrophobia that makes him bark at his wife and babes; insanity that makes him eat grass; war, plague, cholera, famine, indicate a certain ferocity in nature, which, as it had its inlet by human crime, must have its outlet by human suffering. Unhappily no man exists who has not in his own person become to some amount a stockholder in the sin, and so made himself liable to a share in the expiation.

Our culture therefore must not omit the arming of the man. Let him hear in season that he is born into the state of war, and that the commonwealth and his own well-being require that he should not go dancing in the weeds of peace, but warned, self-collected and neither defying nor dreading the thunder, let him take both reputation and life in his hand, and with perfect urbanity dare the gibbet and the mob by the absolute truth of his speech and the rectitude of his behavior.

Towards all this external evil the man within the breast assumes a warlike attitude, and affirms his ability to cope single-handed with the infinite army of enemies. To this military attitude of the soul we give the name of Heroism. Its rudest form is the contempt for safety and ease, which makes the attractiveness of war. It is a self-trust which slights the restraints of prudence, in the plenitude of its energy and power to repair the harms it may suffer. The hero is a mind of such balance that no disturbances can shake his will, but pleasantly and as it were merrily he advances to his own music, alike in frightful alarms and in the tipsy mirth of universal dissoluteness. There is somewhat not philosophical in heroism; there is somewhat not holy in it; it seems not to know that other souls are of one texture with it; it has pride; it is the extreme of individual nature. Nevertheless we must profoundly revere it. There is somewhat in great actions which does not allow us to go behind them. Heroism feels and never reasons, and therefore is always right; and although a different breeding, different religion and greater intellectual activity would have modified or even reversed the particular action, yet for the hero that thing he does is the highest deed, and is not open to the censure of philosophers or divines. It is the avowal of the unschooled man that he finds a quality in him that is negligent of expense, of health, of life, of danger, of hatred, of reproach, and knows that his will is higher and more excellent than all actual and all possible antagonists.

Heroism works in contradiction to the voice of

mankind and in contradiction, for a time, to the voice of the great and good. Heroism is an obedience to a secret impulse of an individual's character. Now to no other man can its wisdom appear as it does to him, for every man must be supposed to see a little farther on his own proper path than any one else. Therefore just and wise men take umbrage at his act, until after some little time be past; then they see it to be in unison with their acts. All prudent men see that the action is clean contrary to a sensual prosperity; for every heroic act measures itself by its contempt of some external good. But it finds its own success at last, and then the prudent also extol.

Self-trust is the essence of heroism. It is the state of the soul at war, and its ultimate objects are the last defiance of falsehood and wrong, and the power to bear all that can be inflicted by evil agents It speaks the truth and it is just, generous, hospitable, temperate, scornful of petty calculations and scornful of being scorned. It persists; it is of an undaunted boldness and of a fortitude not to be wearied out. Its jest is the littleness of common life. That false prudence which dotes on health and wealth is the butt and merriment of heroism. Heroism, like Plotinus, is almost ashamed of its body. What shall it say then to the sugar-plums and cats'-cradles, to the toilet compliments, quar-

rels, cards and custard, which rack the wit of all
society? What joys has kind nature provided for
us dear creatures! There seems to be no interval
between greatness and meanness. When the spirit
is not master of the world, then it is its dupe.
Yet the little man takes the great hoax so innocently, works in it so headlong and believing, is
born red, and dies gray, arranging his toilet, attending on his own health, laying traps for sweet
food and strong wine, setting his heart on a horse
or a rifle, made happy with a little gossip or a little praise, that the great soul cannot choose but
laugh at such earnest nonsense. " Indeed, these
humble considerations make me out of love with
greatness. What a disgrace is it to me to take
note how many pairs of silk stockings thou hast,
namely, these and those that were the peach-col-
ored ones; or to bear the inventory of thy shirts,
as one for superfluity, and one other for use ! "

Citizens, thinking after the laws of arithmetic,
consider the inconvenience of receiving strangers
at their fireside, reckon narrowly the loss of time
and the unusual display; the soul of a better quality thrusts back the unseasonable economy into the
vaults of life, and says, I will obey the God, and
the sacrifice and the fire he will provide. Ibn
Hankal, the Arabian geographer, describes a heroic
extreme in the hospitality of Sogd, in Bukharia.

" When I was in Sogd I saw a great building, like
a palace, the gates of which were open and fixed
back to the wall with large nails. I asked the reason, and was told that the house had not been shut,
night or day, for a hundred years. Strangers may
present themselves at any hour and in whatever
number ; the master has amply provided for the reception of the men and their animals and is never
happier than when they tarry for some time.
Nothing of the kind have I seen in any other country." The magnanimous know very well that they
who give time, or money, or shelter, to the stranger, — so it be done for love and not for ostentation, — do, as it were, put God under obligation to
them. so perfect are the compensations of the universe. In some way the time they seem to lose is
redeemed and the pains they seem to take remuner-
ate themselves. These men fan the flame of human
love and raise the standard of civil virtue among
mankind. But hospitality must be for service and
not for show, or it pulls down the host. The brave
soul rates itself too high to value itself by the
splendor of its table and draperies. It gives what
it hath, and all it hath, but its own majesty can
lend a better grace to bannocks and fair water than
belong to city feasts.

The temperance of the hero proceeds from the
same wish to do no dishonor to the worthiness he

has. But he loves it for its elegancy, not for its austerity. It seems not worth his while to be solemn and denounce with bitterness flesh-eating or wine - drinking, the use of tobacco, or opium, or tea, or silk, or gold. A great man scarcely knows how he dines, how he dresses; but without railing or precision his living is natural and poetic. John Eliot, the Indian Apostle, drank water, and said of wine, — "It is a noble, generous liquor and we should be humbly thankful for it, but, as I remember, water was made before it." Better still is the temperance of King David, who poured out on the ground unto the Lord the water which three of his warriors had brought him to drink, at the peril of their lives.

It is told of Brutus, that when he fell on his sword after the battle of Philippi, he quoted a line of Euripides, — "O Virtue! I have followed thee through life, and I find thee at last but a shade." I doubt not the hero is slandered by this report. The heroic soul does not sell its justice and its nobleness. It does not ask to dine nicely and to sleep warm. The essence of greatness is the perception that virtue is enough. Poverty is its ornament. It does not need plenty, and can very well abide its loss.

But that which takes my fancy most in the heroic class, is the good-humor and hilarity they ex hibit. It is a height to which common duty can very well attain, to suffer and to dare with solemnity. But these rare souls set opinion, success, and life at so cheap a rate that they will not soothe their enemies by petitions, or the show of sorrow, but wear their own habitual greatness. Scipio, charged with peculation, refuses to do himself so great a disgrace as to wait for justification, though he had the scroll of his accounts in his hands, but tears it to pieces before the tribunes. Socrates's condemnation of himself to be maintained in all honor in the Prytaneum, during his life, and Sir Thomas More's playfulness at the scaffold, are of the same strain. In Beaumont and Fletcher's "Sea Voyage," Juletta tells the stout captain and his company, —

> *Jul.* Why, slaves, 'tis in our power to hang ye.
> *Master.*   Very likely,
> 'Tis in our powers, then, to be hanged, and scorn ye.

These replies are sound and whole. Sport is the bloom and glow of a perfect health. The great will not condescend to take any thing seriously; all must be as gay as the song of a canary, though it were the building of cities or the eradication of old and foolish churches and nations which have cumbered the earth long thousands of years. Simple hearts put all the history and customs of this world behind them, and play their own game in innocent

defiance of the Blue-Laws of the world ; and such
would appear, could we see the human race assem-
bled in vision, like little children frolicking together, though to the eyes of mankind at large
they wear a stately and solemn garb of works and
influences.

The interest these fine stories have for us, the
power of a romance over the boy who grasps the
forbidden book under his bench at school, our delight in the hero, is the main fact to our purpose.
All these great and transcendent properties are
ours. If we dilate in beholding the Greek energy,
the Roman pride, it is that we are already domesti-
cating the same sentiment. Let us find room for
this great guest in our small houses. The first
step of worthiness will be to disabuse us of our superstitious associations with places and times, with
number and size. Why should these words, Athe-
nian, Roman, Asia and England, so tingle in the
ear? Where the heart is, there the muses, there
the gods sojourn, and not in any geography of
fame. Massachusetts, Connecticut River and Boston Bay you think paltry places, and the ear loves
names of foreign and classic topography. But
here we are ; and, if we will tarry a little, we may
come to learn that here is best. See to it only that
thyself is here, and art and nature, hope and fate,
friends, angels and the Supreme Being shall not be

absent from the chamber where thou sittest. Epaminondas, brave and affectionate, does not seem to us to need Olympus to die upon, nor the Syrian sunshine. He lies very well where he is. The Jerseys were handsome ground enough for Washington to tread, and London streets for the feet of Milton. A great man makes his climate genial in the imagination of men, and its air the beloved element of all delicate spirits. That country is the fairest which is inhabited by the noblest minds. The pictures which fill the imagination in reading the actions of Pericles, Xenophon, Columbus, Bayard, Sidney, Hampden, teach us how needlessly mean our life is; that we, by the depth of our living, should deck it with more than regal or national splendor, and act on principles that should interest man and nature in the length of our days.

We have seen or heard of many extraordinary young men who never ripened, or whose performance in actual life was not extraordinary. When we see their air and mien, when we hear them speak of society, of books, of religion, we admire their superiority ; they seem to throw contempt on our entire polity and social state ; theirs is the tone of a youthful giant who is sent to work revolutions. But they enter an active profession and the forming Colossus shrinks to the common size of man. The magic they used was the ideal tendencies, which al·

ways make the Actual ridiculous; but the tough
world had its revenge the moment they put their
horses of the sun to plough in its furrow. They
found no example and no companion, and their
heart fainted. What then? The lesson they gave
in their first aspirations is yet true; and a better
valor and a purer truth shall one day organize
their belief. Or why should a woman liken herself to any historical woman, and think, because
Sappho, or Sévigné, or De Staël, or the cloistered
souls who have had genius and cultivation do not
satisfy the imagination and the serene Themis, none
can, — certainly not she? Why not? She has a
new and unattempted problem to solve, perchance
that of the happiest nature that ever bloomed.
Let the maiden, with erect soul, walk serenely on
her way, accept the hint of each new experience,
search in turn all the objects that solicit her eye,
that she may learn the power and the charm of her
new-born being, which is the kindling of a new
dawn in the recesses of space. The fair girl who
repels interference by a decided and proud choice
of influences, so careless of pleasing, so wilful and
lofty, inspires every beholder with somewhat of her
own nobleness. The silent heart encourages her;
O friend, never strike sail to a fear! Come into
port greatly, or sail with God the seas. Not in
vain you live, for every passing eye is cheered and
refined by the vision.

The characteristic of heroism is its persistency.
All men have wandering impulses, fits and starts
of generosity. But when you have chosen your
part, abide by it, and do not weakly try to reconcile
yourself with the world. The heroic cannot be the
common, nor the common the heroic. Yet we have
the weakness to expect the sympathy of people in
those actions whose excellence is that they outrun
sympathy and appeal to a tardy justice. If you
would serve your brother, because it is fit for you
to serve him, do not take back your words when
you find that prudent people do not commend you.
Adhere to your own act, and congratulate yourself
if you have done something strange and extravagant and broken the monotony of a decorous age.
It was a high counsel that I once heard given to a
young person, — " Always do what you are afraid
to do." A simple manly character need never
make an apology, but should regard its past action
with the calmness of Phocion, when he admitted
that the event of the battle was happy, yet did not
regret his dissuasion from the battle.

There is no weakness or exposure for which we
cannot find consolation in the thought — this is a
part of my constitution, part of my relation and office to my fellow-creature. Has nature convenanted
with me that I should never appear to disadvan-
tage, never make a ridiculous figure? Let us be

generous of our dignity as well as of our money.
Greatness once and for ever has done with opinion.
We tell our charities, not because we wish to be
praised for them, not because we think they have
great merit, but for our justification. It is a capital blunder ; as you discover when another man recites his charities.

To speak the truth, even with some austerity, to
live with some rigor of temperance, or some extremes of generosity, seems to be an asceticism
which common good-nature would appoint to those
who are at ease and in plenty, in sign that they
feel a brotherhood with the great multitude of suffering men. And not only need we breathe and
exercise the soul by assuming the penalties of abstinence, of debt, of solitude, of unpopularity, — but
it behooves the wise man to look with a bold eye
into those rarer dangers which sometimes invade
men, and to familiarize himself with disgusting
forms of disease, with sounds of execration, and
the vision of violent death.

Times of heroism are generally times of terror,
but the day never shines in which this element may
not work. The circumstances of man, we say, are
historically somewhat better in this country and at
this hour than perhaps ever before. More freedom
exists for culture. It will not now run against an
axe at the first step out of the beaten track of opin-

ion. But whoso is heroic will always find crises to try his edge. Human virtue demands her champions and martyrs, and the trial of persecution always proceeds. It is but the other day that the brave Lovejoy gave his breast to the bullets of a mob, for the rights of free speech and opinion, and died when it was better not to live.

I see not any road of perfect peace which a man can walk, but after the counsel of his own bosom. Let him quit too much association, let him go home much, and stablish himself in those courses he approves. The unremitting retention of simple and high sentiments in obscure duties is hardening the character to that temper which will work with honor, if need be in the tumult, or on the scaffold, Whatever outrages have happened to men may befall a man again ; and very easily in a republic, if there appear any signs of a decay of religion. Coarse slander, fire, tar and feathers and the gibbet, the youth may freely bring home to his mind and with what sweetness of temper he can, and inquire how fast he can fix his sense of duty, braving such penalties, whenever it may please the next newspaper and a sufficient number of his neighbors to pronounce his opinions incendiary.

It may calm the apprehension of calamity in the most susceptible heart to see how quick a bound Nature has set to the utmost infliction of malice.

We rapidly approach a brink over which no enemy can follow us: —

> " Let them rave :
> Thou art quiet in thy grave."

In the gloom of our ignorance of what shall be, in the hour when we are deaf to the higher voices, who does not envy those who have seen safely to an end their manful endeavor? Who that sees the meanness of our politics but inly congratulates Washington that he is long already wrapped in his shroud, and for ever safe; that he was laid sweet in his grave, the hope of humanity not yet subjugated in him? Who does not sometimes envy the good and brave who are no more to suffer from the tumults of the natural world, and await with curious complacency the speedy term of his own conversation with finite nature? And yet the love that will be annihilated sooner than treacherous has already made death impossible, and affirms itself no mortal but a native of the deeps of absolute and inextinguishable being.

THE OVER-SOUL.

—◆—

"But souls that of his own good life partake,
He loves as his own self ; dear as his eye
They are to Him : He 'll never them forsake :
When they shall die, then God himself shall die
They live, they live in blest eternity."

Henry More

Space is ample, east and west,
But two cannot go abreast,
Cannot travel in it two :
Yonder masterful cuckoo
Crowds every egg out of the nest,
Quick or dead, except its own ;
A spell is laid on sod and stone,
Night and Day 've been tampered with,
Every quality and pith
Surcharged and sultry with a power
That works its will on age and hour.

THE OVER-SOUL.

———◆———

THERE is a difference between one and another hour of life in their authority and subsequent effect. Our faith comes in moments ; our vice is habitual. Yet there is a depth in those brief moments which constrains us to ascribe more reality to them than to all other experiences. For this reason the argument which is always forthcoming to silence those who conceive extraordinary hopes of man, namely the appeal to experience, is for ever invalid and vain. We give up the past to the objector, and yet we hope. He must explain this hope. We grant that human life is mean, but how did we find out that it was mean ? What is the ground of this uneasiness of ours ; of this old discontent ? What is the universal sense of want and ignorance, but the fine innuendo by which the soul makes its enormous claim ? Why do men feel that the natural history of man has never been written, but he is always leaving behind what you have said of him, and t becomes old, and books of metaphysics worthless ?

The philosophy of six thousand years has not searched the chambers and magazines of the soul. In its experiments there has always remained, in the last analysis, a residuum it could not resolve. Man is a stream whose source is hidden. Our being is descending into us from we know not whence. The most exact calculator has no prescience that somewhat incalculable may not balk the very next moment. I am constrained every moment to acknowledge a higher origin for events than the will I call mine.

As with events, so is it with thoughts. When I watch that flowing river, which, out of regions I see not, pours for a season its streams into me, I see that I am a pensioner; not a cause but a surprised spectator of this ethereal water; that I desire and look up and put myself in the attitude of reception, but from some alien energy the visions come.

The Supreme Critic on the errors of the past and the present, and the only prophet of that which must be, is that great nature in which we rest as the earth lies in the soft arms of the atmosphere; that Unity, that Over-soul, within which every man's particular being is contained and made one with all other; that common heart of which all sincere conversation is the worship, to which all right action is submission; that overpowering reality which confutes our tricks and talents, and constrains every

one to pass for what he is, and to speak from his
character and not from his tongue, and which evermore tends to pass into our thought and hand and
become wisdom and virtue and power and beauty.
We live in succession, in division, in parts, in
particles. Meantime within man is the soul of the
whole; the wise silence; the universal beauty, to
which every part and particle is equally related,
the eternal ONE. And this deep power in which
we exist and whose beatitude is all accessible to us,
is not only self-sufficing and perfect in every hour,
but the act of seeing and the thing seen, the seer
and the spectacle, the subject and the object, are
one. We see the world piece by piece, as the sun,
the moon, the animal, the tree; but the whole, of
which these are the shining parts, is the soul. Only
by the vision of that Wisdom can the horoscope of
the ages be read, and by falling back on our better
thoughts, by yielding to the spirit of prophecy
which is innate in every man, we can know what it
saith. Every man's words who speaks from that
life must sound vain to those who do not dwell in
the same thought on their own part. I dare not
speak for it. My words do not carry its august
sense; they fall short and cold. Only itself can inspire whom it will, and behold! their speech shall
be lyrical, and sweet, and universal as the rising of
the wind. Yet I desire, even by profane words, if

I may not use sacred, to indicate the heaven of this deity and to report what hints I have collected of the transcendent simplicity and energy of the High-est Law.

If we consider what happens in conversation, in reveries, in remorse, in times of passion, in surprises, in the instructions of dreams, wherein often we see ourselves in masquerade, — the droll disguises only magnifying and enhancing a real element and forcing it on our distant notice, — we shall catch many hints that will broaden and lighten into knowl-edge of the secret of nature. All goes to show that the soul in man is not an organ, but animates and exercises all the organs ; is not a function, like the power of memory, of calculation, of comparison, but uses these as hands and feet; is not a faculty, but a light ; is not the intellect or the will, but the master of the intellect and the will; is the background of our being, in which they lie, — an immensity not pos-sessed and that cannot be possessed. From within or from behind, a light shines through us upon things and makes us aware that we are nothing, but the light is all. A man is the façade of a temple wherein all wisdom and all good abide. What we commonly call man, the eating, drinking, planting, counting man, does not, as we know him, represent himself, but misrepresents himself. Him we do not re spect, but the soul. whose organ he is, would he let it appear through his action, would make our knees bend. When it breathes through his intellect, it is genius ; when it breathes through his will, it is virtue ; when it flows through his affection, it is love. And the blindness of the intellect begins when it would be something of itself. The weakness of the will begins when the individual would be something of himself. All reform aims in some one particular to let the soul have its way through us ; in other words, to engage us to obey.

Of this pure nature every man is at some time sensible. Language cannot paint it with his colors. It is too subtile. It is undefinable, unmeasurable ; but we know that it prevades and contains us. We know that all spiritual being is in man. A wise old proverb says, " God comes to see us without bell ; " that is, as there is no screen or ceiling between our heads and the infinite heavens, so is there no bar or wall in the soul, where man, the effect, ceases, and God, the cause, begins. The walls are taken away. We lie open on one side to the deeps of spiritual nature, to the attributes of God. Justice we see and know, Love, Freedom, Power. These natures no man ever got above, but they tower over us, and most in the moment when our interests tempt us to wound them.

The sovereignty of this nature whereof we speak is made known by its independency of those limita-

tions which circumscribe us on every hand. The
soul circumscribes all things. As I have said,
it contradicts all experience. In like manner it
abolishes time and space. The influence of the
senses has in most men overpowered the mind to
that degree that the walls of time and space have
come to look real and insurmountable; and to speak
with levity of these limits is, in the world, the sign
of insanity. Yet time and space are but inverse
measures of the force of the soul. The spirit sports
with time, —

> " Can crowd eternity into an hour,
> Or stretch an hour to eternity."

We are often made to feel that there is another
youth and age than that which is measured from
the year of our natural birth. Some thoughts always find us young, and keep us so. Such a thought
is the love of the universal and eternal beauty.
Every man parts from that contemplation with the
feeling that it rather belongs to ages than to mortal
life. The least activity of the intellectual powers
redeems us in a degree from the conditions of time.
In sickness, in languor, give us a strain of poetry
or a profound sentence, and we are refreshed; or
produce a volume of Plato or Shakspeare, or remind us of their names, and instantly we come into
a feeling of longevity. See how the deep divine
thought reduces centuries and millenniums, and

makes itself present through all ages. Is the teaching of Christ less effective now than it was when first his mouth was opened? The emphasis of facts and persons in my thought has nothing to do with time. And so always the soul's scale is one, the scale of the senses and the understanding is another. Before the revelations of the soul, Time, Space and Nature shrink away. In common speech we refer all things to time, as we habitually refer the immensely sundered stars to one concave sphere. And so we say that the Judgment is distant or near, that the Millennium approaches, that a day of certain political, moral, social reforms is at hand, and the like, when we mean that in the nature of things one of the facts we contemplate is external and fugitive, and the other is permanent and connate with the soul. The things we now esteem fixed shall, one by one, detach themselves like ripe fruit from our experience, and fall. The wind shall blow them none knows whither. The landscape, the figures, Boston, London, are facts as fugitive as any institution past, or any whiff of mist or smoke, and so is society, and so is the world. The soul looketh steadily forwards, creating a world before her, leaving worlds behind her. She has no dates, nor rites, nor persons, nor specialties nor men. The soul knows only the soul; the web of events is the flowing robe in which she is clothed.

After its own law and not by arithmetic is the rate of its progress to be computed. The soul's advances are not made by gradation, such as can be represented by motion in a straight line, but rather by ascension of state, such as can be represented by metamorphosis, — from the egg to the worm, from the worm to the fly. The growths of genius are of a certain *total* character, that does not advance the elect individual first over John, then Adam, then Richard, and give to each the pain of discovered inferiority, — but by every throe of growth the man expands there where he works, passing, at each pulsation, classes, populations, of men. With each divine impulse the mind rends the thin rinds of the visible and finite, and comes out into eternity, and inspires and expires its air. It converses with truths that have always been spoken in the world, and becomes conscious of a closer sympathy with Zeno and Arrian than with persons in the house.

This is the law of moral and of mental gain. The simple rise as by specific levity not into a particular virtue, but into the region of all the virtues. They are in the spirit which contains them all. The soul requires purity, but purity is not it; requires justice, but justice is not that; requires beneficence, but is somewhat better: so that there is a kind of descent and accommodation felt when we leave speaking of moral nature to urge a virtue which it enjoins. To the well-born child all the virtues are natural, and not painfully acquired. Speak to his heart, and the man becomes suddenly virtuous.

Within the same sentiment is the germ of intel lectual growth, which obeys the same law. Those who are capable of humility, of justice, of love, of aspiration, stand already on a platform that com mands the sciences and arts, speech and poetry, ac tion and grace. For whoso dwells in this moral beatitude already anticipates those special powers which men prize so highly. The lover has no talent, no skill, which passes for quite nothing with his enamored maiden, however little she may possess of related faculty; and the heart which aban dons itself to the Supreme Mind finds itself related to all its works, and will travel a royal road to particular knowledges and powers. In ascending to this primary and aboriginal sentiment we have come from our remote station on the circumference instantaneously to the centre of the world, where, as in the closet of God, we see causes, and antici pate the universe, which is but a slow effect.

One mode of the divine teaching is the incarna tion of the spirit in a form, — in forms, like my own. I live in society, with persons who answer to thoughts in my own mind, or express a certain obedience to the great instincts to which I live. I see its presence to them. I am certified of a common nature ; and these other souls, these separated selves, draw me as nothing else can. They stir in me the new emotions we call passion ; of love, hatred, fear, admiration, pity ; thence come conversation, competition, persuasion, cities and war. Persons are supplementary to the primary teaching of the soul. In youth we are mad for persons. Childhood and youth see all the world in them. But the larger experience of man discovers the identical nature appearing through them all. Persons themselves acquaint us with the impersonal. In all conversation between two persons tacit reference is made, as to a third party, to a common nature. That third party or common nature is not social; it is impersonal; is God. And so in groups where debate is earnest, and especially on high questions, the company become aware that the thought rises to an equal level in all bosoms, that all have a spiritual property in what was said, as well as the sayer. They all become wiser than they were. It arches over them like a temple, this unity of thought in which every heart beats with nobler sense of power and duty, and thinks and acts with unusual solemnity. All are conscious of attaining to a higher self-possession. It shines for all. There is a certain wisdom of humanity which is common to the greatest men with the lowest, and which our

ordinary education often labors to silence and ob-
struct. The mind is one, and the best minds, who
love truth for its own sake, think much less of
property in truth. They accept it thankfully everywhere, and do not label or stamp it with any man's
name, for it is theirs long beforehand, and from
eternity. The learned and the studious of thought
have no monopoly of wisdom. Their violence of
direction in some degree disqualifies them to think
truly. We owe many valuable observations to people who are not very acute or profound, and who
say the thing without effort which we want and
have long been hunting in vain. The action of the
soul is oftener in that which is felt and left unsaid
than in that which is said in any conversation. It
broods over every society, and they unconsciously
seek for it in each other. We know better than
we do. We do not yet possess ourselves, and we
know at the same time that we are much more. I
feel the same truth how often in my trivial conversation with my neighbors, that somewhat higher in
each of us overlooks this by-play, and Jove nods to
Jove from behind each of us.

Men descend to meet. In their habitual and
mean service to the world, for which they forsake
their native nobleness, they resemble those Arabian
sheiks who dwell in mean houses and affect an external poverty, to escape the rapacity of the Pacha.

and reserve all their display of wealth for their interior and guarded retirements.

As it is present in all persons, so it is in every
period of life. It is adult already in the infant
man. In my dealing with my child, my Latin and
Greek, my accomplishments and my money stead
me nothing ; but as much soul as I have avails. If
I am wilful, he sets his will against mine, one for
one, and leaves me, if I please, the degradation of
beating him by my superiority of strength. But if
I renounce my will and act for the soul, setting
that up as umpire between us two, out of his
young eyes looks the same soul; he reveres and
loves with me.

The soul is the perceiver and revealer of truth.
We know truth when we see it, let skeptic and
scoffer say what they choose. Foolish people ask
you, when you have spoken what they do not
wish to hear, ' How do you know it is truth, and
not an error of your own? ' We know truth
when we see it, from opinion, as we know when we
are awake that we are awake. It was a grand sentence of Emanuel Swedenborg, which would alone
indicate the greatness of that man's perception, —
" It is no proof of a man's understanding to be able
to affirm whatever he pleases ; but to be able to discern that what is true is true, and that what is
false is false, — this is the mark and character of

intelligence." In the book I read, the good thought returns to me, as every truth will, the image of the whole soul. To the bad thought which I find in it, the same soul becomes a discerning, separating sword, and lops it away. We are wiser than we know. If we will not interfere with our thought, but will act entirely, or see how the thing stands in God, we know the particular thing, and every thing, and every man. For the Maker of all things and all persons stands behind us and casts his dread omniscience through us over things.

But beyond this recognition of its own in particular passages of the individual's experience, it also reveals truth. And here we should seek to reinforce ourselves by its very presence, and to speak with a worthier, loftier strain of that advent. For the soul's communication of truth is the highest event in nature, since it then does not give somewhat from itself, but it gives itself, or passes into and becomes that man whom it enlightens ; or, in proportion to that truth he receives, it takes him to itself.

We distinguish the announcements of the soul, its manifestations of its own nature, by the term *Revelation.* These are always attended by the emotion of the sublime. For this communication is an influx of the Divine mind into our mind. It is an ebb of the individual rivulet before the flow

ing surges of the sea of life. Every distinct apprehension of this central commandment agitates
men with awe and delight. A thrill passes through
all men at the reception of new truth, or at the
performance of a great action, which comes out
of the heart of nature. In these communications
the power to see is not separated from the will to
do, but the insight proceeds from obedience, and
the obedience proceeds from a joyful perception.
Every moment when the individual feels himself
invaded by it is memorable. By the necessity of
our constitution a certain enthusiasm attends the
individual's consciousness of that divine presence.
The character and duration of this enthusiasm vary
with the state of the individual, from an ecstasy
and trance and prophetic inspiration, — which is
its rarer appearance, — to the faintest glow of virtuous emotion, in which form it warms, like our
household fires, all the families and associations of
men, and makes society possible. A certain tendency to insanity has always attended the opening
of the religious sense in men, as if they had been
" blasted with excess of light." The trances of
Socrates, the " union " of Plotinus, the vision of
Porphyry, the conversion of Paul, the aurora of
Behmen, the convulsions of George Fox and his
Quakers, the illumination of Swedenborg, are of this
kind. What was in the case of these remarkable

persons a ravishment, has, in innumerable instances in common life, been exhibited in less striking manner. Everywhere the history of religion
betrays a tendency to enthusiasm. The rapture of
the Moravian and Quietist; the opening of the
eternal sense of the Word, in the language of the
New Jerusalem Church; the *revival* of the Calvinistic churches; the *experiences* of the Methodists,
are varying forms of that shudder of awe and delight with which the individual soul always mingles
with the universal soul.

The nature of these revelations is the same;
they are perceptions of the absolute law. They
are solutions of the soul's own questions. They do
not answer the questions which the understanding
asks. The soul answers never by words, but by
the thing itself that is inquired after.

Revelation is the disclosure of the soul. The
popular notion of a revelation is that it is a telling
of fortunes. In past oracles of the soul the understanding seeks to find answers to sensual questions,
and undertakes to tell from God how long men
shall exist, what their hands shall do and who shall
be their company, adding names and dates and
places. But we must pick no locks. We must
check this low curiosity. An answer in words is
delusive; it is really no answer to the questions you
ask. Do not require a description of the countries

towards which you sail. The description does not describe them to you, and to-morrow you arrive there and know them by inhabiting them. Men ask concerning the immortality of the soul, the employments of heaven, the state of the sinner, and so forth. They even dream that Jesus has left replies to precisely these interrogatories. Never a moment did that sublime spirit speak in their *patois*. To truth, justice, love, the attributes of the soul, the idea of immutableness is essentially associated. Jesus, living in these moral sentiments, heedless of sensual fortunes, heeding only the manifestations of these, never made the separation of the idea of duration from the essence of these attributes, nor uttered a syllable concerning the duration of the soul. It was left to his disciples to sever duration from the moral elements, and to teach the immortality of the soul as a doctrine, and maintain it by evidences. The moment the doctrine of the immortality is separately taught, man is already fallen. In the flowing of love, in the adoration of humility, there is no question of continuance. No inspired man ever asks this question or condescends to these evidences. For the soul is true to itself, and the man in whom it is shed abroad cannot wander from the present, which is infinite, to a future which would be finite.

These questions which we lust to ask about the

future are a confession of sin. God has no answer
for them. No answer in words can reply to a question of things. It is not in an arbitrary "decree
of God," but in the nature of man, that a veil shuts
down on the facts of to-morrow; for the soul will
not have us read any other cipher than that of
cause and effect. By this veil which curtains
events it instructs the children of men to live in
to-day. The only mode of obtaining an answer to
these questions of the senses is to forego all low
curiosity, and, accepting the tide of being which
floats us into the secret of nature, work and live,
work and live, and all unawares the advancing soul
has built and forged for itself a new condition, and
the question and the answer are one.

By the same fire, vital, consecrating, celestial,
which burns until it shall dissolve all things into
the waves and surges of an ocean of light, we see
and know each other, and what spirit each is of.
Who can tell the grounds of his knowledge of the
character of the several individuals in his circle of
friends? No man. Yet their acts and words do
not disappoint him. In that man, though he knew
no ill of him, he put no trust. In that other,
though they had seldom met, authentic signs had
yet passed, to signify that he might be trusted as
one who had an interest in his own character. We
know each other very well, — which of us has been

just to himself and whether that which we teach or behold is only an aspiration or is our honest effort also.

We are all discerners of spirits. That diagnosis lies aloft in our life or unconscious power. The intercourse of society, its trade, its religion, its friendships, its quarrels, is one wide judicial investigation of character. In full court, or in small committee, or confronted face to face, accuser and accused, men offer themselves to be judged. Against their will they exhibit those decisive trifles by which character is read. But who judges? and what? Not our understanding. We do not read them by learning or craft. No; the wisdom of the wise man consists herein, that he does not judge them; he lets them judge themselves and merely reads and records their own verdict.

By virtue of this inevitable nature, private will is overpowered, and, maugre our efforts or our imperfections, your genius will speak from you, and mine from me. That which we are, we shall teach, not voluntarily but involuntarily. Thoughts come into our minds by avenues which we never left open, and thoughts go out of our minds through avenues which we never voluntarily opened. Character teaches over our head. The infallible index of true progress is found in the tone the man takes. Neither his age, nor his breeding, nor company, nor books, nor actions, nor talents, nor all together can hinder him from being deferential to a higher spirit than his own. If he have not found his home in God, his manners, his forms of speech, the turn of his sentences, the build, shall I say, of all his opinions will involuntarily confess it, let him brave it out how he will. If he have found his centre, the Deity will shine through him, through all the disguises of ignorance, of ungenial temperament, of unfavorable circumstance. The tone of seeking is one, and the tone of having is another.

The great distinction between teachers sacred or literary, — between poets like Herbert, and poets like Pope, — between philosophers like Spinoza, Kant and Coleridge, and philosophers like Locke, Paley, Mackintosh and Stewart, — between men of the world who are reckoned accomplished talkers, and here and there a fervent mystic, prophesying half insane under the infinitude of his thought, — is that one class speak *from within,* or from experience, as parties and possessors of the fact; and the other class *from without,* as spectators merely, or perhaps as acquainted with the fact on the evidence of third persons. It is of no use to preach to me from without. I can do that too easily myself. Jesus speaks always from within, and in a degree that transcends all others. In that is the miracle. I believe beforehand that it ought so to be. All men stand continually in the expectation of the appearance of such a teacher. But if a man do not speak from within the veil, where the word is one with that it tells of, let him lowly confess it.

The same Omniscience flows into the intellect and makes what we call genius. Much of the wis-dom of the world is not wisdom, and the most il-luminated class of men are no doubt superior to literary fame, and are not writers. Among the multitude of scholars and authors we feel no hallow-ing presence; we are sensible of a knack and skill rather than of inspiration; they have a light and know not whence it comes and call it their own ; their talent is some exaggerated faculty, some over-grown member, so that their strength is a disease. In these instances the intellectual gifts do not make the impression of virtue, but almost of vice ; and we feel that a man's talents stand in the way of his advancement in truth. But genius is religious. It is a larger imbibing of the common heart. It is not anomalous, but more like and not less like other men. There is in all great poets a wisdom of humanity which is superior to any talents they exercise. The author, the wit, the partisan, the fine gentleman, does not take place of the man. Humanity shines in Homer, in Chaucer, in Spen-ser, in Shakspeare, in Milton. They are content

with truth. They use the positive degree. They
seem frigid and phlegmatic to those who have been
spiced with the frantic passion and violent coloring of inferior but popular writers. For they are
poets by the free course which they allow to the informing soul, which through their eyes beholds
again and blesses the things which it hath made.
The soul is superior to its knowledge, wiser than
any of its works. The great poet makes us feel
our own wealth, and then we think less of his compositions. His best communication to our mind is
to teach us to despise all he has done. Shakspeare
carries us to such a lofty strain of intelligent activity as to suggest a wealth which beggars his own ;
and we then feel that the splendid works which he
has created, and which in other hours we extol as a
sort of self-existent poetry, take no stronger hold
of real nature than the shadow of a passing traveller on the rock. The inspiration which uttered itself
in Hamlet and Lear could utter things as good
from day to day for ever. Why then should I
make account of Hamlet and Lear, as if we had
not the soul from which they fell as syllables from
the tongue ?

This energy does not descend into individual life
on any other condition than entire possession. It
comes to the lowly and simple ; it comes to whomsoever will put off what is foreign and proud ; it

comes as insight; it comes as serenity and grandeur. When we see those whom it inhabits, we are
apprised of new degrees of greatness. From that
inspiration the man comes back with a changed
tone. He does not talk with men with an eye to
their opinion. He tries them. It requires of us to
be plain and true. The vain traveller attempts
to embellish his life by quoting my lord and the
prince and the countess, who thus said or did to
him. The ambitious vulgar show you their spoons
and brooches and rings, and preserve their cards
and compliments. The more cultivated, in their
account of their own experience, cull out the pleasing, poetic circumstance, — the visit to Rome, the
man of genius they saw, the brilliant friend they
know; still further on perhaps the gorgeous landscape, the mountain lights, the mountain thoughts
they enjoyed yesterday, — and so seek to throw a
romantic color over their life. But the soul that
ascends to worship the great God is plain and true;
has no rose-color, no fine friends, no chivalry, no
adventures; does not want admiration; dwells in
the hour that now is, in the earnest experience of
the common day, — by reason of the present moment and the mere trifle having become porous to
thought and bibulous of the sea of light.

Converse with a mind that is grandly simple, and
literature looks like word-catching. The simplest

utterances are worthiest to be written, yet are they so cheap and so things of course, that in the infinite riches of the soul it is like gathering a few pebbles off the ground, or bottling a little air in a phial, when the whole earth and the whole atmosphere are ours. Nothing can pass there, or make you one of the circle, but the casting aside your trappings and dealing man to man in naked truth, plain confession and omniscient affirmation.

Souls such as these treat you as gods would, walk as gods in the earth, accepting without any admiration your wit, your bounty, your virtue even, — say rather your act of duty, for your virtue they own as their proper blood, royal as themselves, and over-royal, and the father of the gods. But what rebuke their plain fraternal bearing casts on the mutual flattery with which authors solace each other and wound themselves! These flatter not. I do not wonder that these men go to see Cromwell and Christina and Charles the Second and James the First and the Grand Turk. For they are, in their own elevation, the fellows of kings, and must feel the servile tone of conversation in the world. They must always be a godsend to princes, for they confront them, a king to a king, without ducking or concession, and give a high nature the refreshment and satisfaction of resistance, of plain humanity, of even companionship and of new ideas. They leave them wiser and superior men. Souls like these make us feel that sincerity is more excellent than flattery. Deal so plainly with man and woman as to constrain the utmost sincerity and destroy all hope of trifling with you. It is the highest compliment you can pay. Their "highest praising," said Milton, "is not flattery, and their plainest advice is a kind of praising."

Ineffable is the union of man and God in every act of the soul. The simplest person who in his integrity worships God, becomes God; yet for ever and ever the influx of this better and universal self is new and unsearchable. It inspires awe and astonishment. How dear, how soothing to man, arises the idea of God, peopling the lonely place, effacing the scars of our mistakes and disappointments! When we have broken our god of tradition and ceased from our god of rhetoric, then may God fire the heart with his presence. It is the doubling of the heart itself, nay, the infinite enlargement of the heart with a power of growth to a new infinity on every side. It inspires in man an infallible trust. He has not the conviction, but the sight, that the best is the true, and may in that thought easily dismiss all particular uncertainties and fears, and adjourn to the sure revelation of time the solution of his private riddles. He is sure that his welfare is dear to the heart of being. In the presence of law to his mind he is overflowed with a reliance so universal that it sweeps away all cherished hopes and the most stable projects of mortal condition in its flood. He believes that he cannot escape from his good. The things that are really for thee gravitate to thee. You are running to seek your friend. Let your feet run, but your mind need not. If you do not find him, will you not acquiesce that it is best you should not find him? for there is a power, which, as it is in you, is in him also, and could therefore very well bring you together, if it were for the best. You are preparing with eagerness to go and render a service to which your talent and your taste invite you, the love of men and the hope of fame. Has it not occurred to you that you have no right to go, unless you are equally willing to be prevented from going? O, believe, as thou livest, that every sound that is spoken over the round world, which thou oughtest to hear, will vibrate on thine ear! Every proverb, every book, every byword that belongs to thee for aid or comfort, shall surely come home through open or winding passages. Every friend whom not thy fantastic will but the great and tender heart in thee craveth, shall lock thee in his embrace. And this because the heart in thee is the heart of all; not a valve, not a wall, not an intersection is there anywhere in nature, but one blood rolls uninterruptedly an end

less circulation through all men, as the water of
the globe is all one sea, and, truly seen, its tide is
one.

Let man then learn the revelation of all nature
and all thought to his heart; this, namely; that the
Highest dwells with him; that the sources of nature are in his own mind, if the sentiment of duty
is there. But if he would know what the great
God speaketh, he must ' go into his closet and shut
the door,' as Jesus said. God will not make himself manifest to cowards. He must greatly listen
to himself, withdrawing himself from all the accents
of other men's devotion. Even their prayers are
hurtful to him, until he have made his own. Our
religion vulgarly stands on numbers of believers.
Whenever the appeal is made, — no matter how in-
directly, — to numbers, proclamation is then and
there made that religion is not. He that finds God
a sweet enveloping thought to him never counts his
company. When I sit in that presence, who shall
dare to come in? When I rest in perfect humility,
when I burn with pure love, what can Calvin or
Swedenborg say?

It makes no difference whether the appeal is to
numbers or to one. The faith that stands on authority is not faith. The reliance on authority
measures the decline of religion, the withdrawal of
the soul. The position men have given to Jesus,

now for many centuries of history, is a position of authority. It characterizes themselves. It cannot alter the eternal facts. Great is the soul, and plain. It is no flatterer, it is no follower ; it never appeals from itself. It believes in itself. Before the immense possibilities of man all mere experience, all past biography, however spotless and sainted, shrinks away. Before that heaven which our presentiments foreshow us, we cannot easily praise any form of life we have seen or read of. We not only affirm that we have few great men, but, absolutely speaking, that we have none ; that we have no history, no record of any character or mode of living that entirely contents us. The saints and demigods whom history worships we are constrained to accept with a grain of allowance. Though in our lonely hours we draw a new strength out of their memory, yet, pressed on our attention, as they are by the thoughtless and customary, they fatigue and invade. The soul gives itself, alone, original and pure, to the Lonely, Original and Pure, who, on that condition, gladly inhabits, leads and speaks through it. Then is it glad, young and nimble. It is not wise, but it sees through all things. It is not called religious, but it is innocent. It calls the light its own, and feels that the grass grows and the stone falls by a law inferior to, and dependent on, its nature. Behold, it saith, I am

born into the great, the universal mind. I, the imperfect, adore my own Perfect. I am somehow
receptive of the great soul, and thereby I do over-
look the sun and the stars and feel them to be the
fair accidents and effects which change and pass.
More and more the surges of everlasting nature enter into me, and I become public and human in my
regards and actions. So come I to live in thoughts
and act with energies which are immortal. Thus
revering the soul, and learning, as the ancient said,
that " its beauty is immense," man will come to see
that the world is the perennial miracle which the
soul worketh, and be less astonished at particular
wonders ; he will learn that there is no profane history ; that all history is sacred ; that the universe is
represented in an atom, in a moment of time. He
will weave no longer a spotted life of shreds and
patches, but he will live with a divine unity. He
will cease from what is base and frivolous in his
life and be content with all places and with any
service he can render. He will calmly front the
morrow in the negligency of that trust which carries God with it and so hath already the whole future in the bottom of the heart.

CIRCLES.

——◆——

NATURE centres into balls,
And her proud ephemerals
Fast to surface and outside,
Scan the profile of the sphere,
Knew they what that signified
A new genesis were here.

X.

CIRCLES.

———◆———

THE eye is the first circle; the horizon which it forms is the second; and throughout nature this primary figure is repeated without end. It is the highest emblem in the cipher of the world. St. Augustine described the nature of God as a circle whose centre was everywhere and its circumference nowhere. We are all our lifetime reading the copious sense of this first of forms. One moral we have already deduced in considering the circular or compensatory character of every human action. Another analogy we shall now trace, that every action admits of being outdone. Our life is an apprenticeship to the truth that around every circle another can be drawn; that there is no end in nature, but every end is a beginning; that there is always another dawn risen on mid-noon, and under every deep a lower deep opens.

This fact, as far as it symbolizes the moral fact of the Unattainable, the flying Perfect, around which the hands of man can never meet, at once the inspirer and the condemner of every success, may conveniently serve us to connect many illustrations of human power in every department.

There are no fixtures in nature. The universe is fluid and volatile. Permanence is but a word of degrees. Our globe seen by God is a transparent law, not a mass of facts. The law dissolves the fact and holds it fluid. Our culture is the predominance of an idea which draws after it this train of cities and institutions. Let us rise into another idea, they will disappear. The Greek sculpture is all melted away, as if it had been statues of ice; here and there a solitary figure or fragment remaining, as we see flecks and scraps of snow left in cold dells and mountain clefts in June and July. For the genius that created it creates now somewhat else. The Greek letters last a little longer, but are already passing under the same sentence and tumbling into the inevitable pit which the creation of new thought opens for all that is old. The new continents are built out of the ruins of an old planet; the new races fed out of the decomposition of the foregoing. New arts destroy the old. See the investment of capital in aqueducts, made useless by hydraulics; fortifications, by gunpowder; roads and canals, by railways: sails, by steam; steam by electricity.

You admire this tower of granite, weathering the

hurts of so many ages. Yet a little waving hand built this huge wall, and that which builds is better than that which is built. The hand that built can topple it down much faster. Better than the hand and nimbler was the invisible thought which wrought through it; and thus ever, behind the coarse effect, is a fine cause, which, being narrowly seen, is itself the effect of a finer cause. Every thing looks permanent until its secret is known. A rich estate appears to women a firm and lasting fact; to a merchant, one easily created out of any materials, and easily lost. An orchard, good tillage, good grounds, seem a fixture, like a gold mine, or a river, to a citizen; but to a large farmer, not much more fixed than the state of the crop. Nature looks provokingly stable and secular, but it has a cause like all the rest; and when once I comprehend that, will these fields stretch so immovably wide, these leaves hang so individually considerable? Permanence is a word of degrees. Every thing is medial. Moons are no more bounds to spiritual power than bat-balls.

The key to every man is his thought. Sturdy and defying though he look, he has a helm which he obeys, which is the idea after which all his facts are classified. He can only be reformed by showing him a new idea which commands his own. The life of man is a self-evolving circle, which, from a ring imperceptibly small, rushes on all sides outwards to new and larger circles, and that without end.   The extent to which this generation of circles, wheel without wheel, will go, depends on the force or truth of the individual soul.   For it is the inert effort of each thought, having formed itself into a circular wave of circumstance, — as for instance an empire, rules of an art, a local usage, a religious rite, — to heap itself on that ridge and to solidify and hem in the life.   But if the soul is quick and strong it bursts over that boundary on all sides and expands another orbit on the great deep, which also runs up into a high wave, with attempt again to stop and to bind.   But the heart refuses to be imprisoned ; in its first and narrowest pulses it already tends outward with a vast force and to immense and innumerable expansions.

Every ultimate fact is only the first of a new series.   Every general law only a particular fact of some more general law presently to disclose itself.   There is no outside, no inclosing wall, no circumference to us.   The man finishes his story, — how good ! how final ! how it puts a new face on all things !   He fills the sky.   Lo ! on the other side rises also a man and draws a circle around the circle we had just pronounced the outline of the sphere.   Then already is our first speaker not man, but only a first speaker.   His only redress is forthwith to draw a circle outside of his antagonist. And so men do by themselves. The result of to-day, which haunts the mind and cannot be escaped, will presently be abridged into a word, and the principle that seemed to explain nature will itself be included as one example of a bolder generalization. In the thought of to-morrow there is a power to upheave all thy creed, all the creeds, all the literatures of the nations, and marshal thee to a heaven which no epic dream has yet depicted. Every man is not so much a workman in the world as he is a suggestion of that he should be. Men walk as prophecies of the next age.

Step by step we scale this mysterious ladder; the steps are actions, the new prospect is power. Every several result is threatened and judged by that which follows. Every one seems to be contradicted by the new; it is only limited by the new. The new statement is always hated by the old, and, to those dwelling in the old, comes like an abyss of scepticism. But the eye soon gets wonted to it, for the eye and it are effects of one cause; then its innocency and benefit appear, and presently, all its energy spent, it pales and dwindles before the revelation of the new hour.

Fear not the new generalization. Does the fact look crass and material, threatening to degrade thy theory of spirit? Resist it not; it goes to refine and raise thy theory of matter just as much.

There are no fixtures to men, if we appeal to consciousness. Every man supposes himself not to be fully understood; and if there is any truth in him, if he rests at last on the divine soul, I see not how it can be otherwise. The last chamber, the last closet, he must feel was never opened; there is always a residuum unknown, unanalyzable. That is, every man believes that he has a greater possibility.

Our moods do not believe in each other. To-day I am full of thoughts and can write what I please. I see no reason why I should not have the same thought, the same power of expression, to-morrow. What I write, whilst I write it, seems the most natural thing in the world; but yesterday I saw a dreary vacuity in this direction in which now I see so much; and a month hence, I doubt not, I shall wonder who he was that wrote so many continuous pages. Alas for this infirm faith, this will not strenuous, this vast ebb of a vast flow! I am God in nature; I am a weed by the wall.

The continual effort to raise himself above himself, to work a pitch above his last height, betrays itself in a man's relations. We thirst for approbation, yet cannot forgive the approver. The sweet of nature is love; yet if I have a friend I am tormented by my imperfections. The love of me accuses the other party. If he were high enough to slight

me, then could I love him, and rise by my affection
to new heights. A man's growth is seen in the
successive choirs of his friends. For every friend
whom he loses for truth, he gains a better. I
thought as I walked in the woods and mused on my
friends, why should I play with them this game of
idolatry? I know and see too well, when not voluntarily blind, the speedy limits of persons called
high and worthy. Rich, noble and great they are
by the liberality of our speech, but truth is sad. O
blessed Spirit, whom I forsake for these, they are
not thou! Every personal consideration that we
allow costs us heavenly state. We sell the thrones
of angels for a short and turbulent pleasure.

How often must we learn this lesson? Men
cease to interest us when we find their limitations.
The only sin is limitation. As soon as you once
come up with a man's limitations, it is all over with
him. Has he talents? has he enterprise? has he
knowledge? It boots not. Infinitely alluring and
attractive was he to you yesterday, a great hope, a
sea to swim in; now, you have found his shores,
found it a pond, and you care not if you never see
it again.

Each new step we take in thought reconciles
twenty seemingly discordant facts, as expressions
of one law. Aristotle and Plato are reckoned the
respective heads of two schools. A wise man will

see that Aristotle platonizes. By going one step
farther back in thought, discordant opinions are
reconciled by being seen to be two extremes of one
principle, and we can never go so far back as to
preclude a still higher vision.

Beware when the great God lets loose a thinker
on this planet. Then all things are at risk. It is
as when a conflagration has broken out in a great
city, and no man knows what is safe, or where it
will end. There is not a piece of science but its
flank may be turned to-morrow; there is not any
literary reputation, not the so-called eternal names
of fame, that may not be revised and condemned.
The very hopes of man, the thoughts of his heart,
the religion of nations, the manners and morals of
mankind are all at the mercy of a new generalization. Generalization is always a new influx of the
divinity into the mind. Hence the thrill that at
tends it.

Valor consists in the power of self-recovery, so
that a man cannot have his flank turned, cannot be
out-generalled, but put him where you will, he
stands. This can only be by his preferring truth
to his past apprehension of truth, and his alert acceptance of it from whatever quarter; the intrepid
conviction that his laws, his relations to society,
his Christianity, his world, may at any time be superseded and decease.

There are degrees in idealism. We learn first to play with it academically, as the magnet was once a toy. Then we see in the heyday of youth and poetry that it may be true, that it is true in gleams and fragments. Then its countenance waxes stern and grand, and we see that it must be true. It now shows itself ethical and practical. We learn that God *is ;* that he is in me ; and that all things are shadows of him. The idealism of Berkeley is only a crude statement of the idealism of Jesus, and that again is a crude statement of the fact that all nature is the rapid efflux of goodness executing and organizing itself. Much more obviously is history and the state of the world at any one time directly dependent on the intellectual classification then existing in the minds of men. The things which are dear to men at this hour are so on account of the ideas which have emerged on their mental horizon, and which cause the present order of things, as a tree bears its apples. A new degree of culture would instantly revolutionize the entire system of human pursuits.

Conversation is a game of circles. In conversation we pluck up the *termini* which bound the common of silence on every side. The parties are not to be judged by the spirit they partake and even express under this Pentecost. To-morrow they will have receded from this high-water mark. To-morrow you shall find them stooping under the old pack-saddles. Yet let us enjoy the cloven flame whilst it glows on our walls. When each new speaker strikes a new light, emancipates us from the oppression of the last speaker to oppress us with the greatness and exclusiveness of his own thought, then yields us to another redeemer, we seem to recover our rights, to become men. O, what truths profound and executable only in ages and orbs, are supposed in the announcement of every truth! In common hours, society sits cold and statuesque. We all stand waiting, empty, — knowing, possibly, that we can be full, surrounded by mighty symbols which are not symbols to us, but prose and trivial toys. Then cometh the god and converts the statues into fiery men, and by a flash of his eye burns up the veil which shrouded all things, and the meaning of the very furniture, of cup and saucer, of chair and clock and tester, is manifest. The facts which loomed so large in the fogs of yesterday, — property, climate, breeding, personal beauty and the like, have strangely changed their proportions. All that we reckoned settled shakes and rattles ; and literatures, cities, climates, religions, leave their foundations and dance before our eyes. And yet here again see the swift circumscription! Good as is discourse, si-lence is better, and shames it. The length of th* discourse indicates the distance of thought betwixt the speaker and the hearer. If they were at a perfect understanding in any part, no words would be necessary thereon. If at one in all parts, no words would be suffered.

Literature is a point outside of our hodiernal circle through which a new one may be described. The use of literature is to afford us a platform whence we may command a view of our present life, a purchase by which we may move it. We fill ourselves with ancient learning, install ourselves the best we can in Greek, in Punic, in Roman houses, only that we may wiselier see French, English and American houses and modes of living. In like manner we see literature best from the midst of wild nature, or from the din of affairs, or from a high religion. The field cannot be well seen from within the field. The astronomer must have his diameter of the earth's orbit as a base to find the parallax of any star.

Therefore we value the poet. All the argument and all the wisdom is not in the encyclopædia, or the treatise on metaphysics, or the Body of Divinity, but in the sonnet or the play. In my daily work I incline to repeat my old steps, and do not believe in remedial force, in the power of change and reform. But some Petrarch or Ariosto, filled with the new wine of his imagination, writes me an ode or a brisk romance, full of daring thought and action. He smites and arouses me with his shrill tones, breaks up my whole chain of habits, and I open my eye on my own possibilities. He claps wings to the sides of all the solid old lumber of the world, and I am capable once more of choosing a straight path in theory and practice.

We have the same need to command a view of the religion of the world. We can never see Christianity from the catechism : — from the pastures, from a boat in the pond, from amidst the songs of wood-birds we possibly may. Cleansed by the elemental light and wind, steeped in the sea of beautiful forms which the field offers us, we may chance to cast a right glance back upon biography. Christianity is rightly dear to the best of mankind ; yet was there never a young philosopher whose breeding had fallen into the Christian church by whom that brave text of Paul's was not specially prized : — " Then shall also the Son be subject unto Him who put all things under him, that God may be all in all." Let the claims and virtues of persons be never so great and welcome, the instinct of man presses eagerly onward to the impersonal and illimitable, and gladly arms itself against the dogmatism of bigots with this generous word out of the book itself.

The natural world may be conceived of as a sys

tem of concentric circles, and we now and then detect in nature slight dislocations which apprise us that this surface on which we now stand is not fixed, but sliding. These manifold tenacious qual-ities, this chemistry and vegetation, these metals and animals, which seem to stand there for their own sake, are means and methods only, — are words of God, and as fugitive as other words. Has the naturalist or chemist learned his craft, who has explored the gravity of atoms and the elective affini-ties, who has not yet discerned the deeper law whereof this is only a partial or approximate state-ment, namely that like draws to like, and that the goods which belong to you gravitate to you and need not be pursued with pains and cost? Yet is that statement approximate also, and not final. Omnipresence is a higher fact. Not through subtle subterranean channels need friend and fact be drawn to their counterpart, but, rightly considered, these things proceed from the eternal generation of the soul. Cause and effect are two sides of one fact.

The same law of eternal procession ranges all that we call the virtues, and extinguishes each in the light of a better. The great man will not be prudent in the popular sense ; all his prudence will be so much deduction from his grandeur. But it behooves each to see, when he sacrifices prudence, to what god he devotes it; if to ease and pleasure, he had better be prudent still; if to a great trust he can well spare his mule and panniers who has a winged chariot instead. Geoffrey draws on his boots to go through the woods, that his feet may be safer from the bite of snakes; Aaron never thinks of such a peril. In many years neither is harmed by such an accident. Yet it seems to me that with every precaution you take against such an evil you put yourself into the power of the evil. I suppose that the highest prudence is the lowest prudence. Is this too sudden a rushing from the centre to the verge of our orbit? Think how many times we shall fall back into pitiful calculations before we take up our rest in the great sentiment, or make the verge of to-day the new centre. Besides, your bravest sentiment is familiar to the humblest men. The poor and the low have their way of expressing the last facts of philosophy as well as you. " Blessed be nothing " and " The worse things are, the better they are " are proverbs which express the transcendentalism of common life.

One man's justice is another's injustice; one man's beauty another's ugliness; one man's wisdom another's folly; as one beholds the same objects from a higher point. One man thinks justice consists in paying debts, and has no measure in his abhorrence of another who is very remiss in this duty and makes the creditor wait tediously. But that second man has his own way of looking at things, asks himself Which debt must I pay first, the debt to the rich, or the debt to the poor? the debt of money, or the debt of thought to mankind, of genius to nature? For you, O broker, there is no other principle but arithmetic. For me, commerce is of trivial import; love, faith, truth of character, the aspiration of man, these are sacred; nor can I detach one duty, like you, from all other duties, and concentrate my forces mechanically on the payment of moneys. Let me live onward; you shall find that, though slower, the progress of my character will liquidate all these debts without injustice to higher claims. If a man should dedicate himself to the payment of notes, would not this be injustice? Does he owe no debt but money? And are all claims on him to be postponed to a landlord's or a banker's?

There is no virtue which is final; all are initial. The virtues of society are vices of the saint. The terror of reform is the discovery that we must cast away our virtues, or what we have always esteemed such, into the same pit that has consumed our grosser vices : —

"Forgive his crimes, forgive his virtues too,
Those smaller faults, half converts to the right."

It is the highest power of divine moments that

they abolish our contritions also. I accuse myself of sloth and unprofitableness day by day; but when these waves of God flow into me I no longer reckon lost time. I no longer poorly compute my possible achievement by what remains to me of the month or the year; for these moments confer a sort of omnipresence and omnipotence which asks nothing of duration, but sees that the energy of the mind is commensurate with the work to be done, without time.

And thus, O circular philosopher, I hear some reader exclaim, you have arrived at a fine Pyrrhonism, at an equivalence and indifferency of all actions, and would fain teach us that *if we are true,* forsooth, our crimes may be lively stones out of which we shall construct the temple of the true God!

I am not careful to justify myself. I own I am gladdened by seeing the predominance of the saccharine principle throughout vegetable nature, and not less by beholding in morals that unrestrained inundation of the principle of good into every chink and hole that selfishness has left open, yea into selfishness and sin itself; so that no evil is pure, nor hell itself without its extreme satisfactions. But lest I should mislead any when I have my own head and obey my whims, let me remind the reader that I am only an experimenter. Do not set the least value on what I do, or the least discredit on what I do not, as if I pretended to settle any thing as true or false. I unsettle all things. No facts are to me sacred ; none are profane ; I simply experiment, an endless seeker with no Past at my back.

Yet this incessant movement and progression which all things partake could never become sensible to us but by contrast to some principle of fixture or stability in the soul. Whilst the eternal generation of circles proceeds, the eternal generator abides. That central life is somewhat superior to creation, superior to knowledge and thought, and contains all its circles. Forever it labors to create a life and thought as large and excellent as itself, but in vain, for that which is made instructs how to make a better.

Thus there is no sleep, no pause, no preservation, but all things renew, germinate and spring. Why should we import rags and relics into the new hour ? Nature abhors the old, and old age seems the only disease ; all others run into this one. We call it by many names, — fever, intemperance, insanity, stupidity and crime ; they are all forms of old age ; they are rest, conservatism, appropriation, inertia ; not newness, not the way onward. We grizzle every day. I see no need of it. Whilst we converse with what is above us, we do not grow old, but grow young. Infancy, youth, receptive, aspiring, with religious eye looking upward, counts itself nothing and abandons itself to the instruction flowing from all sides. But the man and woman of seventy assume to know all, they have outlived their hope, they renounce aspiration, accept the actual for the necessary and talk down to the young. Let them then become organs of the Holy Ghost; let them be lovers; let them behold truth; and their eyes are uplifted, their wrinkles smoothed, they are perfumed again with hope and power. This old age ought not to creep on a human mind. In nature every moment is new; the past is always swallowed and forgotten; the coming only is sacred. Nothing is secure but life, transition, the energizing spirit. No love can be bound by oath or covenant to secure it against a higher love. No truth so sublime but it may be trivial to-morrow in the light of new thoughts. People wish to be settled; only as far as they are unsettled is there any hope for them.

Life is a series of surprises. We do not guess to-day the mood, the pleasure, the power of to-morrow, when we are building up our being. Of lower states, of acts of routine and sense, we can tell somewhat; but the masterpieces of God, the total growths and universal movements of the soul, ae hideth, they are incalculable. I can know that

truth is divine and helpful; but how it shall help
me I can have no guess, for *so to be* is the sole inlet of *so to know.* The new position of the advancing man has all the powers of the old, yet has them
all new. It carries in its bosom all the energies of
the past, yet is itself an exhalation of the morning.
I cast away in this new moment all my once
hoarded knowledge, as vacant and vain. Now for
the first time seem I to know any thing rightly.
The simplest words, — we do not know what they
mean except when we love and aspire.

The difference between talents and character is
adroitness to keep the old and trodden round, and
power and courage to make a new road to new and
better goals. Character makes an overpowering
present ; a cheerful, determined hour, which forti-
fies all the company by making them see that much
is possible and excellent that was not thought of.
Character dulls the impression of particular events.
When we see the conqueror we do not think much
of any one battle or success. We see that we had
exaggerated the difficulty. It was easy to him.
The great man is not convulsible or tormentable ;
events pass over him without much impression.
People say sometimes, ' See what I have over-
come ; see how cheerful I am ; see how completely
I have triumphed over these black events.' Not if
they still remind me of the black event. True con-

quest is the causing the calamity to fade and disappear as an early cloud of insignificant result in a
history so large and advancing.

The one thing which we seek with insatiable desire is to forget ourselves, to be surprised out of our
propriety, to lose our sempiternal memory and to
do something without knowing how or why; in
short to draw a new circle. Nothing great was
ever achieved without enthusiasm. The way of
life is wonderful; it is by abandonment. The great
moments of history are the facilities of performance
through the strength of ideas, as the works of genius and religion. " A man " said Oliver Cromwell
" never rises so high as when he knows not whither
he is going." Dreams and drunkenness, the use of
opium and alcohol are the semblance and counterfeit of this oracular genius, and hence their dangerous attraction for men. For the like reason they
ask the aid of wild passions, as in gaming and war,
to ape in some manner these flames and generosi-
ties of the heart.

INTELLECT.

Go, speed the stars of Thought
On to their shining goals ; —
The sower scatters broad his seed
The wheat thou strew'st be souls.

XI.

INTELLECT.

———·———

EVERY substance is negatively electric to that which stands above it in the chemical tables, positively to that which stands below it. Water dissolves wood and iron and salt; air dissolves water; electric fire dissolves air, but the intellect dissolves fire, gravity, laws, method, and the subtlest unnamed relations of nature in its resistless menstruum. Intellect lies behind genius, which is intellect constructive. Intellect is the simple power anterior to all action or construction. Gladly would I unfold in calm degrees a natural history of the intellect, but what man has yet been able to mark the steps and boundaries of that transparent essence? The first questions are always to be asked, and the wisest doctor is gravelled by the inquisitiveness of a child. How can we speak of the action of the mind under any divisions, as of its knowledge, of its ethics, of its works, and so forth, since it melts will into perception, knowledge into act? Each becomes the other. Itself alone is

Its vision is not like the vision of the eye, but is union with the things known.

Intellect and intellection signify to the common ear consideration of abstract truth. The considerations of time and place, of you and me, of profit and hurt tyrannize over most men's minds. Intellect separates the fact considered, from *you*, from all local and personal reference, and discerns it as if it existed for its own sake. Heraclitus looked upon the affections as dense and colored mists. In the fog of good and evil affections it is hard for man to walk forward in a straight line. Intellect is void of affection and sees an object as it stands in the light of science, cool and disengaged. The intellect goes out of the individual, floats over its own personality, and regards it as a fact, and not as *I* and *mine*. He who is immersed in what concerns person or place cannot see the problem of existence. This the intellect always ponders. Nature shows all things formed and bound. The intellect pierces the form, overleaps the wall, detects intrinsic likeness between remote things and reduces all things into a few principles.

The making a fact the subject of thought raises it. All that mass of mental and moral phenomena which we do not make objects of voluntary thought, come within the power of fortune; they constitute the circumstance of daily life; they are subject to change, to fear and hope. Every man beholds his human condition with a degree of melancholy. As a ship aground is battered by the waves, so man, imprisoned in mortal life, lies open to the mercy of coming events. But a truth, separated by the intellect, is no longer a subject of destiny. We behold it as a god upraised above care and fear. And so any fact in our life, or any record of our fancies or reflections, disentangled from the web of our unconsciousness, becomes an object impersonal and immortal. It is the past restored, but embalmed. A better art than that of Egypt has taken fear and corruption out of it. It is eviscerated of care. It is offered for science. What is addressed to us for contemplation does not threaten us but makes us intellectual beings.

The growth of the intellect is spontaneous in every expansion. The mind that grows could not predict the times, the means, the mode of that spontaneity. God enters by a private door into every individual. Long prior to the age of reflection is the thinking of the mind. Out of darkness it came insensibly into the marvellous light of to-day. In the period of infancy it accepted and disposed of all impressions from the surrounding creation after its own way. Whatever any mind doth or saith is after a law, and this native law remains over it after it has come to reflection or conscious thought.

In the most worn, pedantic, introverted self-tormen-
tor's life, the greatest part is incalculable by him,
unforeseen, unimaginable, and must be, until he can
take himself up by his own ears. What am I?
What has my will done to make me that I am?
Nothing. I have been floated into this thought,
this hour, this connection of events, by secret currents of might and mind, and my ingenuity and
wilfulness have not thwarted, have not aided to an
appreciable degree.

Our spontaneous action is always the best. You
cannot with your best deliberation and heed come
so close to any question as your spontaneous glance
shall bring you, whilst you rise from your bed, or
walk abroad in the morning after meditating the
matter before sleep on the previous night. Our
thinking is a pious reception. Our truth of thought
is therefore vitiated as much by too violent direction given by our will, as by too great negligence.
We do not determine what we will think. We
only open our senses, clear away as we can all obstruction from the fact, and suffer the intellect to
see. We have little control over our thoughts.
We are the prisoners of ideas. They catch us up
for moments into their heaven and so fully engage
us that we take no thought for the morrow, gaze
like children, without an effort to make them our
own. By and by we fall out of that rapture, be-

think us where we have been, what we have seen,
and repeat as truly as we can what we have beheld.
As far as we can recall these ecstasies we carry
away in the ineffaceable memory the result, and all
men and all the ages confirm it. It is called
truth. But the moment we cease to report and attempt to correct and contrive, it is not truth.

If we consider what persons have stimulated and
profited us, we shall perceive the superiority of the
spontaneous or intuitive principle over the arithmetical or logical. The first contains the second,
but virtual and latent. We want in every man a
long logic; we cannot pardon the absence of it, but
it must not be spoken. Logic is the procession or
proportionate unfolding of the intuition; but its
virtue is as silent method; the moment it would
appear as propositions and have a separate value, it
is worthless.

In every man's mind, some images, words and
facts remain, without effort on his part to imprint
them, which others forget, and afterwards these il-
lustrate to him important laws. All our progress
is an unfolding, like the vegetable bud. You have
first an instinct, then an opinion, then a knowledge,
as the plant has root, bud and fruit. Trust the instinct to the end, though you can render no reason.
It is vain to hurry it. By trusting it to the end,
it shall ripen into truth and you shall know why
you believe.

Each mind has its own method. A true man never acquires after college rules. What you have aggregated in a natural manner surprises and delights when it is produced. For we cannot oversee each other's secret. And hence the differences between men in natural endowment are insignificant in comparison with their common wealth. Do you think the porter and the cook have no anecdotes, no experiences, no wonders for you? Every body knows as much as the savant. The walls of rude minds are scrawled all over with facts, with thoughts. They shall one day bring a lantern and read the inscriptions. Every man, in the degree in which he has wit and culture, finds his curiosity inflamed concerning the modes of living and thinking of other men, and especially of those classes whose minds have not been subdued by the drill of school education.

This instinctive action never ceases in a healthy mind, but becomes richer and more frequent in its informations through all states of culture. At last comes the era of reflection, when we not only observe, but take pains to observe; when we of set purpose sit down to consider an abstract truth; when we keep the mind's eye open whilst we converse, whilst we read, whilst we act, intent to learn the secret law of some class of facts.

What is the hardest task in the world? To

think. I would put myself in the attitude to look in the eye an abstract truth, and I cannot. I blench and withdraw on this side and on that. I seem to know what he meant who said, No man can see God face to face and live. For example, a man explores the basis of civil government. Let him intend his mind without respite, without rest, in one direction. His best heed long time avails him nothing. Yet thoughts are flitting before him. We all but apprehend, we dimly forebode the truth. We say I will walk abroad, and the truth will take form and clearness to me. We go forth, but cannot find it. It seems as if we needed only the stillness and composed attitude of the library to seize the thought. But we come in, and are as far from it as at first. Then, in a moment, and unannounced, the truth appears. A certain wandering light appears, and is the distinction, the principle, we wanted. But the oracle comes because we had previously laid siege to the shrine. It seems as if the law of the intellect resembled that law of nature by which we now inspire, now expire the breath; by which the heart now draws in, then hurls out the blood, — the law of undulation. So now you must labor with your brains, and now you must forbear your activity and see what the great Soul showeth.

The immortality of man is as legitimately

preached from the intellections as from the moral volitions. Every intellection is mainly prospective. Its present value is its least. Inspect what delights you in Plutarch, in Shakspeare, in Cervantes. Each truth that a writer acquires is a lantern which he turns full on what facts and thoughts lay already in his mind, and behold, all the mats and rubbish which had littered his garret become precious. Every trivial fact in his private biography becomes an illustration of this new principle, revisits the day, and delights all men by its piquancy and new charm. Men say, Where did he get this? and think there was something divine in his life. But no; they have myriads of facts just as good, would they only get a lamp to ransack their attics withal.

We are all wise. The difference between persons is not in wisdom but in art. I knew, in an academical club, a person who always deferred to me; who, seeing my whim for writing, fancied that my experiences had somewhat superior; whilst I saw that his experiences were as good as mine. Give them to me and I would make the same use of them. He held the old; he holds the new; I had the habit of tacking together the old and the new which he did not use to exercise. This may hold in the great examples. Perhaps, if we should meet Shakspeare we should not be conscious of any steep inferiority; no, but of a great equality, — only that

he possessed a strange skill of using, of classify-
ing his facts, which we lacked. For notwithstanding our utter incapacity to produce anything like
Hamlet and Othello, see the perfect reception this
wit and immense knowledge of life and liquid eloquence find in us all.

If you gather apples in the sunshine, or make
hay, or hoe corn, and then retire within doors and
shut your eyes and press them with your hand, you
shall still see apples hanging in the bright light
with boughs and leaves thereto, or the tasselled
grass, or the corn-flags, and this for five or six
hours afterwards. There lie the impressions on
the retentive organ, though you knew it not. So
lies the whole series of natural images with which
your life has made you acquainted, in your memory, though you know it not ; and a thrill of passion flashes light on their dark chamber, and the
active power seizes instantly the fit image, as the
word of its momentary thought.

It is long ere we discover how rich we are.
Our history, we are sure, is quite tame : we have
nothing to write, nothing to infer. But our wiser
years still run back to the despised recollections of
childhood, and always we are fishing up some wonderful article out of that pond ; until by and by we
begin to suspect that the biography of the one foolish person we know is, in reality, nothing less than

the miniature paraphrase of the hundred volumes of the Universal History.

In the intellect constructive, which we popularly designate by the word Genius, we observe the same balance of two elements as in intellect receptive. The constructive intellect produces thoughts, sentences, poems, plans, designs, systems. It is the generation of the mind, the marriage of thought with nature. To genius must always go two gifts, the thought and the publication. The first is revelation, always a miracle, which no frequency of occurrence or incessant study can ever familiarize, but which must always leave the inquirer stupid with wonder. It is the advent of truth into the world, a form of thought now for the first time bursting into the universe, a child of the old eternal soul, a piece of genuine and immeasurable greatness. It seems, for the time, to inherit all that has yet existed and to dictate to the unborn. It affects every thought of man and goes to fashion every institution. But to make it available it needs a vehicle or art by which it is conveyed to men. To be communicable it must become picture or sensible object. We must learn the language of facts. The most wonderful inspirations die with their subject if he has no hand to paint them to the senses. The ray of light passes invisible through space and only when it falls on an object is it seen.

When the spiritual energy is directed on something outward, then it is a thought. The relation between it and you first makes you, the value of you, apparent to me. The rich inventive genius of the painter must be smothered and lost for want of the power of drawing, and in our happy hours we should be inexhaustible poets if once we could break through the silence into adequate rhyme. As all men have some access to primary truth, so all have some art or power of communication in their head, but only in the artist does it descend into the hand. There is an inequality, whose laws we do not yet know, between two men and between two moments of the same man, in respect to this faculty. In common hours we have the same facts as in the uncommon or inspired, but they do not sit for their portraits ; they are not detached, but lie in a web. The thought of genius is spontaneous ; but the power of picture or expression, in the most enriched and flowing nature, implies a mixture of will, a certain control over the spontaneous states, without which no production is possible. It is a conversion of all nature into the rhetoric of thought, under the eye of judgment, with a strenuous exercise of choice. And yet the imaginative vocabulary seems to be spontaneous also. It does not flow from experience only or mainly, but from a richer source. Not by any con-

scious imitation of particular forms are the grand
strokes of the painter executed, but by repairing to
the fountain-head of all forms in his mind.   Who
is the first drawing-master? Without instruction
we know very well the ideal of the human form.
A child knows if an arm or a leg be distorted in a
picture; if the attitude be natural or grand or
mean; though he has never received any instruction in drawing or heard any conversation on the
subject, nor can himself draw with correctness a
single feature.   A good form strikes all eyes pleasantly, long before they have any science on the
subject, and a beautiful face sets twenty hearts in
palpitation, prior to all consideration of the mechanical proportions of the features and head. We
may owe to dreams some light on the fountain of
this skill; for as soon as we let our will go and let
the unconscious states ensue, see what cunning
draughtsmen we are! We entertain ourselves with
wonderful forms of men, of women, of animals, of
gardens, of woods and of monsters, and the mystic
pencil wherewith we then draw has no awkward-
ness or inexperience, no meagreness or poverty; it
can design well and group well; its composition is
full of art, its colors are well laid on and the whole
canvas which it paints is lifelike and apt to touch
us with terror, with tenderness, with desire and
with grief.   Neither are the artist's copies from ex-

perience ever mere copies, but always touched and softened by tints from this ideal domain.

The conditions essential to a constructive mind do not appear to be so often combined but that a good sentence or verse remains fresh and memorable for a long time. Yet when we write with ease and come out into the free air of thought, we seem to be assured that nothing is easier than to continue this communication at pleasure. Up, down, around, the kingdom of thought has no inclosures, but the Muse makes us free of her city. Well, the world has a million writers. One would think then that good thought would be as familiar as air and water, and the gifts of each new hour would exclude the last. Yet we can count all our good books; nay, I remember any beautiful verse for twenty years. It is true that the discerning intellect of the world is always much in advance of the creative, so that there are many competent judges of the best book, and few writers of the best books. But some of the conditions of intellectual construction are of rare occurrence. The intellect is a whole and demands integrity in every work. This is resisted equally by a man's devotion to a single thought and by his ambition to combine too many.

Truth is our element of life, yet if a man fasten his attention on a single aspect of truth and appiy

himself to that alone for a long time, the truth becomes distorted and not itself but falsehood; herein
resembling the air, which is our natural element
and the breath of our nostrils, but if a stream of
the same be directed on the body for a time, it
causes cold, fever, and even death. How wearisome
the grammarian, the phrenologist, the political or
religious fanatic, or indeed any possessed mortal
whose balance is lost by the exaggeration of a single topic. It is incipient insanity. Every thought
is a prison also. I cannot see what you see, because I am caught up by a strong wind and blown
so far in one direction that I am out of the hoop of
your horizon.

Is it any better if the student, to avoid this offence and to liberalize himself, aims to make a mechanical whole of history, or science, or philosophy,
by a numerical addition of all the facts that fall
within his vision? The world refuses to be analyzed by addition and subtraction. When we are
young we spend much time and pains in filling our
note-books with all definitions of Religion, Love,
Poetry, Politics, Art, in the hope that in the course
of a few years we shall have condensed into our encyclopædia the net value of all the theories at which
the world has yet arrived. But year after year our
tables get no completeness, and at last we discover
that our curve is a parabola, whose arcs will never
meet.

Neither by detachment neither by aggregation is the integrity of the intellect transmitted to its works, but by a vigilance which brings the intellect in its greatness and best state to operate every moment. It must have the same wholeness which nature has. Although no diligence can rebuild the universe in a model by the best accumulation or disposition of details, yet does the world reappear in miniature in every event, so that all the laws of nature may be read in the smallest fact. The intellect must have the like perfection in its apprehension and in its works. For this reason, an index or mercury of intellectual proficiency is the perception of identity. We talk with accomplished persons who appear to be strangers in nature. The cloud, the tree, the turf, the bird, are not theirs, have nothing of them; the world is only their lodging and table. But the poet, whose verses are to be spheral and complete, is one whom Nature cannot deceive, whatsoever face of strangeness she may put on. He feels a strict consanguinity, and detects more likeness than variety in all her changes. We are stung by the desire for new thought; but when we receive a new thought it is only the old thought with a new face, and though we make it our own we instantly crave another; we are not really enriched. For the truth was in us before it was reflected to us from natural objects; and the

profound genius will cast the likeness of all creatures into every product of his wit.

But if the constructive powers are rare and it is
given to few men to be poets, yet every man is a
receiver of this descending holy ghost, and may
well study the laws of its influx. Exactly parallel
is the whole rule of intellectual duty to the rule of
moral duty. A self-denial no less austere than the
saint's is demanded of the scholar. He must worship truth, and forego all things for that, and
choose defeat and pain, so that his treasure in
thought is thereby augmented.

God offers to every mind its choice between truth
and repose. Take which you please, — you can
never have both. Between these, as a pendulum,
man oscillates. He in whom the love of repose predominates will accept the first creed, the first philosophy, the first political party he meets, — most
likely his father's. He gets rest, commodity and
reputation; but he shuts the door of truth. He in
whom the love of truth predominates will keep himself aloof from all moorings, and afloat. He will
abstain from dogmatism, and recognize all the opposite negations between which, as walls, his being
is swung. He submits to the inconvenience of sus-
pense and imperfect opinion, but he is a candidate
for truth, as the other is not, and respects the highest law of his being.

The circle of the green earth he must measure
with his shoes to find the man who can yield him
truth. He shall then know that there is somewhat
more blessed and great in hearing than in speaking.
Happy is the hearing man; unhappy the speaking
man. As long as I hear truth I am bathed by a
beautiful element and am not conscious of any limits to my nature. The suggestions are thousand-
fold that I hear and see. The waters of the great
deep have ingress and egress to the soul. But if I
speak, I define, I confine and am less. When Socrates speaks, Lysis and Menexenus are afflicted by
no shame that they do not speak. They also are
good. He likewise defers to them, loves them,
whilst he speaks. Because a true and natural man
contains and is the same truth which an eloquent
man articulates; but in the eloquent man, because
he can articulate it, it seems something the less to
reside, and he turns to these silent beautiful with
the more inclination and respect. The ancient sentence said, Let us be silent, for so are the gods.
Silence is a solvent that destroys personality, and
gives us leave to be great and universal. Every
man's progress is through a succession of teachers,
each of whom seems at the time to have a superlative influence, but it at last gives place to a new.
Frankly let him accept it all. Jesus says, Leave
father, mother, house and lands, and follow me.

Who leaves all, receives more. This is as true intellectually as morally. Each new mind we approach seems to require an abdication of all our past and present possessions. A new doctrine seems at first a subversion of all our opinions, tastes, and manner of living. Such has Swedenborg, such has Kant, such has Coleridge, such has Hegel or his interpreter Cousin seemed to many young men in this country. Take thankfully and heartily all they can give. Exhaust them, wrestle with them, let them not go until their blessing be won, and after a short season the dismay will be overpast, the excess of influence withdrawn, and they will be no longer an alarming meteor, but one more bright star shining serenely in your heaven and blending its light with all your day.

But whilst he gives himself up unreservedly to that which draws him, because that is his own, he is to refuse himself to that which draws him not, whatsoever fame and authority may attend it, because it is not his own. Entire self-reliance belongs to the intellect. One soul is a counterpoise of all souls, as a capillary column of water is a balance for the sea. It must treat things and books and sovereign genius as itself also a sovereign. If Æschylus be that man he is taken for, he has not yet done his office when he has educated the learned of Europe for a thousand years. He is now to approve himself a master of delight to me also. It he cannot do that, all his fame shall avail him nothing with me. I were a fool not to sacrifice a thousand Æschyluses to my intellectual integrity. Especially take the same ground in regard to abstract truth, the science of the mind. The Bacon, the Spinoza, the Hume, Schelling, Kant, or whosoever propounds to you a philosophy of the mind, is only a more or less awkward translator of things in your consciousness which you have also your way of seeing, perhaps of denominating. Say then, instead of too timidly poring into his obscure sense, that he has not succeeded in rendering back to you your consciousness. He has not succeeded; now let another try. If Plato cannot, perhaps Spinoza will. If Spinoza cannot, then perhaps Kant. Anyhow, when at last it is done, you will find it is no recondite, but a simple, natural, common state which the writer restores to you.

But let us end these didactics. I will not, though the subject might provoke it, speak to the open question between Truth and Love. I shall not presume to interfere in the old politics of the skies;— " The cherubim know most; the seraphim love most." The gods shall settle their own quarrels. But I cannot recite, even thus rudely, laws of the intellect, without remembering that lofty and sequestered class who have been its prophets and oracles, the high-priesthood of the pure reason, the *Trismegisti*, the expounders of the principles of thought from age to age. When at long intervals we turn over their abstruse pages, wonderful seems the calm and grand air of these few, these great spiritual lords who have walked in the world, — these of the old religion, — dwelling in a worship which makes the sanctities of Christianity look *parvenues* and popular; for "persuasion is in soul, but necessity is in intellect." This band of grandees, Hermes, Heraclitus, Empedocles, Plato, Plotinus, Olympiodorus, Proclus, Synesius and the rest, have somewhat so vast in their logic, so primary in their thinking, that it seems antecedent to all the ordinary distinctions of rhetoric and literature, and to be at once poetry and music and dancing and astronomy and mathematics. I am present at the sowing of the seed of the world. With a geometry of sunbeams the soul lays the foundations of nature. The truth and grandeur of their thought is proved by its scope and applicability, for it commands the entire schedule and inventory of things for its illustration. But what marks its elevation and has even a comic look to us, is the innocent serenity with which these babe-like Jupiters sit in their clouds, and from age to age prattle to each other and to no contemporary. Well assured that their speech is intelligible and the most natural thing in the world, they add thesis to thesis, without a moment's heed of the universal astonishment of the human race below, who do not comprehend their plainest argument; nor do they ever relent so much as to insert a popular or explaining sentence, nor testify the least displeasure or petulance at the dulness of their amazed auditory. The angels are so enamored of the language that is spoken in heaven that they will not distort their lips with the hissing and unmusical dialects of men, but speak their own, whether there be any who understand *it* or not.

ART.

Give to barrows trays and pans
Grace and glimmer of romance,
Bring the moonlight into noon
Hid in gleaming piles of stone ;
On the city's paved street
Plant gardens lined with lilac sweet,
Let spouting fountains cool the air,
Singing in the sun-baked square.
Let statue, picture, park and hall,
Ballad, flag and festival,
The past restore, the day adorn
And make each morrow a new morn
So shall the drudge in dusty frock
Spy behind the city clock
Retinues of airy kings,
Skirts of angels, starry wings,
His fathers shining in bright fables,
His children fed at heavenly tables.
' T is the privilege of Art
Thus to play its cheerful part,
Man in Earth to acclimate
And bend the exile to his fate,
And, moulded of one element
With the days and firmament,
Teach him on these as stairs to climb
And live on even terms with Time ;
Whilst upper life the slender rill
Of human sense doth overfill.

XII.

ART.

———◆———

BECAUSE the soul is progressive, it never quite repeats itself, but in every act attempts the production of a new and fairer whole. This appears in works both of the useful and fine arts, if we employ the popular distinction of works according to their aim either at use or beauty. Thus in our fine arts, not imitation but creation is the aim. In landscapes the painter should give the suggestion of a fairer creation than we know. The details, the prose of nature he should omit and give us only the spirit and splendor. He should know that the landscape has beauty for his eye because it expresses a thought which is to him good; and this because the same power which sees through his eyes is seen in that spectacle; and he will come to value the expression of nature and not nature itself, and so exalt in his copy the features that please him. He will give the gloom of gloom and the sunshine of sunshine. In a portrait he must inscribe the character and not the features, and must esteem the man who sits to him as himself only an imperfect picture or likeness of the aspiring original within.

What is that abridgment and selection we observe in all spiritual activity, but itself the creative impulse? for it is the inlet of that higher illumination which teaches to convey a larger sense by simpler symbols. What is a man but nature's finer success in self-explication? What is a man but a finer and compacter landscape than the horizon figures, — nature's eclecticism? and what is his speech, his love of painting, love of nature, but a still finer success, — all the weary miles and tons of space and bulk left out, and the spirit or moral of it contracted into a musical word, or the most cunning stroke of the pencil?

But the artist must employ the symbols in use in his day and nation to convey his enlarged sense to his fellow-men. Thus the new in art is always formed out of the old. The Genius of the Hour sets his ineffaceable seal on the work and gives it an inexpressible charm for the imagination. As far as the spiritual character of the period overpowers the artist and finds expression in his work, so far it will retain a certain grandeur, and will represent to future beholders the Unknown, the Inevitable, the Divine. No man can quite exclude this element of Necessity from his labor. No man can quite emancipate himself from his age and country, or produce a model in which the education, the religion, the politics, usages and arts of his times shall have no share. Though he were never so original, never so wilful and fantastic, he cannot wipe out of his work every trace of the thoughts amidst which it grew. The very avoidance betrays the usage he avoids. Above his will and out of his sight he is necessitated by the air he breathes and the idea on which he and his contemporaries live and toil, to share the manner of his times, without knowing what that manner is. Now that which is inevitable in the work has a higher charm than individual talent can ever give, inasmuch as the artist's pen or chisel seems to have been held and guided by a gigantic hand to inscribe a line in the history of the human race. This circumstance gives a value to the Egyptian hieroglyphics, to the Indian, Chinese and Mexican idols, however gross and shapeless. They denote the height of the human soul in that hour, and were not fantastic, but sprung from a necessity as deep as the world. Shall I now add that the whole extant product of the plastic arts has herein its highest value, *as history ;* as a stroke drawn in the portrait of that fate, perfect and beautiful, according to whose ordinations all beings advance to their beatitude ?

Thus, historically viewed, it has been the office of art to educate the perception of beauty. We are

immersed in beauty, but our eyes have no clear vision. It needs, by the exhibition of single traits, to
assist and lead the dormant taste. We carve and
paint, or we behold what is carved and painted, as
students of the mystery of Form. The virtue of
art lies in detachment, in sequestering one object
from the embarrassing variety. Until one thing
comes out from the connection of things, there can
be enjoyment, contemplation, but no thought. Our
happiness and unhappiness are unproductive. The
infant lies in a pleasing trance, but his individual
character and his practical power depend on his
daily progress in the separation of things, and dealing with one at a time. Love and all the passions
concentrate all existence around a single form. It
is the habit of certain minds to give an all-exclud-
ing fulness to the object, the thought, the word
they alight upon, and to make that for the time the
deputy of the world. These are the artists, the or-
ators, the leaders of society. The power to detach
and to magnify by detaching is the essence of rhetoric in the hands of the orator and the poet. This
rhetoric, or power to fix the momentary eminency
of an object, — so remarkable in Burke, in Byron,
in Carlyle, — the painter and sculptor exhibit in
color and in stone. The power depends on the
depth of the artist's insight of that object he con-
templates. For every object has its roots in cen-

tral nature, and may of course be so exhibited to
us as to represent the world. Therefore each work
of genius is the tyrant of the hour and concentrates
attention on itself. For the time, it is the only
thing worth naming to do that, — be it a sonnet, an
opera, a landscape, a statue, an oration, the plan
of a temple, of a campaign, or of a voyage of discovery. Presently we pass to some other object,
which rounds itself into a whole as did the first ;
for example a well-laid garden ; and nothing seems
worth doing but the laying out of gardens. I
should think fire the best thing in the world, if I
were not acquainted with air, and water, and earth.
For it is the right and property of all natural objects, of all genuine talents, of all native properties
whatsoever, to be for their moment the top of the
world. A squirrel leaping from bough to bough
and making the wood but one wide tree for his
pleasure, fills the eye not less than a lion, — is
beautiful, self-sufficing, and stands then and there
for nature. A good ballad draws my ear and
heart whilst I listen, as much as an epic has done
before. A dog, drawn by a master, or a litter of
pigs, satisfies and is a reality not less than than the
frescoes of Angelo. From this succession of excellent objects we learn at last the immensity of the
world, the opulence of human nature, which can
run out to infinitude in any direction. But I also

learn that what astonished and fascinated me in the first work, astonished me in the second work also; that excellence of all things is one.

The office of painting and sculpture seems to be merely initial. The best pictures can easily tell us their last secret. The best pictures are rude draughts of a few of the miraculous dots and lines and dyes which make up the ever-changing "landscape with figures" amidst which we dwell. Painting seems to be to the eye what dancing is to the limbs. When that has educated the frame to self-possession, to nimbleness, to grace, the steps of the dancing-master are better forgotten; so painting teaches me the splendor of color and the expression of form, and as I see many pictures and higher genius in the art, I see the boundless opulence of the pencil, the indifferency in which the artist stands free to choose out of the possible forms. If he can draw every thing, why draw any thing? and then is my eye opened to the eternal picture which nature paints in the street, with moving men and children, beggars and fine ladies, draped in red and green and blue and gray; long-haired, grizzled, white-faced, black-faced, wrinkled, giant, dwarf, expanded, elfish, — capped and based by heaven, earth and sea.

A gallery of sculpture teaches more austerely the same lesson. As picture teaches the coloring, so sculpture the anatomy of form. When I have seen fine statues and afterwards enter a public assembly, I understand well what he meant who said, " When I have been reading Homer, all men look like giants." I too see that painting and sculpture are gymnastics of the eye, its training to the niceties and curiosities of its function. There is no statue like this living man, with his infinite advantage over all ideal sculpture, of perpetual variety. What a gallery of art have I here ! No mannerist made these varied groups and diverse original single figures. Here is the artist himself improvising, grim and glad, at his block. Now one thought strikes him, now another, and with each moment he alters the whole air, attitude and expression of his clay. Away with your nonsense of oil and easels, of marble and chisels ; except to open your eyes to the masteries of eternal art, they are hypocritical rubbish.

The reference of all production at last to an aboriginal Power explains the traits common to all works of the highest art, — that they are universally intelligible ; that they restore to us the simplest states of mind, and are religious. Since what skill is therein shown is the reappearance of the original soul, a jet of pure light, it should produce a similar impression to that made by natural objects. In happy hours, nature appears to us one with art

art perfected, — the work of genius. And the individual in whom simple tastes and susceptibility
to all the great human influences overpower the accidents of a local and special culture, is the best
critic of art. Though we travel the world over to
find the beautiful, we must carry it with us, or we
find it not. The best of beauty is a finer charm
than skill in surfaces, in outlines, or rules of art can
ever teach, namely a radiation from the work of
art, of human character, — a wonderful expression
through stone, or canvas, or musical sound, of the
deepest and simplest attributes of our nature, and
therefore most intelligible at last to those souls
which have these attributes. In the sculptures of
the Greeks, in the masonry of the Romans, and in
the pictures of the Tuscan and Venetian masters,
the highest charm is the universal language they
speak. A confession of moral nature, of purity,
love, and hope, breathes from them all. That
which we carry to them, the same we bring back
more fairly illustrated in the memory. The traveller who visits the Vatican and passes from chamber to chamber through galleries of statues, vases,
sarcophagi and candelabra, through all forms of
beauty cut in the richest materials, is in danger
of forgetting the simplicity of the principles out of
which they all sprung, and that they had their origin from thoughts and laws in his own breast. He

studies the technical rules on these wonderful remains, but forgets that these works were not always thus constellated ; that they are the contribu-
tions of many ages and many countries ; that each
came out of the solitary workshop of one artist,
who toiled perhaps in ignorance of the existence
of other sculpture, created his work without other
model save life, household life, and the sweet and
smart of personal relations, of beating hearts, and
meeting eyes; of poverty and necessity and hope
and fear. These were his inspirations, and these
are the effects he carries home to your heart and
mind. In proportion to his force, the artist will
find in his work an outlet for his proper character.
He must not be in any manner pinched or hindered by his material, but through his necessity of
imparting himself the adamant will be wax in his
hands, and will allow an adequate communication
of himself, in his full stature and proportion. He
need not cumber himself with a conventional nature and culture, nor ask what is the mode in Rome
or in Paris, but that house and weather and manner
of living which poverty and the fate of birth have
made at once so odious and so dear, in the gray un-
painted wood cabin, on the corner of a New Hampshire farm, or in the log-hut of the backwoods, or
in the narrow lodging where he has endured the
constraints and seeming of a city poverty, will

serve as well as any other condition as the symbol of a thought which pours itself indifferently through all.

I remember when in my younger days I had heard of the wonders of Italian painting, I fancied the great pictures would be great strangers; some surprising combination of color and form; a foreign wonder, barbaric pearl and gold, like the spontoons and standards of the militia, which play such pranks in the eyes and imaginations of school-boys. I was to see and acquire I knew not what. When I came at last to Rome and saw with eyes the pictures, I found that genius left to novices the gay and fantastic and ostentatious, and itself pierced directly to the simple and true; that it was familiar and sincere; that it was the old, eternal fact I had met already in so many forms, — unto which I lived; that it was the plain *you and me* I knew so well, — had left at home in so many conversations. I had the same experience already in a church at Naples. There I saw that nothing was changed with me but the place, and said to myself — 'Thou foolish child, hast thou come out hither, over four thousand miles of salt water, to find that which was perfect to thee there at home?' That fact I saw again in the Academmia at Naples, in the chambers of sculpture, and yet again when I came to Rome and to the paintings of Raphael, Angelo,

Sacchi, Titian, and Leonardo da Vinci. "What, old mole! workest thou in the earth so fast?" It had travelled by my side; that which I fancied I had left in Boston was here in the Vatican, and again at Milan and at Paris, and made all travelling ridiculous as a treadmill. I now require this of all pictures, that they domesticate me, not that they dazzle me. Pictures must not be too picturesque. Nothing astonishes men so much as common-sense and plain dealing. All great actions have been simple, and all great pictures are.

The Transfiguration, by Raphael, is an eminent example of this peculiar merit. A calm benignant beauty shines over all this picture, and goes directly to the heart. It seems almost to call you by name. The sweet and sublime face of Jesus is beyond praise, yet how it disappoints all florid expectations! This familiar, simple, home-speaking countenance is as if one should meet a friend. The knowledge of picture-dealers has its value, but listen not to their criticism when your heart is touched by genius. It was not painted for them, it was painted for you; for such as had eyes capable of being touched by simplicity and lofty emotions.

Yet when we have said all our fine things about the arts, we must end with a frank confession that the arts, as we know them, are but initial. Our

best praise is given to what they aimed and promised, not to the actual result. He has conceived
meanly of the resources of man, who believes that
the best age of production is past. The real value
of the Iliad or the Transfiguration is as signs of
power; billows or ripples they are of the stream
of tendency; tokens of the everlasting effort to produce, which even in its worst estate the soul betrays.
Art has not yet come to its maturity if it do not
put itself abreast with the most potent influences of
the world, if it is not practical and moral, if it do
not stand in connection with the conscience, if it do
not make the poor and uncultivated feel that it addresses them with a voice of lofty cheer. There is
higher work for Art than the arts. They are abor-
tive births of an imperfect or vitiated instinct. Art
is the need to create; but in its essence, immense
and universal, it is impatient of working with lame
or tied hands, and of making cripples and monsters, such as all pictures and statues are. Nothing
less than the creation of man and nature is its end.
A man should find in it an outlet for his whole energy. He may paint and carve only as long as he
can do that. Art should exhilarate, and throw
down the walls of circumstance on every side,
awakening in the beholder the same sense of universal relation and power which the work evinced
in the artist, and its highest effect is to make new
artists.

Already History is old enough to witness the old age and disappearance of particular arts. The art of sculpture is long ago perished to any real effect. It was originally a useful art, a mode of writing, a savage's record of gratitude or devotion, and among a people possessed of a wonderful perception of form this childish carving was refined to the utmost splendor of effect. But it is the game of a rude and youthful people, and not the manly labor of a wise and spiritual nation. Under an oak-tree loaded with leaves and nuts, under a sky full of eternal eyes, I stand in a thoroughfare; but in the works of our plastic arts and especially of sculpture, creation is driven into a corner. I cannot hide from myself that there is a certain appearance of paltriness, as of toys and the trumpery of a theatre, in sculpture. Nature transcends all our moods of thought, and its secret we do not yet find. But the gallery stands at the mercy of our moods, and there is a moment when it becomes frivolous. I do not wonder that Newton, with an attention habitually engaged on the paths of planets and suns, should have wondered what the Earl of Pembroke found to admire in "stone dolls." Sculpture may serve to teach the pupil how deep is the secret of form, how purely the spirit can translate its meanings into that eloquent dialect. But the statue will look cold and false before that new activity which needs to roll through all things, and is impatient of counterfeits and things not alive. Picture and sculpture are the celebrations and festivities of form. But true art is never fixed, but always flowing. The sweetest music is not in the oratorio, but in the human voice when it speaks from its instant life tones of tenderness, truth, or courage. The oratorio has already lost its relation to the morning, to the sun, and the earth, but that persuading voice is in tune with these. All works of art should not be detached, but extempore performances. A great man is a new statue in every attitude and action. A beautiful woman is a picture which drives all beholders nobly mad. Life may be lyric or epic, as well as a poem or a romance.

A true announcement of the law of creation, if a man were found worthy to declare it, would carry art up into the kingdom of nature, and destroy its separate and contrasted existence. The fountains of invention and beauty in modern society are all but dried up. A popular novel, a theatre, or a ball-room makes us feel that we are all paupers in the almshouse of this world, without dignity, without skill or industry. Art is as poor and low. The old tragic Necessity, which lowers on the brows even of the Venuses and the Cupids of the antique, and furnishes the sole apology for the intrusion of such anomalous figures into nature, —

namely that they were inevitable ; that the artist was drunk with a passion for form which he could not resist, and which vented itself in these fine extravagances, — no longer dignifies the chisel or the pencil. But the artist and the connoisseur now seek in art the exhibition of their talent, or an asy-lum from the evils of life. Men are not well pleased with the figure they make in their own imaginations, and they flee to art, and convey their better sense in an oratorio, a statue, or a picture. Art makes the same effort which a sensual prosperity makes ; namely to detach the beautiful from the useful, to do up the work as unavoidable, and, hating it, pass on to enjoyment. These solaces and compensations, this division of beauty from use, the laws of nature do not permit. As soon as beauty is sought, not from religion and love but for pleasure, it degrades the seeker. High beauty is no longer attainable by him in canvas or in stone, in sound, or in lyrical construction ; an effeminate, prudent, sickly beauty, which is not beauty, is all that can be formed ; for the hand can never execute any thing higher than the character can inspire.

The art that thus separates is itself first separated. Art must not be a superficial talent, but must begin farther back in man. Now men do not see nature to be beautiful, and they go to make a

statue which shall be. They abhor men as taste
less, dull, and inconvertible, and console themselves
with color-bags and blocks of marble. They reject
life as prosaic, and create a death which they call
poetic. They despatch the day's weary chores, and
fly to voluptuous reveries. They eat and drink,
that they may afterwards execute the ideal. Thus
is art vilified; the name conveys to the mind its
secondary and bad senses; it stands in the imagination as somewhat contrary to nature, and struck
with death from the first. Would it not be better
to begin higher up, — to serve the ideal before they
eat and drink; to serve the ideal in eating and
drinking, in drawing the breath, and in the functions of life? Beauty must come back to the useful arts, and the distinction between the fine and
the useful arts be forgotten. If history were truly
told, if life were nobly spent, it would be no
longer easy or possible to distinguish the one from
the other. In nature, all is useful, all is beautiful.
It is therefore beautiful because it is alive, moving,
reproductive; it is therefore useful because it is
symmetrical and fair. Beauty will not come at the
call of a legislature, nor will it repeat in England or America its history in Greece. It will
come, as always, unannounced, and spring up between the feet of brave and earnest men. It is in
vain that we look for genius to reiterate its mira-

cies in the old arts; it is its instinct to find beauty
and holiness in new and necessary facts, in the
field and road-side, in the shop and mill. Pro
ceeding from a religious heart it will raise to a di=
vine use the railroad, the insurance office, the joint-
stock company; our law, our primary assemblies.
our commerce, the galvanic battery, the electric jar,
the prism, and the chemist's retort; in which we
seek now only an economical use. Is not the selfish and even cruel aspect which belongs to our
great mechanical works, to mills, railways, and
machinery, the effect of the mercenary impulses
which these works obey? When its errands are
noble and adequate, a steamboat bridging the Atlantic between Old and New England and arriving
at its ports with the punctuality of a planet, is a
step of man into harmony with nature. The boat
at St. Petersburg, which plies along the Lena by
magnetism, needs little to make it sublime. When
science is learned in love, and its powers are
wielded by love, they will appear the supplements
and continuations of the material creation.

ESSAYS

SECOND SERIES

Olympian bards who sung
　Divine ideas below,
Which always find us young,
　And always keep us so.

THE POET.

THOSE who are esteemed umpires of taste are often persons who have acquired some knowledge of admired pictures or sculptures, and have an inclination for whatever is elegant; but if you inquire whether they are beautiful souls, and whether their own acts are like fair pictures, you learn that they are selfish and sensual. Their cultivation is local, as if you should rub a log of dry wood in one spot to produce fire, all the rest remaining cold. Their knowledge of the fine arts is some study of rules and particulars, or some limited judgment of color or form, which is exercised for amusement or for show. It is a proof of the shallowness of the doctrine of beauty as it lies in the minds of our amateurs, that men seem to have lost the perception of the instant dependence of form upon soul. There is no doctrine of forms in our philosophy. We were put into our bodies, as fire is put into a pan to be carried about; but there is no accurate adjustment between the spirit and the organ, much

less is the latter the germination of the former. So
in regard to other forms, the intellectual men do
not believe in any essential dependence of the material world on thought and volition. Theologians
think it a pretty air-castle to talk of the spiritual
meaning of a ship or a cloud, of a city or a contract, but they prefer to come again to the solid
ground of historical evidence; and even the poets
are contented with a civil and conformed manner
of living, and to write poems from the fancy, at a
safe distance from their own experience. But the
highest minds of the world have never ceased to
explore the double meaning, or shall I say the
quadruple or the centuple or much more manifold
meaning, of every sensuous fact; Orpheus, Empedocles, Heraclitus, Plato, Plutarch, Dante, Swedenborg, and the masters of sculpture, picture, and
poetry. For we are not pans and barrows, nor
even porters of the fire and torch-bearers, but children of the fire, made of it, and only the same divinity transmuted and at two or three removes,
when we know least about it. And this hidden
truth, that the fountains whence all this river of
Time and its creatures floweth are intrinsically
ideal and beautiful, draws us to the consideration
of the nature and functions of the Poet, or the
man of Beauty; to the means and materials he
uses, and to the general aspect of the art in the
present time.

The breadth of the problem is great, for the poet is representative. He stands among partial men for the complete man, and apprises us not of his wealth, but of the common wealth. The young man reveres men of genius, because, to speak truly, they are more himself than he is. They receive of the soul as he also receives, but they more. Nature enhances her beauty, to the eye of loving men, from their belief that the poet is beholding her shows at the same time. He is isolated among his contemporaries by truth and by his art, but with this consolation in his pursuits, that they will draw all men sooner or later. For all men live by truth and stand in need of expression. In love, in art, in avarice, in politics, in labor, in games, we study to utter our painful secret. The man is only half himself, the other half is his expression.

Notwithstanding this necessity to be published, adequate expression is rare. I know not how it is that we need an interpreter, but the great majority of men seem to be minors, who have not yet come into possession of their own, or mutes, who cannot report the conversation they have had with nature. There is no man who does not anticipate a supersensual utility in the sun and stars, earth and water. These stand and wait to render him a peculiar service. But there is some obstruction or some excess of phlegm in our constitution, which does not suffer them to yield the due effect. Too feeble fall the impressions of nature on us to make us artists. Every touch should thrill. Every man should be so much an artist that he could report in conversation what had befallen him. Yet, in our experience, the rays or appulses have sufficient force to arrive at the senses, but not enough to reach the quick and compel the reproduction of themselves in speech. The poet is the person in whom these powers are in balance, the man without impediment, who sees and handles that which others dream of, traverses the whole scale of experience, and is representative of man, in virtue of being the largest power to receive and to impart.

For the Universe has three children, born at one time, which reappear under different names in every system of thought, whether they be called cause, operation, and effect; or, more poetically, Jove, Pluto, Neptune; or, theologically, the Father, the Spirit, and the Son; but which we will call here the Knower, the Doer, and the Sayer. These stand respectively for the love of truth, for the love of good, and for the love of beauty. These three are equal. Each is that which he is, essentially, so that he cannot be surmounted or analyzed, and each of these three has the power of the others latent in him, and his own, patent.

The poet is the sayer, the namer, and represents beauty. He is a sovereign, and stands on the centre. For the world is not painted or adorned, but is from the beginning beautiful; and God has not made some beautiful things, but Beauty is the creator of the universe. Therefore the poet is not any permissive potentate, but is emperor in his own right. Criticism is infested with a cant of materialism, which assumes that manual skill and activity is the first merit of all men, and disparages such as say and do not, overlooking the fact that some men, namely poets, are natural sayers, sent into the world to the end of expression, and confounds them with those whose province is action but who quit it to imitate the sayers. But Homer's words are as costly and admirable to Homer as Agamemnon's victories are to Agamemnon. The poet does not wait for the hero or the sage, but, as they act and think primarily, so he writes primarily what will and must be spoken, reckoning the others, though primaries also, yet, in respect to him, secondaries and servants; as sitters or models in the studio of a painter, or as assistants who bring building-materials to an architect.

For poetry was all written before time was, and whenever we are so finely organized that we can penetrate into that region where the air is music, we hear those primal warblings and attempt to

write them down, but we lose ever and anon a word
or a verse and substitute something of our own,
and thus miswrite the poem. The men of more
delicate ear write down these cadences more faithfully, and these transcripts, though imperfect, become the songs of the nations. For nature is as
truly beautiful as it is good, or as it is reasonable,
and must as much appear as it must be done, or be
known. Words and deeds are quite indifferent
modes of the divine energy. Words are also actions, and actions are a kind of words.

The sign and credentials of the poet are that he
announces that which no man foretold. He is the
true and only doctor; he knows and tells; he is
the only teller of news, for he was present and privy
to the appearance which he describes. He is a beholder of ideas and an utterer of the necessary and
causal. For we do not speak now of men of poetical
talents, or of industry and skill in metre, but of the
true poet. I took part in a conversation the other
day concerning a recent writer of lyrics, a man of
subtle mind, whose head appeared to be a music-
box of delicate tunes and rhythms, and whose skill
and command of language we could not sufficiently
praise. But when the question arose whether he
was not only a lyrist but a poet, we were obliged to
confess that he is plainly a contemporary, not an
eternal man. He does not stand out of our low

limitations, like a Chimborazo under the line, running up from a torrid base through all the climates
of the globe, with belts of the herbage of every latitude on its high and mottled sides; but this genius is the landscape - garden of a modern house,
adorned with fountains and statues, with well-bred
men and women standing and sitting in the walks
and terraces. We hear, through all the varied
music, the ground-tone of conventional life. Our
poets are men of talents who sing, and not the children of music. The argument is secondary, the
finish of the verses is primary.

For it is not metres, but a metre-making argument that makes a poem, — a thought so passionate
and alive that like the spirit of a plant or an animal it has an architecture of its own, and adorns
nature with a new thing. The thought and the
form are equal in the order of time, but in the order of genesis the thought is prior to the form. The
poet has a new thought; he has a whole new experience to unfold; he will tell us how it was with
him, and all men will be the richer in his fortune.
For the experience of each new age requires a new
confession, and the world seems always waiting for
its poet. I remember when I was young how much
I was moved one morning by tidings that genius
had appeared in a youth who sat near me at table.
He had left his work and gone rambling none knew

whither, and had written hundreds of lines, but
could not tell whether that which was in him was
therein told; he could tell nothing but that all
was changed, — man, beast, heaven, earth and sea.
How gladly we listened! how credulous! Society
seemed to be compromised. We sat in the aurora
of a sunrise which was to put out all the stars.
Boston seemed to be at twice the distance it had
the night before, or was much farther than that.
Rome, — what was Rome? Plutarch and Shakspeare were in the yellow leaf, and Homer no more
should be heard of. It is much to know that poetry has been written this very day, under this very
roof, by your side. What! that wonderful spirit
has not expired! These stony moments are still
sparkling and animated! I had fancied that the
oracles were all silent, and nature had spent her
fires; and behold! all night, from every pore, these
fine auroras have been streaming. Every one has
some interest in the advent of the poet, and no one
knows how much it may concern him. We know
that the secret of the world is profound, but who or
what shall be our interpreter, we know not. A
mountain ramble, a new style of face, a new person,
may put the key into our hands. Of course the
value of genius to us is in the veracity of its report.
Talent may frolic and juggle; genius realizes and
adds. Mankind in good earnest have availed so far

.n understanding themselves and their work, that the foremost watchman on the peak announces his news. It is the truest word ever spoken, and the phrase will be the fittest, most musical, and the unerring voice of the world for that time.

All that we call sacred history attests that the birth of a poet is the principal event in chronology. Man, never so often deceived, still watches for the arrival of a brother who can hold him steady to a truth until he has made it his own. With what joy I begin to read a poem which I confide in as an inspiration! And now my chains are to be broken; I shall mount above these clouds and opaque airs in which I live, — opaque, though they seem transparent, — and from the heaven of truth I shall see and comprehend my relations. That will reconcile me to life and renovate nature, to see trifles animated by a tendency, and to know what I am doing. Life will no more be a noise; now I shall see men and women, and know the signs by which they may be discerned from fools and satans. This day shall be better than my birthday: then I became an animal; now I am invited into the science of the real. Such is the hope, but the fruition is postponed. Oftener it falls that this winged man, who will carry me into the heaven, whirls me into mists, then leaps and frisks about with me as it were from cloud to cloud, still affirming that he is bound heavenward:

and I, being myself a novice, am slow in perceiving
that he does not know the way into the heavens, and
is merely bent that I should admire his skill to rise
like a fowl or a flying fish, a little way from the
ground or the water; but the all-piercing, all-feed-
ing, and ocular air of heaven that man shall never
inhabit. I tumble down again soon into my old
nooks, and lead the life of exaggerations as before,
and have lost my faith in the possibility of any
guide who can lead me thither where I would be.

But, leaving these victims of vanity, let us, with
new hope, observe how nature, by worthier impulses, has insured the poet's fidelity to his office
of announcement and affirming, namely by the
beauty of things, which becomes a new and higher
beauty when expressed. Nature offers all her creatures to him as a picture-language. Being used as
a type, a second wonderful value appears in the object, far better than its old value; as the carpenter's stretched cord, if you hold your ear close
enough, is musical in the breeze. " Things more
excellent than every image," says Jamblichus, " are
expressed through images." Things admit of being used as symbols because nature is a symbol, in
the whole, and in every part. Every line we can
draw in the sand has expression; and there is no
body without its spirit or genius. All form is an
effect of character; all condition, of the quality of

the life; all harmony, of health; and for this reason a perception of beauty should be sympathetic,
or proper only to the good. The beautiful rests on
the foundations of the necessary. The soul makes
the body, as the wise Spenser teaches : —

> "So every spirit, as it is more pure,
> And hath in it the more of heavenly light,
> So it the fairer body doth procure
> To habit in, and it more fairly dight,
> With cheerful grace and amiable sight.
> For, of the soul, the body form doth take,
> For soul is form, and doth the body make."

Here we find ourselves suddenly not in a critical
speculation but in a holy place, and should go very
warily and reverently. We stand before the secret
of the world, there where Being passes into Appearance and Unity into Variety.

The Universe is the externization of the soul.
Wherever the life is, that bursts into appearance
around it. Our science is sensual, and therefore
superficial. The earth and the heavenly bodies,
physics, and chemistry, we sensually treat, as if
they were self-existent ; but these are the retinue of
that Being we have. "The mighty heaven," said
Proclus, "exhibits, in its transfigurations, clear
images of the splendor of intellectual perceptions;
being moved in conjunction with the unapparent
periods of intellectual natures." Therefore science

always goes abreast with the just elevation of the man, keeping step with religion and metaphysics; or the state of science is an index of our self-knowledge. Since every thing in nature answers to a moral power, if any phenomenon remains brute and dark it is because the corresponding faculty in the observer is not yet active.

No wonder then, if these waters be so deep, that we hover over them with a religious regard. The beauty of the fable proves the importance of the sense; to the poet, and to all others; or, if you please, every man is so far a poet as to be susceptible of these enchantments of nature; for all men have the thoughts whereof the universe is the celebration. I find that the fascination resides in the symbol. Who loves nature? Who does not? Is it only poets, and men of leisure and cultivation, who live with her? No; but also hunters, farmers, grooms, and butchers, though they express their affection in their choice of life and not in their choice of words. The writer wonders what the coachman or the hunter values in riding, in horses and dogs. It is not superficial qualities. When you talk with him he holds these at as slight a rate as you. His worship is sympathetic; he has no definitions, but he is commanded in nature by the living power which he feels to be there present. No imitation or playing of these things would content him; he loves the earnest of the north wind, of rain, of stone, and wood, and iron. A beauty not explicable is dearer than a beauty which we can see to the end of. It is nature the symbol, nature certifying the supernatural, body overflowed by life which he worships with coarse but sincere rites.

The inwardness and mystery of this attachment drive men of every class to the use of emblems. The schools of poets and philosophers are not more intoxicated with their symbols than the populace with theirs. In our political parties, compute the power of badges and emblems. See the great ball which they roll from Baltimore to Bunker Hill! In the political processions, Lowell goes in a loom, and Lynn in a shoe, and Salem in a ship. Witness the cider-barrel, the log-cabin, the hickory-stick, the palmetto, and all the cognizances of party. See the power of national emblems. Some stars, lilies, leopards, a crescent, a lion, an eagle, or other figure which came into credit God knows how, on an old rag of bunting, blowing in the wind on a fort at the ends of the earth, shall make the blood tingle under the rudest or the most conventional exterior. The people fancy they hate poetry, and they are all poets and mystics!

Beyond this universality of the symbolic language, we are apprised of the divineness of this superior use of things, whereby the world is a temple whose

walls are covered with emblems, pictures, and commandments of the Deity, — in this, that there is no
fact in nature which does not carry the whole sense
of nature; and the distinctions which we make in
events and in affairs, of low and high, honest and
base, disappear when nature is used as a symbol.
Thought makes everything fit for use. The vocabulary of an omniscient man would embrace words
and images excluded from polite conversation.
What would be base, or even obscene, to the obscene, becomes illustrious, spoken in a new connection of thought. The piety of the Hebrew prophets
purges their grossness. The circumcision is an example of the power of poetry to raise the low and
offensive. Small and mean things serve as well as
great symbols. The meaner the type by which a
law is expressed, the more pungent it is, and the
more lasting in the memories of men; just as we
choose the smallest box or case in which any needful utensil can be carried. Bare lists of words
are found suggestive to an imaginative and excited
mind; as it is related of Lord Chatham that he was
accustomed to read in Bailey's Dictionary when he
was preparing to speak in Parliament. The poor-
est experience is rich enough for all the purposes of
expressing thought. Why covet a knowledge of
new facts? Day and night, house and garden, a
few books, a few actions, serve us as well as would

all trades and all spectacles. We are far from
having exhausted the significance of the few symbols we use. We can come to use them yet with a
terrible simplicity. It does not need that a poem
should be long. Every word was once a poem.
Every new relation is a new word. Also we use
defects and deformities to a sacred purpose, so ex
pressing our sense that the evils of the world are
such only to the evil eye. In the old mythology,
mythologists observe, defects are ascribed to divine
natures, as lameness to Vulcan, blindness to Cupid,
and the like, — to signify exuberances.

For as it is dislocation and detachment from the
life of God that makes things ugly, the poet, who
re-attaches things to nature and the Whole, — re-
attaching even artificial things and violations of
nature, to nature, by a deeper insight, — disposes
very easily of the most disagreeable facts. Readers of poetry see the factory-village and the railway, and fancy that the poetry of the landscape is
broken up by these; for these works of art are not
yet consecrated in their reading; but the poet sees
them fall within the great Order not less than the
beehive or the spider's geometrical web. Nature
adopts them very fast into her vital circles, and the
gliding train of cars she loves like her own. Be
sides, in a centred mind, it signifies nothing how
many mechanical inventions you exhibit. Though

you add millions, and never so surprising, the fact
of mechanics has not gained a grain's weight. The
spiritual fact remains unalterable, by many or by
few particulars; as no mountain is of any appreciable height to break the curve of the sphere. A
shrewd country-boy goes to the city for the first
time, and the complacent citizen is not satisfied
with his little wonder. It is not that he does not
see all the fine houses and know that he never saw
such before, but he disposes of them as easily as
the poet finds place for the railway. The chief
value of the new fact is to enhance the great and
constant fact of Life, which can dwarf any and
every circumstance, and to which the belt of wam-
pum and the commerce of America are alike.

The world being thus put under the mind for
verb and noun, the poet is he who can articulate it.
For though life is great, and fascinates and absorbs;
and though all men are intelligent of the symbols
through which it is named; yet they cannot originally use them. We are symbols and inhabit symbols; workmen, work, and tools, words and things,
birth and death, all are emblems; but we sympathize with the symbols, and being infatuated with
the economical uses of things, we do not know that
they are thoughts. The poet, by an ulterior intellectual perception, gives them a power which makes
their old use forgotten, and puts eyes and a tongue

Into every dumb and inanimate object. He perceives the independence of the thought on the symbol, the stability of the thought, the accidency and
fugacity of the symbol. As the eyes of Lyncæus
were said to see through the earth, so the poet turns
the world to glass, and shows us all things in their
right series and procession. For through that better perception he stands one step nearer to things,
and sees the flowing or metamorphosis ; perceives
that thought is multiform ; that within the form of
every creature is a force impelling it to ascend into
a higher form ; and following with his eyes the life,
uses the forms which express that life, and so his
speech flows with the flowing of nature. All the
facts of the animal economy, sex, nutriment, ges-
tation, birth, growth, are symbols of the passage of
the world into the soul of man, to suffer there a
change and reappear a new and higher fact. He
uses forms according to the life, and not according
to the form. This is true science. The poet alone
knows astronomy, chemistry, vegetation and anima-
tion, for he does not stop at these facts, but employs
them as signs. He knows why the plain or meadow
of space was strown with these flowers we call suns
and moons and stars ; why the great deep is adorned
with animals, with men, and gods ; for in every
word he speaks he rides on them as the horses of
thought.

By virtue of this science the poet is the Namer
or Language-maker, naming things sometimes after
their appearance, sometimes after their essence, and
giving to every one its own name and not another's,
thereby rejoicing the intellect, which delights in
detachment or boundary. The poets made all the
words, and therefore language is the archives of
history, and, if we must say it, a sort of tomb of
the muses. For though the origin of most of our
words is forgotten, each word was at first a stroke
of genius, and obtained currency because for the
moment it symbolized the world to the first speaker
and to the hearer. The etymologist finds the dead-
est word to have been once a brilliant picture.
Language is fossil poetry. As the limestone of the
continent consists of infinite masses of the shells of
animalcules, so language is made up of images or
tropes, which now, in their secondary use, have long
ceased to remind us of their poetic origin. But the
poet names the thing because he sees it, or comes
one step nearer to it than any other. This expression or naming is not art, but a second nature,
grown out of the first, as a leaf out of a tree. What
we call nature is a certain self-regulated motion or
change; and nature does all things by her own
hands, and does not leave another to baptize her
but baptizes herself; and this through the metamorphosis again. I remember that a certain poet
described it to me thus : —

Genius is the activity which repairs the decay of things, whether wholly or partly of a material and finite kind. Nature, through all her kingdoms, insures herself. Nobody cares for planting the poor fungus; so she shakes down from the gills of one agaric countless spores, any one of which, being preserved, transmits new billions of spores to-morrow or next day. The new agaric of this hour has a chance which the old one had not. This atom of seed is thrown into a new place, not subject to the accidents which destroyed its parent two rods off. She makes a man; and having brought him to ripe age, she will no longer run the risk of losing this wonder at a blow, but she detaches from him a new self, that the kind may be safe from accidents to which the individual is exposed. So when the soul of the poet has come to ripeness of thought, she detaches and sends away from it its poems or songs, — a fearless, sleepless, deathless progeny, which is not exposed to the accidents of the weary kingdom of time; a fearless, vivacious offspring, clad with wings (such was the virtue of the soul out of which they came) which carry them fast and far, and infix them irrecoverably into the hearts of men. These wings are the beauty of the poet's soul. The songs, thus flying immortal from their mortal parent, are pursued by clamorous flights of censures, which swarm in far

greater numbers and threaten to devour them; bu.
these last are not winged. At the end of a very
short leap they fall plump down and rot, having re.
ceived from the souls out of which they came no
beautiful wings. But the melodies of the poet as
cend and leap and pierce into the deeps of infinite
time.

So far the bard taught me, using his freer
speech. But nature has a higher end, in the production of new individuals, than security, namely
ascension, or the passage of the soul into higher
forms. I knew in my younger days the sculptor
who made the statue of the youth which stands in
the public garden. He was, as I remember, unable
to tell directly what made him happy or unhappy,
but by wonderful indirections he could tell. He
rose one day, according to his habit, before the
dawn, and saw the morning break, grand as the
eternity out of which it came, and for many days
after, he strove to express this tranquillity, and lo!
his chisel had fashioned out of marble the form of
a beautiful youth, Phosphorus, whose aspect is such
that it is said all persons who look on it become
silent. The poet also resigns himself to his mood,
and that thought which agitated him is expressed,
but *alter idem*, in a manner totally new. The expression is organic, or the new type which things

themselves take when liberated. As, in the sun, ob
jects paint their images on the retina of the eye, so
they, sharing the aspiration of the whole universe,
tend to paint a far more delicate copy of their essence in his mind. Like the metamorphosis of
things into higher organic forms is their change
into melodies. Over everything stands its dæmon
or soul, and, as the form of the thing is reflected
by the eye, so the soul of the thing is reflected by a
melody. The sea, the mountain-ridge, Niagara, and
every flower-bed, pre-exist, or super-exist, in pre-can-
tations, which sail like odors in the air, and when
any man goes by with an ear sufficiently fine, he
overhears them and endeavors to write down the
notes without diluting or depraving them. And
herein is the legitimation of criticism, in the mind's
faith that the poems are a corrupt version of some
text in nature with which they ought to be made to
tally. A rhyme in one of our sonnets should not
be less pleasing than the iterated nodes of a sea-
shell, or the resembling difference of a group of
flowers. The pairing of the birds is an idyl, not
tedious as our idyls are ; a tempest is a rough ode,
without falsehood or rant ; a summer, with its
harvest sown, reaped, and stored, is an epic song,
subordinating how many admirably executed parts.
Why should not the symmetry and truth that mod-
ulate these, glide into our spirits, and we partici-
pate the invention of nature ?

This insight, which expresses itself by what is called Imagination, is a very high sort of seeing, which does not come by study, but by the intellect being where and what it sees; by sharing the path or circuit of things through forms, and so making them translucid to others. The path of things is silent. Will they suffer a speaker to go with them? A spy they will not suffer; a lover, a poet, is the transcendency of their own nature, — him they will suffer. The condition of true naming, on the poet's part, is his resigning himself to the divine *aura* which breathes through forms, and accompanying that.

It is a secret which every intellectual man quickly learns, that beyond the energy of his possessed and conscious intellect he is capable of a new energy (as of an intellect doubled on itself), by abandonment to the nature of things; that beside his privacy of power as an individual man, there is a great public power on which he can draw, by unlocking, at all risks, his human doors, and suffering the ethereal tides to roll and circulate through him; then he is caught up into the life of the Universe, his speech is thunder, his thought is law, and his words are universally intelligible as the plants and animals. The poet knows that he speaks adequately then only when he speaks somewhat wildly, or " with the flower of the mind; " not with the in tellect used as an organ, but with the intellect released from all service and suffered to take its direction from its celestial life; or as the ancients were wont to express themselves, not with intellect alone but with the intellect inebriated by nectar. As the traveller who has lost his way throws his reins on his horse's neck and trusts to the instinct of the animal to find his road, so must we do with the divine animal who carries us through this world. For if in any manner we can stimulate this instinct, new passages are opened for us into nature; the mind flows into and through things hardest and highest, and the metamorphosis is possible.

This is the reason why bards love wine, mead, narcotics, coffee, tea, opium, the fumes of sandalwood and tobacco, or whatever other procurers of animal exhilaration. All men avail themselves of such means as they can, to add this extraordinary power to their normal powers; and to this end they prize conversation, music, pictures, sculpture, dancing, theatres, travelling, war, mobs, fires, gaming, politics, or love, or science, or animal intoxication, — which are several coarser or finer *quasi*-mechanical substitutes for the true nectar, which is the ravishment of the intellect by coming nearer to the fact. These are auxiliaries to the centrifugal tendency of a man, to his passage out into free space, and they help him to escape the custody of that body

in which he is pent up, and of that jail-yard of individual relations in which he is enclosed. Hence
a great number of such as were professionally ex-
pressers of Beauty, as painters, poets, musicians,
and actors, have been more than others wont to lead
a life of pleasure and indulgence; all but the few
who received the true nectar; and, as it was a spurious mode of attaining freedom, as it was an emancipation not into the heavens but into the freedom
of baser places, they were punished for that advantage they won, by a dissipation and deterioration.
But never can any advantage be taken of nature by
a trick. The spirit of the world, the great calm
presence of the Creator, comes not forth to the sor-
ceries of opium or of wine. The sublime vision
comes to the pure and simple soul in a clean and
chaste body. That is not an inspiration, which we
owe to narcotics, but some counterfeit excitement
and fury. Milton says that the lyric poet may
drink wine and live generously, but the epic poet,
he who shall sing of the gods and their descent
unto men, must drink water out of a wooden bowl.
For poetry is not 'Devil's wine,' but God's wine.
It is with this as it is with toys. We fill the hands
and nurseries of our children with all manner of
dolls, drums, and horses; withdrawing their eyes
from the plain face and sufficing objects of nature,
the sun, and moon, the animals, the water, and

stones, which should be their toys. So the poet's habit of living should be set on a key so low that the common influences should delight him. His cheerfulness should be the gift of the sunlight; the air should suffice for his inspiration, and he should be tipsy with water. That spirit which suffices quiet hearts, which seems to come forth to such from every dry knoll of sere grass, from every pine-stump and half-imbedded stone on which the dull March sun shines, comes forth to the poor and hungry, and such as are of simple taste. If thou fill thy brain with Boston and New York, with fashion and covetousness, and wilt stimulate thy jaded senses with wine and French coffee, thou shalt find no radiance of wisdom in the lonely waste of the pinewoods.

If the imagination intoxicates the poet, it is not inactive in other men. The metamorphosis excites in the beholder an emotion of joy. The use of symbols has a certain power of emancipation and exhilaration for all men. We seem to be touched by a wand which makes us dance and run about happily, like children. We are like persons who come out of a cave or cellar into the open air. This is the effect on us of tropes, fables, oracles, and all poetic forms. Poets are thus liberating gods. Men have really got a new sense, and found within their world another world, or nest of worlds;

for, the metamorphosis once seen, we divine that it
does not stop. I will not now consider how much
this makes the charm of algebra and the mathemat
ics, which also have their tropes, but it is felt in
every definition; as when Aristotle defines *space*
to be an immovable vessel in which things are contained; — or when Plato defines a *line* to be a flowing point; or *figure* to be a bound of solid ; and
many the like. What a joyful sense of freedom
we have when Vitruvius announces the old opinion
of artists that no architect can build any house
well who does not know something of anatomy.
When Socrates, in Charmides, tells us that the
soul is cured of its maladies by certain incantations,
and that these incantations are beautiful reasons,
from which temperance is generated in souls; when
Plato calls the world an animal, and Timæus affirms that the plants also are animals ; or affirms
a man to be a heavenly tree, growing with his root,
which is his head, upward ; and, as George Chap-
man, following him, writes, —

> " So in our tree of man, whose nervie root
> Springs in his top; " —

when Orpheus speaks of hoariness as "that white
flower which marks extreme old age ; " when Proclus calls the universe the statue of the intellect;
when Chaucer, in his praise of 'Gentilesse,' com-

pares good blood in mean condition to fire, which, though carried to the darkest house betwixt this and the mount of Caucasus, will yet hold its natural office and burn as bright as if twenty thousand men did it behold ; when John saw, in the Apoca lypse, the ruin of the world through evil, and the stars fall from heaven as the figtree casteth her untimely fruit; when Æsop reports the whole cat-alogue of common daily relations through the mas-querade of birds and beasts ; — we take the cheer-ful hint of the immortality of our essence and its versatile habit and escapes, as when the gypsies say of themselves "it is in vain to hang them, they cannot die."

The poets are thus liberating gods. The ancient British bards had for the title of their order, " Those who are free throughout the world." They are free, and they make free. An imaginative book renders us much more service at first, by stim-ulating us through its tropes, than afterward when we arrive at the precise sense of the author. I think nothing is of any value in books excepting the transcendental and extraordinary. If a man is inflamed and carried away by his thought, to that degree that he forgets the authors and the public and heeds only this one dream which holds him like an insanity, let me read his paper, and you may have all the arguments and histories and criticism. All the value which attaches to Pythagoras, Paracelsus, Cornelius Agrippa, Cardan, Kepler, Swedenborg, Schelling, Oken, or any other who introduces questionable facts into his cosmogony, as angels, devils, magic, astrology, palmistry, mesmerism, and so on, is the certificate we have of departure from routine, and that here is a new witness. That also is the best success in conversation, the magic of liberty, which puts the world like a ball in our hands. How cheap even the liberty then seems; how mean to study, when an emotion communicates to the intellect the power to sap and upheave nature ; how great the perspective ! nations, times, systems, enter and disappear like threads in tapestry of large figure and many colors; dream delivers us to dream, and while the drunkenness lasts we will sell our bed, our philosophy, our religion, in our opulence.

There is good reason why we should prize this liberation. The fate of the poor shepherd, who, blinded and lost in the snow-storm, perishes in a drift within a few feet of his cottage door, is an emblem of the state of man. On the brink of the waters of life and truth, we are miserably dying. The inaccessibleness of every thought but that we are in, is wonderful. What if you come near to it; you are as remote when you are nearest as when you are farthest. Every thought is also a prison ;

every heaven is also a prison. Therefore we love
the poet, the inventor, who in any form, whether in
an ode or in an action or in looks and behavior
has yielded us a new thought. He unlocks our
chains and admits us to a new scene.

This emancipation is dear to all men, and the
power to impart it, as it must come from greater
depth and scope of thought, is a measure of intellect. Therefore all books of the imagination endure, all which ascend to that truth that the writer
sees nature beneath him, and uses it as his exponent. Every verse or sentence possessing this virtue will take care of its own immortality. The religions of the world are the ejaculations of a few
imaginative men.

But the quality of the imagination is to flow, and
not to freeze. The poet did not stop at the color
or the form, but read their meaning; neither may
he rest in this meaning, but he makes the same objects exponents of his new thought. Here is the
difference betwixt the poet and the mystic, that the
last nails a symbol to one sense, which was a true
sense for a moment, but soon becomes old and
false. For all symbols are fluxional; all language
is vehicular and transitive, and is good, as ferries
and horses are, for conveyance, not as farms and
houses are, for homestead. Mysticism consists in
the mistake of an accidental and individual symbol

for an universal one. The morning-redness happens to be the favorite meteor to the eyes of Jacob
Behmen, and comes to stand to him for truth and
faith; and, he believes, should stand for the same
realities to every reader. But the first reader pre-
fers as naturally the symbol of a mother and child,
or a gardener and his bulb, or a jeweller polishing
a gem. Either of these, or of a myriad more, are
equally good to the person to whom they are significant. Only they must be held lightly, and be
very willingly translated into the equivalent terms
which others use. And the mystic must be steadily
told, — All that you say is just as true without the
tedious use of that symbol as with it. Let us have
a little algebra, instead of this trite rhetoric, —
universal signs, instead of these village symbols, —
and we shall both be gainers. The history of
hierarchies seems to show that all religious error
consisted in making the symbol too stark and solid,
and was at last nothing but an excess of the organ
of language.

Swedenborg, of all men in the recent ages, stands
eminently for the translator of nature into thought.
I do not know the man in history to whom things
stood so uniformly for words. Before him the
metamorphosis continually plays. Everything on
which his eye rests, obeys the impulses of moral
nature. The figs become grapes whilst he eats

them. When some of his angels affirmed a truth, the laurel twig which they held blossomed in their hands. The noise which at a distance appeared like gnashing and thumping, on coming nearer was found to be the voice of disputants. The men in one of his visions, seen in heavenly light, appeared like dragons, and seemed in darkness; but to each other they appeared as men, and when the light from heaven shone into their cabin, they complained of the darkness, and were compelled to shut the window that they might see.

There was this perception in him which makes the poet or seer an object of awe and terror, namely that the same man or society of men may wear one aspect to themselves and their companions, and a different aspect to higher intelligences. Certain priests, whom he describes as conversing very learnedly together, appeared to the children who were at some distance, like dead horses; and many the like misappearances. And instantly the mind inquires whether these fishes under the bridge, yonder oxen in the pasture, those dogs in the yard, are immutably fishes, oxen, and dogs, or only so appear to me, and perchance to themselves appear upright men; and whether I appear as a man to all eyes. The Bramins and Pythagoras propounded the same question, and if any poet has witnessed the transformation he doubtless found it in harmony with various experiences. We have all seen changes as considerable in wheat and caterpillars. He is the poet and shall draw us with love and terror, who sees through the flowing vest the firm nature, and can declare it.

I look in vain for the poet whom I describe We do not with sufficient plainness or sufficient profoundness address ourselves to life, nor dare we chaunt our own times and social circumstance. If we filled the day with bravery, we should not shrink from celebrating it. Time and nature yield us many gifts, but not yet the timely man, the new religion, the reconciler, whom all things await. Dante's praise is that he dared to write his autobiography in colossal cipher, or into universality. We have yet had no genius in America, with tyrannous eye, which knew the value of our incomparable materials, and saw, in the barbarism and materialism of the times, another carnival of the same gods whose picture he so much admires in Homer ; then in the Middle Age ; then in Calvinism. Banks and tariffs, the newspaper and caucus, Methodism and Unitarianism, are flat and dull to dull people, but rest on the same foundations of wonder as the town of Troy and the temple of Delphi, and are as swiftly passing away. Our logrolling, our stumps and their politics, our fisheries, our Negroes and Indians, our boats and our repu diations, the wrath of rogues and the pusillanimity of honest men, the northern trade, the southern planting, the western clearing, Oregon and Texas, are yet unsung. Yet America is a poem in our eyes ; its ample geography dazzles the imagination, and it will not wait long for metres. If I have not found that excellent combination of gifts in my countrymen which I seek, neither could I aid myself to fix the idea of the poet by reading now and then in Chalmers's collection of five centuries of English poets. These are wits more than poets, though there have been poets among them. But when we adhere to the ideal of the poet, we have our difficulties even with Milton and Homer. Milton is too literary, and Homer too literal and historical.

But I am not wise enough for a national criticism, and must use the old largeness a little longer, to discharge my errand from the muse to the poet concerning his art.

Art is the path of the creator to his work. The paths or methods are ideal and eternal, though few men ever see them ; not the artist himself for years, or for a lifetime, unless he come into the conditions. The painter, the sculptor, the composer, the epic rhapsodist, the orator, all partake one desire, namely to express themselves symmetrically and abundantly, not dwarfishly and fragmentarily. They found or put themselves in certain conditions, as, the painter and sculptor before some impressive human figures; the orator, into the assembly of the people; and the others in such scenes as each has found exciting to his intellect; and each presently feels the new desire. He hears a voice, he sees a beckoning. Then he is apprised, with wonder, what herds of dæmons hem him in. He can no more rest; he says, with the old painter, " By God it is in me and must go forth of me." He pursues a beauty, half seen, which flies before him. The poet pours out verses in every solitude. Most of the things he says are conventional, no doubt; but by and by he says something which is original and beautiful. That charms him. He would say nothing eise but such things. In our way of talking we say ' That is yours, this is mine;' but the poet knows well that it is not his; that it is as strange and beautiful to him as to you; he would fain hear the like eloquence at length. Once having tasted this immortal ichor, he cannot have enough of it, and as an admirable creative power exists in these intellections, it is of the last importance that these things get spoken. What a little of all we know is said! What drops of all the sea of our science are baled up! and by what accident it is that these are exposed, when so many secrets sleep in nature! Hence the necessity of speech and song; hence

these throbs and heart-beatings in the orator, at
the door of the assembly, to the end namely that
thought may be ejaculated as Logos, or Word.

Doubt not, O poet, but persist. Say ' It is in
ne, and shall out.' Stand there, balked and dumb,
stuttering and stammering, hissed and hooted, stand
ind strive, until at last rage draw out of thee that
lream-power which every night shows thee is thine
own ; a power transcending all limit and privacy,
and by virtue of which a man is the conductor of
the whole river of electricity. Nothing walks, or
creeps, or grows, or exists, which must not in turn
arise and walk before him as exponent of his meaning. Comes he to that power, his genius is no
longer exhaustible. All the creatures by pairs and
by tribes pour into his mind as into a Noah's ark,
to come forth again to people a new world. This
is like the stock of air for our respiration or for
the combustion of our fireplace ; not a measure of
gallons, but the entire atmosphere if wanted. And
therefore the rich poets, as Homer, Chaucer, Shakspeare, and Raphael, have obviously no limits to
their works except the limits of their lifetime, and
resemble a mirror carried through the street, ready
to render an image of every created thing.

O poet ! a new nobility is conferred in groves
and pastures, and not in castles or by the sword-
blade any longer. The conditions are hard, but

equal. Thou shalt leave the world, and know the
muse only. Thou shalt not know any longer the
times, customs, graces, politics, or opinions of men,
but shalt take all from the muse. For the time of
towns is tolled from the world by funereal chimes,
but in nature the universal hours are counted by
succeeding tribes of animals and plants, and by
growth of joy on joy. God wills also that thou ab-
dicate a manifold and duplex life, and that thou be
content that others speak for thee. Others shall
be thy gentlemen and shall represent all courtesy
and worldly life for thee ; others shall do the great
and resounding actions also. Thou shalt lie close
hid with nature, and canst not be afforded to the
Capitol or the Exchange. The world is full of re-
nunciations and apprenticeships, and this is thine ;
thou must pass for a fool and a churl for a long
season. This is the screen and sheath in which
Pan has protected his well-beloved flower, and thou
shalt be known only to thine own, and they shall
console thee with tenderest love. And thou shalt
not be able to rehearse the names of thy friends in
thy verse, for an old shame before the holy ideal.
And this is the reward; that the ideal shall be real
to thee, and the impressions of the actual world
shall fall like summer rain, copious, but not troublesome to thy invulnerable essence. Thou shalt have
the whole land for thy park and manor, the sea for

thy bath and navigation, without tax and without envy; the woods and the rivers thou shalt own, and thou shalt possess that wherein others are only tenants and boarders. Thou true land-lord! sea-lord! air-lord! Wherever snow falls or water flows or birds fly, wherever day and night meet in twilight, wherever the blue heaven is hung by clouds or sown with stars, wherever are forms with transparent boundaries, wherever are outlets into celestial space, wherever is danger, and awe, and love, — there is Beauty, plenteous as rain, shed for thee, and though thou shouldst walk the world over thou shalt not be able to find a condition inopportune or ignoble.

EXPERIENCE.

The lords of life, the lords of life,—
I saw them pass,
In their own guise,
Like and unlike,
Portly and grim,
Use and Surprise,
Surface and Dream,
Succession swift, and spectral Wrong,
Temperament without a tongue,
And the inventor of the game
Omnipresent without name ; —
Some to see, some to be guessed,
They marched from east to west:
Little man, least of all,
Among the legs of his guardians tall,
Walked about with puzzled look : —
Him by the hand dear Nature took ;
Dearest Nature, strong and kind,
Whispered, ' Darling, never mind !
To-morrow they will wear another face,
The founder thou ! these are thy race !

II.

EXPERIENCE.

———•———

WHERE do we find ourselves? In a series of which we do not know the extremes, and believe that it has none. We wake and find ourselves on a stair; there are stairs below us, which we seem to have ascended; there are stairs above us, many a one, which go upward and out of sight. But the Genius which according to the old belief stands at the door by which we enter, and gives us the lethe to drink, that we may tell no tales, mixed the cup too strongly, and we cannot shake off the lethargy now at noonday. Sleep lingers all our lifetime about our eyes, as night hovers all day in the boughs of the fir-tree. All things swim and glitter. Our life is not so much threatened as our perception. Ghostlike we glide through nature, and should not know our place again. Did our birth fall in some fit of indigence and frugality in nature, that she was so sparing of her fire and so liberal of her earth that it appears to us that we lack the affirmative principle, and though we have health and reason,

yet we have no superfluity of spirit for new creation ?
We have enough to live and bring the year about,
but not an ounce to impart or to invest. Ah that
our Genius were a little more of a genius! We are
like millers on the lower levels of a stream, when
the factories above them have exhausted the water
We too fancy that the upper people must have raised
their dams.

If any of us knew what we were doing, or where
we are going, then when we think we best know!
We do not know to-day whether we are busy or idle.
In times when we thought ourselves indolent, we
have afterwards discovered that much was accomplished and much was begun in us. All our days are
so unprofitable while they pass, that 't is wonderful
where or when we ever got anything of this which
we call wisdom, poetry, virtue. We never got it
on any dated calendar day. Some heavenly days
must have been intercalated somewhere, like those
that Hermes won with dice of the Moon, that Osiris
might be born. It is said all martyrdoms looked
mean when they were suffered. Every ship is a
romantic object, except that we sail in. Embark,
and the romance quits our vessel and hangs on
every other sail in the horizon. Our life looks
trivial, and we shun to record it. Men seem to
have learned of the horizon the art of perpetual re-
treating and reference. ' Yonder uplands are rich

pasturage, and my neighbor has fertile meadow, but my field,' says the querulous farmer, ' only holds the world together.' I quote another man's saying; unluckily that other withdraws himself in the same way, and quotes me. 'T is the trick of nature thus to degrade to-day; a good deal of buzz, and somewhere a result slipped magically in. Every roof is agreeable to the eye until it is lifted; then we find tragedy and moaning women and hard-eyed husbands and deluges of lethe, and the men ask, 'What's the news?' as if the old were so bad. How many individuals can we count in society? how many actions? how many opinions? So much of our time is preparation, so much is routine, and so much retrospect, that the pith of each man's genius contracts itself to a very few hours. The history of literature — take the net result of Tiraboschi, Warton, or Schlegel — is a sum of very few ideas and of very few original tales; all the rest being variation of these. So in this great society wide lying around us, a critical analysis would find very few spontaneous actions. It is almost all custom and gross sense. There are even few opinions, and these seem organic in the speakers, and do not disturb the universal necessity.

What opium is instilled into all disaster! It shows formidable as we approach it, but there is at last no rough rasping friction, but the most slippery

sliding surfaces; we fall soft on a thought; *Atta
Dea* is gentle, —

"Over men's heads walking aloft,
    With tender feet treading so soft."

People grieve and bemoan themselves, but it is not
half so bad with them as they say.   There are moods
in which we court suffering, in the hope that here
at least we shall find reality, sharp peaks and edges
of truth.   But it turns out to be scene-painting and
counterfeit.   The only thing grief has taught me is
to know how shallow it is.   That, like all the rest,
plays about the surface, and never introduces me
into the reality, for contact with which we would
even pay the costly price of sons and lovers.   Was
it Boscovich who found out that bodies never come
in contact?   Well, souls never touch their objects.
An innavigable sea washes with silent waves between us and the things we aim at and converse
with.   Grief too will make us idealists.   In the
death of my son, now more than two years ago, I
seem to have lost a beautiful estate, — no more.   I
cannot get it nearer to me.   If to-morrow I should
be informed of the bankruptcy of my principal
debtors, the loss of my property would be a great
inconvenience to me, perhaps, for many years ; but
it would leave me as it found me, — neither better
nor worse.   So is it with this calamity; it does not

touch me ; something which I fancied was a part of
me, which could not be torn away without tear-
ing me nor enlarged without enriching me, falls off
from me and leaves no scar. It was caducous. I
grieve that grief can teach me nothing, nor carry
me one step into real nature. The Indian who was
laid under a curse that the wind should not blow
on him, nor water flow to him, nor fire burn him, is
a type of us all. The dearest events are summer-
rain, and we the Para coats that shed every drop.
Nothing is left us now but death. We look to that
with a grim satisfaction, saying There at least is
reality that will not dodge us.

I take this evanescence and lubricity of all objects, which lets them slip through our fingers then
when we clutch hardest, to be the most unhand-
some part of our condition. Nature does not like
to be observed, and likes that we should be her
fools and playmates. We may have the sphere for
our cricket-ball, but not a berry for our philosophy.
Direct strokes she never gave us power to make ;
all our blows glance, all our hits are accidents.
Our relations to each other are oblique and casual.

Dream delivers us to dream, and there is no end
to illusion. Life is a train of moods like a string
of beads, and as we pass through them they prove

to be many-colored lenses which paint the world their own hue, and each shows only what lies in its focus. From the mountain you see the mountain. We animate what we can, and we see only what we animate. Nature and books belong to the eyes that see them. It depends on the mood of the man whether he shall see the sunset or the fine poem. There are always sunsets, and there is always genius; but only a few hours so serene that we can relish nature or criticism. The more or less depends on structure or temperament. Temperament is the iron wire on which the beads are strung. Of what use is fortune or talent to a cold and defective nature? Who cares what sensibility or discrimination a man has at some time shown, if he falls asleep in his chair? or if he laugh and giggle? or if he apologize? or is infected with egotism? or thinks of his dollar? or cannot go by food? or has gotten a child in his boyhood? Of what use is genius, if the organ is too convex or too concave and cannot find a focal distance within the actual horizon of human life? Of what use, if the brain is too cold or too hot, and the man does not care enough for results to stimulate him to experiment, and hold him up in it? or if the web is too finely woven, too irritable by pleasure and pain, so that life stagnates from too much reception without due outlet? Of what use to make heroic vows of

amendment, if the same old law-breaker is to keep
them? What cheer can the religious sentiment
yield, when that is suspected to be secretly dependent on the seasons of the year and the state of the
blood? I knew a witty physician who found the
creed in the biliary duct, and used to affirm that if
there was disease in the liver, the man became a
Calvinist, and if that organ was sound, he became
a Unitarian. Very mortifying is the reluctant experience that some unfriendly excess or imbecility
neutralizes the promise of genius. We see young
men who owe us a new world, so readily and lav-
ishly they promise, but they never acquit the debt;
they die young and dodge the account; or if they
live they lose themselves in the crowd.

Temperament also enters fully into the system
of illusions and shuts us in a prison of glass which
we cannot see. There is an optical illusion about
every person we meet. In truth they are all creatures of given temperament, which will appear in a
given character, whose boundaries they will never
pass; but we look at them, they seem alive, and we
presume there is impulse in them. In the moment
it seems impulse; in the year, in the lifetime, it
turns out to be a certain uniform tune which the
revolving barrel of the music-box must play. Men
resist the conclusion in the morning, but adopt it
as the evening wears on, that temper prevails over

everything of time, place, and condition, and is in consumable in the flames of religion. Some modifications the moral sentiment avails to impose, but the individual texture holds its dominion, if not to bias the moral judgments, yet to fix the measure of activity and of enjoyment.

I thus express the law as it is read from the platform of ordinary life, but must not leave it without noticing the capital exception. For temperament is a power which no man willingly hears any one praise but himself. On the platform of physics we cannot resist the contracting influences of so-called science. Temperament puts all divinity to rout. I know the mental proclivity of physicians. I hear the chuckle of the phrenologists. Theoretic kidnappers and slave-drivers, they esteem each man the victim of another, who winds him round his finger by knowing the law of his being; and, by such cheap signboards as the color of his beard or the slope of his occiput, reads the inventory of his fortunes and character. The grossest ignorance does not disgust like this impudent knowingness. The physicians say they are not materialists; but they are: — Spirit is matter reduced to an extreme thinness: O *so* thin! — But the definition of *spiritual* should be, *that which is its own evidence.* What notions do they attach to love! what to religion! One would not willingly pronounce these words in their hearing, and give them the occasion to profane them. I saw a gracious gentleman who adapts his conversation to the form of the head of the man he talks with! I had fancied that the value of life lay in its inscrutable possibilities; in the fact that I never know, in addressing myself to a new individual, what may befall me. I carry the keys of my castle in my hand, ready to throw them at the feet of my lord, whenever and in what disguise soever he shall appear. I know he is in the neighborhood, hidden among vagabonds. Shall I preclude my future by taking a high seat and kindly adapting my conversation to the shape of heads? When I come to that, the doctors shall buy me for a cent. —— ' But, sir, medical history; the report to the Institute; the proven facts!' — I distrust the facts and the inferences. Temperament is the veto or limitation-power in the constitution, very justly applied to restrain an opposite excess in the constitution, but absurdly offered as a bar to original equity. When virtue is in presence, all subordinate powers sleep. On its own level, or in view of nature, temperament is final. I see not, if one be once caught in this trap of so-called sciences, any escape for the man from the links of the chain of physical necessity. Given such an embryo, such a history must follow. On this platform one lives in a sty of sensualism, and would soon come to suicide. But it is impossible, that the creative power should exclude itself. Into every intelligence there is a door which is never closed, through which the creator passes. The intellect, seeker of absolute truth, or the heart, lover of absolute good, intervenes for our succor, and at one whisper of these high powers we awake from ineffectual struggles with this nightmare. We hurl it into its own hell, and cannot again contract ourselves to so base a state.

The secret of the illusoriness is in the necessity of a succession of moods or objects. Gladly we would anchor, but the anchorage is quicksand. This onward trick of nature is too strong for us: *Pero si muove.* When at night I look at the moon and stars, I seem stationary, and they to hurry. Our love of the real draws us to permanence, but health of body consists in circulation, and sanity of mind in variety or facility of association. We need change of objects. Dedication to one thought is quickly odious. We house with the insane, and must humor them; then conversation dies out. Once I took such delight in Montaigne that I thought I should not need any other book; before that, in Shakspeare; then in Plutarch; then in Plotinus; at one time in Bacon; afterwards in Goethe; even in Bettine; but now I turn the

pages of either of them languidly, whilst I still
cherish their genius. So with pictures ; each will
bear an emphasis of attention once, which it cannot
retain, though we fain would continue to be pleased
in that manner. How strongly I have felt of pictures that when you have seen one well, you must
take your leave of it ; you shall never see it again.
I have had good lessons from pictures which I have
since seen without emotion or remark. A deduction must be made from the opinion which even the
wise express on a new book or occurrence. Their
opinion gives me tidings of their mood, and some
vague guess at the new fact, but is nowise to be
trusted as the lasting relation between that intellect
and that thing. The child asks, 'Mamma, why
don't I like the story as well as when you told it
me yesterday ?' Alas ! child it is even so with the
oldest cherubim of knowledge. But will it answer
thy question to say, Because thou wert born to a
whole and this story is a particular ? The reason
of the pain this discovery causes us (and we make
it late in respect to works of art and intellect), is
the plaint of tragedy which murmurs from it in regard to persons, to friendship and love.

That immobility and absence of elasticity which
we find in the arts, we find with more pain in the
artist. There is no power of expansion in men.
Our friends early appear to us as representatives of

certain ideas which they never pass or exceed. They stand on the brink of the ocean of thought and power, but they never take the single step that would bring them there. A man is like a bit of Labrador spar, which has no lustre as you turn it in your hand until you come to a particular angle; then it shows deep and beautiful colors. There is no adaptation or universal applicability in men, but each has his special talent, and the mastery of successful men consists in adroitly keeping themselves where and when that turn shall be oftenest to be practised. We do what we must, and call it by the best names we can, and would fain have the praise of having intended the result which ensues. I cannot recall any form of man who is not superfluous sometimes. But is not this pitiful? Life is not worth the taking, to do tricks in.

Of course it needs the whole society to give the symmetry we seek. The party-colored wheel must revolve very fast to appear white. Something is earned too by conversing with so much folly and defect. In fine, whoever loses, we are always of the gaining party. Divinity is behind our failures and follies also. The plays of children are nonsense, but very educative nonsense. So it is with the largest and solemnest things, with commerce, government, church, marriage, and so with the history of every man's bread, and the ways by which he is to come by it. Like a bird which alights no where, but hops perpetually from bough to bough, is the Power which abides in no man and in no woman, but for a moment speaks from this one, and for another moment from that one.

But what help from these fineries or pedantries? What help from thought? Life is not dialectics. We, I think, in these times, have had lessons enough of the futility of criticism. Our young people have thought and written much on labor and reform, and for all that they have written, neither the world nor themselves have got on a step. Intellectual tasting of life will not supersede muscular activity. If a man should consider the nicety of the passage of a piece of bread down his throat, he would starve. At Education-Farm the noblest theory of life sat on the noblest figures of young men and maidens, quite powerless and melancholy. It would not rake or pitch a ton of hay; it would not rub down a horse; and the men and maidens it left pale and hungry. A political orator wittily compared our party prom- ises to western roads, which opened stately enough, with planted trees on either side to tempt the trav- eller, but soon became narrow and narrower and ended in a squirrel-track and ran up a tree. So does culture with us; it ends in headache. Un- speakably sad and barren does life look to those

who a few months ago were dazzled with the splendor of the promise of the times. "There is now
no longer any right course of action nor any self-
devotion left among the Iranis." Objections and
criticism we have had our fill of. There are objections to every course of life and action, and the
practical wisdom infers an indifferency, from the
omnipresence of objection. The whole frame of
things preaches indifferency. Do not craze yourself with thinking, but go about your business anywhere. Life is not intellectual or critical, but
sturdy. Its chief good is for well-mixed people
who can enjoy what they find, without question.
Nature hates peeping, and our mothers speak her
very sense when they say, "Children, eat your vict-
uals, and say no more of it." To fill the hour, —
that is happiness; to fill the hour and leave no crev-
ice for a repentance or an approval. We live amid
surfaces, and the true art of life is to skate well on
them. Under the oldest mouldiest conventions a
man of native force prospers just as well as in the
newest world, and that by skill of handling and
treatment. He can take hold anywhere. Life itself is a mixture of power and form, and will not
bear the least excess of either. To finish the moment, to find the journey's end in every step of the
road, to live the greatest number of good hours, is
wisdom. It is not the part of men, but of fanatics,

or of mathematicians if you will, to say that the
shortness of life considered, it is not worth caring
whether for so short a duration we were sprawling
in want or sitting high. Since our office is with
moments, let us husband them. Five minutes of to-
day are worth as much to me as five minutes in the
next millennium. Let us be poised, and wise, and
our own, to-day. Let us treat the men and women
well; treat them as if they were real; perhaps they
are. Men live in their fancy, like drunkards whose
hands are too soft and tremulous for successful labor. It is a tempest of fancies, and the only bal-
last I know is a respect to the present hour. With
out any shadow of doubt, amidst this vertigo of
shows and politics, I settle myself ever the firmer in
the creed that we should not postpone and refer and
wish, but do broad justice where we are, by whom
soever we deal with, accepting our actual compan
ions and circumstances, however humble or odious
as the mystic officials to whom the universe has
delegated its whole pleasure for us. If these are
mean and malignant, their contentment, which is
the last victory of justice, is a more satisfying echo
to the heart than the voice of poets and the casual
sympathy of admirable persons. I think that however a thoughtful man may suffer from the defects
and absurdities of his company, he cannot without
affectation deny to any set of men and women a

sensibility to extraordinary merit. The coarse and frivolous have an instinct of superiority, if they have not a sympathy, and honor it in their blind capricious way with sincere homage.

The fine young people despise life, but in me, and in such as with me are free from dyspepsia, and to whom a day is a sound and solid good, it is a great excess of politeness to look scornful and to cry for company. I am grown by sympathy a little eager and sentimental, but leave me alone and I should relish every hour and what it brought me, the potluck of the day, as heartily as the oldest gossip in the bar-room. I am thankful for small mercies. I compared notes with one of my friends who expects everything of the universe and is disappointed when anything is less than the best, and I found that I begin at the other extreme, expecting nothing, and am always full of thanks for moderate goods. I accept the clangor and jangle of contrary tendencies. I find my account in sots and bores also. They give a reality to the circumjacent picture which such a vanishing meteorous appearance can ill spare. In the morning I awake and find the old world, wife, babes, and mother, Concord and Boston, the dear old spiritual world and even the dear old devil not far off. If we will take the good we find, asking no questions, we shall have heaping measures. The great gifts are not got by analysis.

Everything good is on the highway. The middle region of our being is the temperate zone. We may climb into the thin and cold realm of pure geometry and lifeless science, or sink into that of sensation. Between these extremes is the equator of life, of thought, of spirit, of poetry, — a narrow belt. Moreover, in popular experience everything good is on the highway. A collector peeps into all the picture-shops of Europe for a landscape of Poussin, a crayon-sketch of Salvator; but the Transfiguration, the Last Judgment, the Communion of St. Jerome, and what are as transcendent as these, are on the walls of the Vatican, the Uffizii, or the Louvre, where every footman may see them; to say nothing of Nature's pictures in every street, of sunsets and sunrises every day, and the sculpture of the human body never absent. A collector recently bought at public auction, in London, for one hundred and fifty-seven guineas, an autograph of Shakspeare; but for nothing a school-boy can read Hamlet and can detect secrets of highest concernment yet unpublished therein. I think I will never read any but the commonest books, — the Bible, Homer, Dante, Shakspeare, and Milton. Then we are impatient of so public a life and planet, and run hither and thither for nooks and secrets. The imagination delights in the woodcraft of Indians, trappers, and bee-hunters. We fancy that we are strangers, and not so intimately domesticated in the planet as the wild man and the wild beast and bird. But the exclusion reaches them also; reaches the climbing, flying, gliding, feathered and four-footed man. Fox and woodchuck, hawk and snipe and bittern, when nearly seen, have no more root in the deep world than man, and are just such superficial tenants of the globe. Then the new molecular philosophy shows astronomical interspaces betwixt atom and atom, shows that the world is all outside; it has no inside.

The mid-world is best. Nature, as we know her, is no saint. The lights of the church, the ascetics, Gentoos, and corn-eaters, she does not distinguish by any favor. She comes eating and drinking and sinning. Her darlings, the great, the strong, the beautiful, are not children of our law; do not come out of the Sunday School, nor weigh their food, nor punctually keep the commandments. If we will be strong with her strength we must not harbor such disconsolate consciences, borrowed too from the consciences of other nations. We must set up the strong present tense against all the rumors of wrath, past or to come. So many things are unsettled which it is of the first importance to settle; — and, pending their settlement, we will do as we do. Whilst the debate goes forward on the equity of commerce, and will not be closed for a century or two, New and Old England may keep shop. Law of copyright and international copyright is to be discussed, and in the interim we will sell our books for the most we can. Expediency of literature, reason of literature, lawfulness of writing down a thought, is questioned; much is to say on both sides, and, while the fight waxes hot, thou, dearest scholar, stick to thy foolish task, add a line every hour, and between whiles add a line. Right to hold land, right of property, is disputed, and the conventions convene, and before the vote is taken, dig away in your garden, and spend your earnings as a waif or godsend to all serene and beautiful purposes. Life itself is a bubble and a skepticism, and a sleep within a sleep. Grant it, and as much more as they will, — but thou, God's darling! heed thy private dream; thou wilt not be missed in the scorning and skepticism; there are enough of them; stay there in thy closet and toil until the rest are agreed what to do about it. Thy sickness, they say, and thy puny habit require that thou do this or avoid that, but know that thy life is a flitting state, a tent for a night, and do thou, sick or well, finish that stint. Thou art sick, but shalt not be worse, and the universe, which holds thee dear, shall be the better.

Human life is made up of the two elements, power and form, and the proportion must be inva riably kept if we would have it sweet and sound. Each of these elements in excess makes a mischief as hurtful as its defect. Everything runs to excess ; every good quality is noxious if unmixed, and, to carry the danger to the edge of ruin, nature causes each man's peculiarity to superabound. Here, among the farms, we adduce the scholars as examples of this treachery. They are nature's victims of expression. You who see the artist, the orator, the poet, too near, and find their life no more excellent than that of mechanics or farmers, and themselves victims of partiality, very hollow and haggard, and pronounce them failures, not heroes, but quacks, — conclude very reasonably that these arts are not for man, but are disease. Yet nature will not bear you out. Irresistible nature made men such, and makes legions more of such, every day. You love the boy reading in a book, gazing at a drawing or a cast; yet what are these millions who read and behold, but incipient writers and sculptors ? Add a little more of that quality which now reads and sees, and they will seize the pen and chisel. And if one remembers how innocently he began to be an artist, he perceives that nature joined with his enemy. A man is a golden impossibility. The line he must walk is a hair's breadth. The wise through excess of wisdom is made a fool.

How easily, if fate would suffer it, we might keep forever these beautiful limits, and adjust ourselves, once for all, to the perfect calculation of the kingdom of known cause and effect. In the street and in the newspapers, life appears so plain a business that manly resolution and adherence to the multiplication-table through all weathers will insure success. But ah! presently comes a day, or is it only a half-hour, with its angel-whispering, — which discomfits the conclusions of nations and of years! To-morrow again every thing looks real and angular, the habitual standards are reinstated, common sense is as rare as genius, — is the basis of genius, and experience is hands and feet to every enterprise; — and yet, he who should do his business on this understanding would be quickly bankrupt. Power keeps quite another road than the turnpikes of choice and will; namely the subterranean and invisible tunnels and channels of life. It is ridiculous that we are diplomatists, and doctors, and considerate people; there are no dupes like these. Life is a series of surprises, and would not be worth taking or keeping if it were not. God delights to isolate us every day, and hide from us the past and the future. We would look about us, but with grand politeness he draws down before us an impenetrable screen of purest sky, and another behind us of purest sky. ' You will not remember,' he seems to say, 'and you will not expect.' All good conversation, manners, and action, come from a spontaneity which forgets usages and makes the moment great. Nature hates calculators ; her methods are saltatory and impulsive. Man lives by pulses ; our organic movements are such ; and the chemical and ethereal agents are undulatory and alternate ; and the mind goes antagonizing on, and never prospers but by fits. We thrive by casualties. Our chief experiences have been casual. The most attractive class of people are those who are powerful obliquely and not by the direct stroke; men of genius, but not yet accredited ; one gets the cheer of their light without paying too great a tax. Theirs is the beauty of the bird or the morning light, and not of art. In the thought of genius there is always a surprise ; and the moral sentiment is well called " the newness," for it is never other ; as new to the oldest intelligence as to the young child ; — " the kingdom that cometh without observation." In like manner, for practical success, there must not be too much design. A man will not be observed in doing that which he can do best. There is a certain magic about his properest action which stupefies your powers of observation, so that though it is done before you, you wist not of it. The art of life has a pudency, and will not be exposed. Every man is an impossibility until

he is born ; every thing impossible until we see a
success. The ardors of piety agree at last with the
coldest skepticism, — that nothing is of us or our
works, — that all is of God. Nature will not spare
us the smallest leaf of laurel. All writing comes
by the grace of God, and all doing and having. I
would gladly be moral and keep due metes and
bounds, which I dearly love, and allow the most to
the will of man; but I have set my heart on honesty
in this chapter, and I can see nothing at last, in
success or failure, than more or less of vital force
supplied from the Eternal. The results of life are
uncalculated and uncalculable. The years teach
much which the days never know. The persons
who compose our company, converse, and come and
go, and design and execute many things, and somewhat comes of it all, but an unlooked-for result.
The individual is always mistaken. He designed
many things, and drew in other persons as coadju-
tors, quarrelled with some or all, blundered much,
and something is done; all are a little advanced,
but the individual is always mistaken. It turns
out somewhat new and very unlike what he promised himself.

The ancients, struck with this irreducibleness of
the elements of human life to calculation, exalted
Chance into a divinity; but that is to stay too long

at the spark, which glitters truly at one point, but the universe is warm with the latency of the same fire. The miracle of life which will not be expounded but will remain a miracle, introduces a new element. In the growth of the embryo, Sir Everard Home I think noticed that the evolution was not from one central point, but coactive from three or more points. Life has no memory. That which proceeds in succession might be remembered, but that which is coexistent, or ejaculated from a deeper cause, as yet far from being conscious, knows not its own tendency. So is it with us, now skeptical or without unity, because immersed in forms and effects all seeming to be of equal yet hostile value, and now religious, whilst in the reception of spiritual law. Bear with these distractions, with this coetaneous growth of the parts; they will one day be *members*, and obey one will. On that one will, on that secret cause, they nail our attention and hope. Life is hereby melted into an expectation or a religion. Underneath the inharmonious and trivial particulars, is a musical perfection; the Ideal journeying always with us, the heaven without rent or seam. Do but observe the mode of our illumination. When I converse with a profound mind, or if at any time being alone I have good thoughts, I do not at once arrive at satisfactions, as when, being thirsty, I drink water; or

go to the fire, being cold; no! but I am at first apprised of my vicinity to a new and excellent region
of life. By persisting to read or to think, this region gives further sign of itself, as it were in
flashes of light, in sudden discoveries of its profound beauty and repose, as if the clouds that covered it parted at intervals and showed the approaching traveller the inland mountains, with the
tranquil eternal meadows spread at their base,
whereon flocks graze and shepherds pipe and dance.
But every insight from this realm of thought is
felt as initial, and promises a sequel. I do not
make it; I arrive there, and behold what was there
already. I make! O no! I clap my hands in
infantine joy and amazement before the first opening to me of this august magnificence, old with the
love and homage of innumerable ages, young with
the life of life, the sunbright Mecca of the desert.
And what a future it opens! I feel a new heart
beating with the love of the new beauty. I am
ready to die out of nature and be born again into
this new yet unapproachable America I have found
in the West : —

> "Since neither now nor yesterday began
> These thoughts, which have been ever, nor yet can
> A man be found who their first entrance knew."

If I have described life as a flux of moods, I must
now add that there is that in us which changes not

and which ranks all sensations and states of mind.
The consciousness in each man is a sliding scale,
which identifies him now with the First Cause, and
now with the flesh of his body; life above life, in
infinite degrees. The sentiment from which it
sprung determines the dignity of any deed, and the
question ever is, not what you have done or for-
borne, but at whose command you have done or for-
borne it.

Fortune, Minerva, Muse, Holy Ghost, — these
are quaint names, too narrow to cover this un-
bounded substance. The baffled intellect must still
kneel before this cause, which refuses to be named,
— ineffable cause, which every fine genius has es-
sayed to represent by some emphatic symbol, as,
Thales by water, Anaximenes by air, Anaxagoras
by (Νοῦς) thought, Zoroaster by fire, Jesus and the
moderns by love; and the metaphor of each has
become a national religion. The Chinese Mencius
has not been the least successful in his generalization. "I fully understand language," he said,
"and nourish well my vast-flowing vigor." — "I
beg to ask what you call vast-flowing vigor?" —
said his companion. "The explanation," replied
Mencius, "is difficult. This vigor is supremely
great, and in the highest degree unbending. Nourish it correctly and do it no injury, and it will fill
up the vacancy between heaven and earth. This

vigor accords with and assists justice and reason,
and leaves no hunger." — In our more correct writing we give to this generalization the name of Being, and thereby confess that we have arrived as far
as we can go. Suffice it for the joy of the universe
that we have not arrived at a wall, but at intermi-
nable oceans. Our life seems not present so much
as prospective; not for the affairs on which it is
wasted, but as a hint of this vast-flowing vigor.
Most of life seems to be mere advertisement of faculty; information is given us not to sell ourselves
cheap; that we are very great. So, in particulars,
our greatness is always in a tendency or direction,
not in an action. It is for us to believe in the rule,
not in the exception. The noble are thus known
from the ignoble. So in accepting the leading of
the sentiments, it is not what we believe concerning
the immortality of the soul or the like, but *the universal impulse to believe*, that is the material circumstance and is the principal fact in the history
of the globe. Shall we describe this cause as that
which works directly? The spirit is not helpless
or needful of mediate organs. It has plentiful
powers and direct effects. I am explained without
explaining, I am felt without acting, and where I
am not. Therefore all just persons are satisfied
with their own praise. They refuse to explain
themselves, and are content that new actions should

do them that office. They believe that we communicate without speech and above speech, and
that no right action of ours is quite unaffecting to
our friends, at whatever distance; for the influence
of action is not to be measured by miles. Why
should I fret myself because a circumstance has
occurred which hinders my presence where I was
expected? If I am not at the meeting, my presence where I am should be as useful to the commonwealth of friendship and wisdom, as would be
my presence in that place. I exert the same quality of power in all places. Thus journeys the
mighty Ideal before us; it never was known to fall
into the rear. No man ever came to an experience
which was satiating, but his good is tidings of a
better. Onward and onward! In liberated moments we know that a new picture of life and duty
is already possible; the elements already exist in
many minds around you of a doctrine of life which
shall transcend any written record we have. The
new statement will comprise the skepticisms as well
as the faiths of society, and out of unbeliefs a creed
shall be formed. For skepticisms are not gratui-
tous or lawless, but are limitations of the affirmative statement, and the new philosophy must take
them in and make affirmations outside of them,
just as much as it must include the oldest beliefs.

It is very unhappy, but too late to be helped, the

discovery we have made that we exist. That discovery is called the Fall of Man. Ever afterwards
we suspect our instruments. We have learned that
we do not see directly, but mediately, and that we
have no means of correcting these colored and dis-
torting lenses which we are, or of computing the
amount of their errors. Perhaps these subject-
lenses have a creative power; perhaps there are no
objects. Once we lived in what we saw; now, the
rapaciousness of this new power, which threatens
to absorb all things, engages us. Nature, art, persons, letters, religions, objects, successively tumble
in, and God is but one of its ideas. Nature and
literature are subjective phenomena; every evil and
every good thing is a shadow which we cast. The
street is full of humiliations to the proud. As the
fop contrived to dress his bailiffs in his livery and
make them wait on his guests at table, so the chagrins which the bad heart gives off as bubbles, at
once take form as ladies and gentlemen in the
street, shopmen or bar-keepers in hotels, and
threaten or insult whatever is threatenable and
insultable in us. 'T is the same with our idolatries.
People forget that it is the eye which makes the
horizon, and the rounding mind's eye which makes
this or that man a type or representative of humanity, with the name of hero or saint. Jesus, the
"providential man," is a good man on whom many

people are agreed that these optical laws shall take effect. By love on one part and by forbearance to press objection on the other part, it is for a time settled that we will look at him in the centre of the horizon, and ascribe to him the properties that will attach to any man so seen. But the longest love or aversion has a speedy term. The great and crescive self, rooted in absolute nature, supplants all relative existence and ruins the kingdom of mortal friendship and love. Marriage (in what is called the spiritual world) is impossible, because of the inequality between every subject and every object. The subject is the receiver of Godhead, and at every comparison must feel his being enhanced by that cryptic might. Though not in energy, yet by presence, this magazine of substance cannot be otherwise than felt; nor can any force of intellect attribute to the object the proper deity which sleeps or wakes forever in every subject. Never can love make consciousness and ascription equal in force. There will be the same gulf between every me and thee as between the original and the picture. The universe is the bride of the soul. All private sympathy is partial. Two human beings are like globes, which can touch only in a point, and whilst they remain in contact all other points of each of the spheres are inert; their turn must also come, and the longer a particular union lasts the more energy of appetency the parts not in union acquire.

Life will be imaged, but cannot be divided nor doubled. Any invasion of its unity would be chaos. The soul is not twin-born but the only begotten, and though revealing itself as child in time, child in appearance, is of a fatal and universal power, admitting no co-life. Every day, every act betrays the ill-concealed deity. We believe in ourselves as we do not believe in others. We permit all things to ourselves, and that which we call sin in others is experiment for us. It is an instance of our faith in ourselves that men never speak of crime as lightly as they think ; or every man thinks a latitude safe for himself which is nowise to be indulged to another. The act looks very differently on the inside and on the outside ; in its quality and in its consequences. Murder in the murderer is no such ruinous thought as poets and romancers will have it ; it does not unsettle him or fright him from his ordinary notice of trifles ; it is an act quite easy to be contemplated ; but in its sequel it turns out to be a horrible jangle and confounding of all relations. Especially the crimes that spring from love seem right and fair from the actor's point of view, but when acted are found destructive of society. No man at last believes that he can be lost, or that the crime in him is as

black as in the felon. Because the intellect qual-
ifies in our own case the moral judgments. For
there is no crime to the intellect. That is antino-
mian or hypernomian, and judges law as well as
fact. "It is worse than a crime, it is a blunder,"
said Napoleon, speaking the language of the intellect. To it, the world is a problem in mathematics
or the science of quantity, and it leaves out praise
and blame and all weak emotions. All stealing is
comparative. If you come to absolutes, pray who
does not steal? Saints are sad, because they behold
sin (even when they speculate), from the point of
view of the conscience, and not of the intellect; a
confusion of thought. Sin, seen from the thought,
is a diminution, or *less;* seen from the conscience
or will, it is pravity or *bad.* The intellect names
it shade, absence of light, and no essence. The
conscience must feel it as essence, essential evil.
This it is not; it has an objective existence, but no
subjective.

Thus inevitably does the universe wear our color,
and every object fall successively into the subject
itself. The subject exists, the subject enlarges; all
things sooner or later fall into place. As I am, so
I see; use what language we will, we can never say
anything but what we are; Hermes, Cadmus, Columbus, Newton, Bonaparte, are the mind's ministers. Instead of feeling a poverty when we encoun-

ter a great man, let us treat the new comer like a
travelling geologist who passes through our estate
and shows us good slate, or limestone, or anthracite,
in our brush pasture. The partial action of each
strong mind in one direction is a telescope for the
objects on which it is pointed. But every other
part of knowledge is to be pushed to the same ex-
travagance, ere the soul attains her due sphericity.
Do you see that kitten chasing so prettily her own
tail? If you could look with her eyes you might
see her surrounded with hundreds of figures performing complex dramas, with tragic and comic issues, long conversations, many characters, many ups
and downs of fate, — and meantime it is only puss
and her tail. How long before our masquerade will
end its noise of tambourines, laughter, and shout-
ing, and we shall find it was a solitary performance?
A subject and an object, — it takes so much to
make the galvanic circuit complete, but magnitude
adds nothing. What imports it whether it is Kepler and the sphere, Columbus and America, a reader
and his book, or puss with her tail?

It is true that all the muses and love and religion
hate these developments, and will find a way to
punish the chemist who publishes in the parlor the
secrets of the laboratory. And we cannot say too
little of our constitutional necessity of seeing things
under private aspects, or saturated with our humors.

And yet is the God the native of these bleak rocks. That need makes in morals the capital virtue of self-trust. We must hold hard to this poverty, however scandalous, and by more vigorous self-recoveries, after the sallies of action, possess our axis more firmly. The life of truth is cold and so far mournful; but it is not the slave of tears, contritions and perturbations. It does not attempt another's work, nor adopt another's facts. It is a main lesson of wisdom to know your own from another's. I have learned that I cannot dispose of other people's facts; but I possess such a key to my own as persuades me, against all their denials, that they also have a key to theirs. A sympathetic person is placed in the dilemma of a swimmer among drowning men, who all catch at him, and if he give so much as a leg or a finger they will drown him. They wish to be saved from the mischiefs of their vices, but not from their vices. Charity would be wasted on this poor waiting on the symptoms. A wise and hardy physician will say, *Come out of that*, as the first condition of advice.

In this our talking America we are ruined by our good nature and listening on all sides. This compliance takes away the power of being greatly useful. A man should not be able to look other than directly and forthright. A preoccupied attention is the only answer to the importunate frivolity of

other people; an attention, and to an aim which
makes their wants frivolous. This is a divine answer, and leaves no appeal and no hard thoughts.
In Flaxman's drawing of the Eumenides of Æschylus, Orestes supplicates Apollo, whilst the Furies
sleep on the threshold. The face of the god expresses a shade of regret and compassion, but is calm
with the conviction of the irreconcilableness of the
two spheres. He is born into other politics, into
the eternal and beautiful. The man at his feet asks
for his interest in turmoils of the earth, into which
his nature cannot enter. And the Eumenides there
lying express pictorially this disparity. The god is
surcharged with his divine destiny.

Illusion, Temperament, Succession, Surface, Surprise, Reality, Subjectiveness, — these are threads
on the loom of time, these are the lords of life. I
dare not assume to give their order, but I name
them as I find them in my way. I know better than
to claim any completeness for my picture. I am a
fragment, and this is a fragment of me. I can very
confidently announce one or another law, which
throws itself into relief and form, but I am too
young yet by some ages to compile a code. I gossip for my hour concerning the eternal politics.
I have seen many fair pictures not in vain. A won.
derful time I have lived in. I am not the novice I

was fourteen, nor yet seven years ago. Let who will ask Where is the fruit? I find a private fruit sufficient. This is a fruit, — that I should not ask for a rash effect from meditations, counsels and the hiving of truths. I should feel it pitiful to demand a result on this town and county, an overt effect on the instant month and year. The effect is deep and secular as the cause. It works on periods in which mortal lifetime is lost. All I know is reception; I am and I have: but I do not get, and when I have fancied I had gotten anything, I found I did not. I worship with wonder the great Fortune. My reception has been so large, that I am not annoyed by receiving this or that superabundantly. I say to the Genius, if he will pardon the proverb, *In for a mill, in for a million.* When I receive a new gift, I do not macerate my body to make the account square, for if I should die I could not make the account square. The benefit overran the merit the first day, and has overrun the merit ever since. The merit itself, so-called, I reckon part of the receiving.

Also that hankering after an overt or practical effect seems to me an apostasy. In good earnest I am willing to spare this most unnecessary deal of doing. Life wears to me a visionary face. Hardest roughest action is visionary also. It is but a choice between soft and turbulent dreams. People

disparage knowing and the intellectual life, and
urge doing. I am very content with knowing, if
only I could know. That is an august entertainment, and would suffice me a great while. To
know a little would be worth the expense of this
world. I hear always the law of Adrastia, " that
every soul which had acquired any truth, should be
safe from harm until another period."

I know that the world I converse with in the city
and in the farms, is not the world I *think*. I observe that difference, and shall observe it. One
day I shall know the value and law of this dis-
crepance. But I have not found that much was
gained by manipular attempts to realize the world
of thought. Many eager persons successively make
an experiment in this way, and make themselves
ridiculous. They acquire democratic manners, they
foam at the mouth, they hate and deny. Worse,
I observe that in the history of mankind there is
never a solitary example of success, — taking
their own tests of success. I say this polemically,
or in reply to the inquiry, Why not realize your
world ? But far be from me the despair which
prejudges the law by a paltry empiricism ;— since
there never was a right endeavor but it succeeded.
Patience and patience, we shall win at the last.
We must be very suspicious of the deceptions
of the element of time. It takes a good deal of

time to eat or to sleep, or to earn a hundred dollars, and a very little time to entertain a hope and an insight which becomes the light of our life. We dress our garden, eat our dinners, discuss the household with our wives, and these things make no impression, are forgotten next week; but, in the solitude to which every man is always returning, he has a sanity and revelations which in his passage into new worlds he will carry with him. Never mind the ridicule, never mind the defeat; up again, old heart! — it seems to say, — there is victory yet for all justice; and the true romance which the world exists to realize will be the transformation of genius into practical power.

CHARACTER.

—◆—

The sun set; but set not his hope:
Stars rose; his faith was earlier up:
Fixed on the enormous galaxy,
Deeper and older seemed his eye:
And matched his sufferance sublime
The taciturnity of time.
He spoke, and words more soft than rain
Brought the Age of Gold again:
His action won such reverence sweet,
As hid all measure of the feat.

Work of his hand
He nor commends nor grieves
Pleads for itself the fact ;
As unrepenting Nature leaves
Her every act.

III.

CHARACTER.

I HAVE read that those who listened to Lord Chatham felt that there was something finer in the man than any thing which he said. It has been complained of our brilliant English historian of the French Revolution that when he has told all his facts about Mirabeau, they do not justify his estimate of his genius. The Gracchi, Agis, Cleomenes, and others of Plutarch's heroes, do not in the record of facts equal their own fame. Sir Philip Sidney, the Earl of Essex, Sir Walter Raleigh, are men of great figure and of few deeds. We cannot find the smallest part of the personal weight of Washington in the narrative of his exploits. The authority of the name of Schiller is too great for his books. This inequality of the reputation to the works or the anecdotes is not accounted for by saying that the reverberation is longer than the thunder-clap, but somewhat resided in these men which begot an expectation that outran all their performance. The largest part of

their power was latent. This is that which we call
Character, — a reserved force, which acts directly
by presence and without means. It is conceived
of as a certain undemonstrable force, a Familiar or
Genius, by whose impulses the man is guided but
whose counsels he cannot impart; which is company for him, so that such men are often solitary,
or if they chance to be social, do not need society
but can entertain themselves very well alone. The
purest literary talent appears at one time great, at
another time small, but character is of a stellar and
undiminishable greatness. What others effect by
talent or by eloquence, this man accomplishes by
some magnetism. "Half his strength he put not
forth." His victories are by demonstration of superiority, and not by crossing of bayonets. He
conquers because his arrival alters the face of affairs. "O Iole! how did you know that Hercules
was a god?" "Because," answered Iole, "I was
content the moment my eyes fell on him. When
I beheld Theseus, I desired that I might see him
offer battle, or at least guide his horses in the char.
iot-race; but Hercules did not wait for a contest;
he conquered whether he stood, or walked, or sat, or
whatever thing he did." Man, ordinarily a pen-
dant to events, only half attached, and that awk-
wardly, to the world he lives in, in these examples
appears to share the life of things, and to be an ex-

pression of the same laws which control the tides
and the sun, numbers and quantities.

But to use a more modest illustration and nearer
home, I observe that in our political elections,
where this element, if it appears at all, can only
occur in its coarsest form, we sufficiently understand its incomparable rate. The people know
that they need in their representative much more
than talent, namely the power to make his talent
trusted. They cannot come at their ends by sending to Congress a learned, acute, and fluent speaker,
if he be not one who, before he was appointed by
the people to represent them, was appointed by
Almighty God to stand for a fact, — invincibly
persuaded of that fact in himself, — so that the
most confident and the most violent persons learn
that here is resistance on which both impudence
and terror are wasted, namely faith in a fact. The
men who carry their points do not need to inquire
of their constituents what they should say, but are
themselves the country which they represent ; nowhere are its emotions or opinions so instant and
true as in them; nowhere so pure from a selfish
infusion. The constituency at home hearkens to
their words, watches the color of their cheek, and
therein, as in a glass, dresses its own. Our public
assemblies are pretty good tests of manly force.
Our frank countrymen of the west and south have

a taste for character, and like to know whether the
New Englander is a substantial man, or whether
the hand can pass through him.

The same motive force appears in trade. There
are geniuses in trade, as well as in war, or the
State, or letters ; and the reason why this or that
man is fortunate is not to be told. It lies in the
man ; that is all anybody can tell you about it.
See him and you will know as easily why he suc-
ceeds, as, if you see Napoleon, you would comprehend his fortune. In the new objects we recognize
the old game, the habit of fronting the fact, and not
dealing with it at second hand, through the perceptions of somebody else. Nature seems to authorize
trade, as soon as you see the natural merchant, who
appears not so much a private agent as her factor
and Minister of Commerce. His natural probity
combines with his insight into the fabric of society
to put him above tricks, and he communicates to
all his own faith that contracts are of no private
interpretation. The habit of his mind is a reference to standards of natural equity and public advantage ; and he inspires respect and the wish to
deal with him, both for the quiet spirit of honor
which attends him, and for the intellectual pastime
which the spectacle of so much ability affords.
This immensely stretched trade, which makes the
capes of the Southern Ocean his wharves and the

Atlantic Sea his familiar port, centres in his brain
only ; and nobody in the universe can make his
place good. In his parlor I see very well that he
has been at hard work this morning, with that
knitted brow and that settled humor, which all his
desire to be courteous cannot shake off. I see
plainly how many firm acts have been done; how
many valiant *noes* have this day been spoken,
when others would have uttered ruinous *yeas*. I
see, with the pride of art and skill of masterly
arithmetic and power of remote combination, the
consciousness of being an agent and playfellow of
the original laws of the world. He too believes
that none can supply him, and that a man must be
born to trade or he cannot learn it.

This virtue draws the mind more when it appears in action to ends not so mixed. It works
with most energy in the smallest companies and in
private relations. In all cases it is an extraordinary and incomputable agent. The excess of physical strength is paralyzed by it. Higher natures
overpower lower ones by affecting them with a certain sleep. The faculties are locked up, and offer
no resistance. Perhaps that is the universal law.
When the high cannot bring up the low to itself,
it benumbs it, as man charms down the resistance
of the lower animals. Men exert on each other a
similar occult power. How often has the influence

of a true master realized all the tales of magic! A
river of command seemed to run down from his
eyes into all those who beheld him, a torrent of
strong sad light, like an Ohio or Danube, which
pervaded them with his thoughts and colored all
events with the hue of his mind. " What means
did you employ ? " was the question asked of the
wife of Concini, in regard to her treatment of Mary
of Medici; and the answer was, " Only that influence which every strong mind has over a weak
one." Cannot Cæsar in irons shuffle off the irons
and transfer them to the person of Hippo or Thra-
so the turnkey? Is an iron handcuff so immutable a bond? Suppose a slaver on the coast of
Guinea should take on board a gang of negroes
which should contain persons of the stamp of Tous-
saint L'Ouverture : or, let us fancy, under these
swarthy masks he has a gang of Washingtons in
chains. When they arrive at Cuba, will the relative order of the ship's company be the same? Is
there nothing but rope and iron? Is there no love,
no reverence? Is there never a glimpse of right
in a poor slave-captain's mind; and cannot these be
supposed available to break or elude or in any
manner overmatch the tension of an inch or two of
iron ring?

This is a natural power, like light and heat, and
all nature coöperates with it. The reason why we

feel one man's presence and do not feel another's is as simple as gravity. Truth is the summit of being; justice is the application of it to affairs. All individual natures stand in a scale, according to the purity of this element in them. The will of the pure runs down from them into other natures as water runs down from a higher into a lower vessel. This natural force is no more to be withstood than any other natural force. We can drive a stone upward for a moment into the air, but it is yet true that all stones will forever fall; and whatever instances can be quoted of unpunished theft, or of a lie which somebody credited, justice must prevail, and it is the privilege of truth to make itself believed. Character is this moral order seen through the medium of an individual nature. An individual is an encloser. Time and space, liberty and necessity, truth and thought, are left at large no longer. Now, the universe is a close or pound. All things exist in the man tinged with the manners of his soul. With what quality is in him he infuses all nature that he can reach; nor does he tend to lose himself in vastness, but, at how long a curve soever, all his regards return into his own good at last. He animates all he can, and he sees only what he animates. He encloses the world, as the patriot does his country, as a material basis for his character, and a theatre for action. A healthy

soul stands united with the Just and the True, as
the magnet arranges itself with the pole; so that he
stands to all beholders like a transparent object betwixt them and the sun, and whoso journeys towards the sun, journeys towards that person. He
is thus the medium of the highest influence to all
who are not on the same level. Thus men of character are the conscience of the society to which they
belong.

The natural measure of this power is the resistance of circumstances. Impure men consider life
as it is reflected in opinions, events, and persons.
They cannot see the action until it is done. Yet
its moral element preëxisted in the actor, and its
quality as right or wrong it was easy to predict.
Everything in nature is bipolar, or has a positive
and a negative pole. There is a male and a female,
a spirit and a fact, a north and a south. Spirit is
the positive, the event is the negative. Will is the
north, action the south pole. Character may be
ranked as having its natural place in the north. It
shares the magnetic currents of the system. The
feeble souls are drawn to the south or negative
pole. They look at the profit or hurt of the action.
They never behold a principle until it is lodged in
a person. They do not wish to be lovely, but to be
loved. Men of character like to hear of their faults;
the other class do not like to hear of faults; they

worship events; secure to them a fact, a connection, a certain chain of circumstances, and they will ask no more. The hero sees that the event is ancillary; it must follow *him*. A given order of events has no power to secure to him the satisfaction which the imagination attaches to it; the soul of goodness escapes from any set of circumstances; whilst prosperity belongs to a certain mind, and will introduce that power and victory which is its natural fruit, into any order of events. No change of circumstances can repair a defect of character. We boast our emancipation from many superstitions; but if we have broken any idols it is through a transfer of the idolatry. What have I gained, that I no longer immolate a bull to Jove or to Neptune, or a mouse to Hecate; that I do not tremble before the Eumenides, or the Catholic Purgatory, or the Calvinistic Judgment-day, — if I quake at opinion, the public opinion as we call it; or at the threat of assault, or contumely, or bad neighbors, or poverty, or mutilation, or at the rumor of revolution, or of murder? If I quake, what matters it what I quake at? Our proper vice takes form in one or another shape, according to the sex, age, or temperament of the person, and, if we are capable of fear, will readily find terrors. The covetousness or the malignity which saddens me when I ascribe it to society, is my own. I am always environed by myself

On the other part, rectitude is a perpetual victory,
celebrated not by cries of joy but by serenity, which
is joy fixed or habitual. It is disgraceful to fly
to events for confirmation of our truth and worth.
The capitalist does not run every hour to the broker
to coin his advantages into current money of the
realm ; he is satisfied to read in the quotations of
the market that his stocks have risen. The same
transport which the occurrence of the best events in
the best order would occasion me, I must learn to
taste purer in the perception that my position is
every hour meliorated, and does already command
those events I desire. That exultation is only to
be checked by the foresight of an order of things
so excellent as to throw all our prosperities into
the deepest shade.

The face which character wears to me is self-
sufficingness. I revere the person who is riches ;
so that I cannot think of him as alone, or poor, or
exiled, or unhappy, or a client, but as perpetual pa-
tron, benefactor, and beatified man. Character is
centrality, the impossibility of being displaced or
overset. A man should give us a sense of mass.
Society is frivolous, and shreds its day into scraps,
its conversation into ceremonies and escapes. But
if I go to see an ingenious man I shall think myself poorly entertained if he give me nimble pieces
of benevolence and etiquette ; rather he shall stand

stoutly in his place and let me apprehend if it were
only his resistance ; know that I have encountered
a new and positive quality ; — great refreshment
for both of us. It is much that he does not accept
the conventional opinions and practices. That nonconformity will remain a goad and remembrancer,
and every inquirer will have to dispose of him, in
the first place. There is nothing real or useful
that is not a seat of war. Our houses ring with
laughter and personal and critical gossip, but it
helps little. But the uncivil, unavailable man, who
is a problem and a threat to society, whom it cannot let pass in silence but must either worship or
hate, — and to whom all parties feel related, both
the leaders of opinion and the obscure and eccentric, — he helps ; he puts America and Europe in
the wrong, and destroys the skepticism which says,
'man is a doll, let us eat and drink, 't is the best
we can do,' by illuminating the untried and unknown. Acquiescence in the establishment and
appeal to the public, indicate infirm faith, heads
which are not clear, and which must see a house
built, before they can comprehend the plan of it.
The wise man not only leaves out of his thought
the many, but leaves out the few. Fountains, the
self-moved, the absorbed, the commander because
he is commanded, the assured, the primary, — they
are good ; for these announce the instant presence
of supreme power.

Our action should rest mathematically on our substance. In nature there are no false valuations. A pound of water in the ocean - tempest has no more gravity than in a midsummer pond. All things work exactly according to their quality and according to their quantity; attempt nothing they cannot do, except man only. He has pretension; he wishes and attempts things beyond his force. I read in a book of English memoirs, " Mr. Fox (afterwards Lord Holland) said, he must have the Treasury; he had served up to it, and would have it." Xenophon and his Ten Thousand were quite equal to what they attempted, and did it; so equal, that it was not suspected to be a grand and inimitable exploit. Yet there stands that fact unrepeated, a high-water mark in military history. Many have attempted it since, and not been equal to it. It is only on reality that any power of action can be based. No institution will be better than the institutor. I knew an amiable and accomplished person who undertook a practical reform, yet I was never able to find in him the enterprise of love he took in hand. He adopted it by ear and by the understanding from the books he had been reading. All his action was tentative, a piece of the city carried out into the fields, and was the city still, and no new fact, and could not inspire enthusiasm. Had there been something latent in the man, a terrible undemonstrated genius agitating and embarrassing his demeanor, we had watched for its advent. It is not enough that the intellect should see the evils and their remedy. We shall still postpone our existence, nor take the ground to which we are entitled, whilst it is only a thought and not a spirit that incites us. We have not yet served up to it.

These are properties of life, and another trait is the notice of incessant growth. Men should be intelligent and earnest. They must also make us feel that they have a controlling happy future opening before them, whose early twilights already kindle in the passing hour. The hero is misconceived and misreported; he cannot therefore wait to unravel any man's blunders; he is again on his road, adding new powers and honors to his domain and new claims on your heart, which will bankrupt you if you have loitered about the old things and have not kept your relation to him by adding to your wealth. New actions are the only apologies and explanations of old ones which the noble can bear to offer or to receive. If your friend has displeased you, you shall not sit down to consider it, for he has already lost all memory of the passage, and has doubled his power to serve you, and ere you can rise up again will burden you with blessings.

We have no pleasure in thinking of a benevolence that is only measured by its works. Love is inexhaustible, and if its estate is wasted, its granary emptied, still cheers and enriches, and the man, though he sleep, seems to purify the air and his house to adorn the landscape and strengthen the laws. People always recognize this difference. We know who is benevolent, by quite other means than the amount of subscription to soup-societies. It is only low merits that can be enumerated. Fear, when your friends say to you what you have done well, and say it through; but when they stand with uncertain timid looks of respect and half-dislike, and must suspend their judgment for years to come, you may begin to hope. Those who live to the future must always appear selfish to those who live to the present. Therefore it was droll in the good Riemer, who has written memoirs of Goethe, to make out a list of his donations and good deeds, as, so many hundred thalers given to Stilling, to Hegel, to Tischbein; a lucrative place found for Professor Voss, a post under the Grand Duke for Herder, a pension for Meyer, two professors recommended to foreign universities; &c., &c. The longest list of specifications of benefit would look very short. A man is a poor creature if he is to be measured so. For all these of course are exceptions, and the rule and hodiernal life of a good man is benefaction. The true charity of Goethe is to be inferred from the account he gave Dr. Eckermann of the

way in which he had spent his fortune. "Each
bon-mot of mine has cost a purse of gold. Half a
million of my own money, the fortune I inherited,
my salary and the large income derived from my
writings for fifty years back, have been expended
to instruct me in what I now know. I have besides
seen," &c.

I own it is but poor chat and gossip to go to
enumerate traits of this simple and rapid power,
and we are painting the lightning with charcoal;
but in these long nights and vacations I like to
console myself so. Nothing but itself can copy it.
A word warm from the heart enriches me. I surrender at discretion. How death-cold is literary
genius before this fire of life! These are the
touches that reanimate my heavy soul and give it
eyes to pierce the dark of nature. I find, where
I thought myself poor, there was I most rich.
Thence comes a new intellectual exaltation, to be
again rebuked by some new exhibition of character. Strange alternation of attraction and repulsion! Character repudiates intellect, yet excites
it; and character passes into thought, is published
so, and then is ashamed before new flashes of moral
worth.

Character is nature in the highest form. It is
of no use to ape it or to contend with it. Somewhat is possible of resistance, and of persistence,

and of creation, to this power, which will foil all emulation.

This masterpiece is best where no hands but nature's have been laid on it. Care is taken that the greatly-destined shall slip up into life in the shade, with no thousand-eyed Athens to watch and blazon every new thought, every blushing emotion of young genius. Two persons lately, very young children of the most high God, have given me occasion for thought. When I explored the source of their sanctity and charm for the imagination, it seemed as if each answered, 'From my nonconformity; I never listened to your people's law, or to what they call their gospel, and wasted my time. I was content with the simple rural poverty of my own; hence this sweetness; my work never reminds you of that; — is pure of that.' And nature advertises me in such persons that in democratic America she will not be democratized. How cloistered and constitutionally sequestered from the market and from scandal! It was only this morning that I sent away some wild flowers of these wood-gods. They are a relief from literature, — these fresh draughts from the sources of thought and sentiment; as we read, in an age of polish and criticism, the first lines of written prose and verse of a nation. How captivating is their devotion to their favorite books, whether Æschylus, Dante, Shakspeare, or Scott, as feeling that they have a stake in that book; who touches that, touches them; — and especially the total solitude of the critic, the Patmos of thought from which he writes, in unconsciousness of any eyes that shall ever read this writing. Could they dream on still, as angels, and not wake to comparisons and to be flattered! Yet some natures are too good to be spoiled by praise, and wherever the vein of thought reaches down into the profound, there is no danger from vanity. Solemn friends will warn them of the danger of the head's being turned by the flourish of trumpets, but they can afford to smile. I remember the indignation of an eloquent Methodist at the kind admonitions of a Doctor of Divinity, — 'My friend, a man can neither be praised nor insulted.' But forgive the counsels; they are very natural. I remember the thought which occurred to me when some ingenious and spiritual foreigners came to America, was, Have you been victimized in being brought hither? — or, prior to that, answer me this, ' Are you victimizable?'

As I have said, Nature keeps these sovereignties in her own hands, and however pertly our sermons and disciplines would divide some share of credit, and teach that the laws fashion the citizen, she goes her own gait and puts the wisest in the wrong. She makes very light of gospels and prophets, as

one who has a great many more to produce and no
excess of time to spare on any one. There is a class
of men, individuals of which appear at long intervals, so eminently endowed with insight and virtue
that they have been unanimously saluted as *divine,*
and who seem to be an accumulation of that power
we consider. Divine persons are character born,
or, to borrow a phrase from Napoleon, they are
victory organized. They are usually received with
ill-will, because they are new and because they set
a bound to the exaggeration that has been made of
the personality of the last divine person. Nature
never rhymes her children, nor makes two men
alike. When we see a great man we fancy a resemblance to some historical person, and predict
the sequel of his character and fortune ; a result
which he is sure to disappoint. None will ever
solve the problem of his character according to our
prejudice, but only in his own high unprecedented
way. Character wants room ; must not be crowded
on by persons nor be judged from glimpses got
in the press of affairs or on few occasions. It
needs perspective, as a great building. It may not,
probably does not, form relations rapidly; and we
should not require rash explanation, either on the
popular ethics, or on our own, of its action.

I look on Sculpture as history. I do not think
the Apollo and the Jove impossible in flesh and

blood. Every trait which the artist recorded in stone he had seen in life, and better than his copy. We have seen many counterfeits, but we are born believers in great men. How easily we read in old books, when men were few, of the smallest action of the patriarchs. We require that a man should be so large and columnar in the landscape, that it should deserve to be recorded that he arose, and girded up his loins, and departed to such a place. The most credible pictures are those of majestic men who prevailed at their entrance, and convinced the senses; as happened to the eastern magian who was sent to test the merits of Zertusht or Zoroaster. When the Yunani sage arrived at Balkh, the Persians tell us, Gushtasp appointed a day on which the Mobeds of every country should assemble, and a golden chair was placed for the Yunani sage. Then the beloved of Yezdam, the prophet Zertusht, advanced into the midst of the assembly. The Yunani sage, on seeing that chief, said, " This form and this gait cannot lie, and nothing but truth can proceed from them." Plato said it was impossible not to believe in the children of the gods, " though they should speak without probable or necessary arguments." I should think myself very unhappy in my associates if I could not credit the best things in history. " John Bradshaw," says Milton, " appears like a consul, from whom the

fasces are not to depart with the year; so that not
on the tribunal only, but throughout his life, you
would regard him as sitting in judgment upon
kings." I find it more credible, since it is anterior
information, that one man should *know heaven*, as
the Chinese say, than that so many men should
know the world. "The virtuous prince confronts
the gods, without any misgiving. He waits a hundred ages till a sage comes, and does not doubt.
He who confronts the gods, without any misgiving,
knows heaven; he who waits a hundred ages until
a sage comes, without doubting, knows men. Hence
the virtuous prince moves, and for ages shows empire the way." But there is no need to seek remote
examples. He is a dull observer whose experience
has not taught him the reality and force of magic, as
well as of chemistry. The coldest precisian cannot
go abroad without encountering inexplicable influences. One man fastens an eye on him and the
graves of the memory render up their dead; the
secrets that make him wretched either to keep or to
betray must be yielded; — another, and he cannot
speak, and the bones of his body seem to lose their
cartilages; the entrance of a friend adds grace,
boldness, and eloquence to him; and there are persons he cannot choose but remember, who gave a
transcendent expansion to his thought, and kindled
another life in his bosom.

What is so excellent as strict relations of amity, when they spring from this deep root? The sufficient reply to the skeptic who doubts the power and the furniture of man, is in that possibility of joyful intercourse with persons, which makes the faith and practice of all reasonable men. I know nothing which life has to offer so satisfying as the profound good understanding which can subsist, after much exchange of good offices, between two virtuous men, each of whom is sure of himself and sure of his friend. It is a happiness which postpones all other gratifications, and makes politics, and commerce, and churches, cheap. For when men shall meet as they ought, each a benefactor, a shower of stars, clothed with thoughts, with deeds, with accomplishments, it should be the festival of nature which all things announce. Of such friendship, love in the sexes is the first symbol, as all other things are symbols of love. Those relations to the best men, which, at one time, we reckoned the romances of youth, become, in the progress of the character, the most solid enjoyment.

If it were possible to live in right relations with men! — if we could abstain from asking anything of them, from asking their praise, or help, or pity, and content us with compelling them through the virtue of the eldest laws! Could we not deal with a few persons, — with one person, — after

the unwritten statutes, and make an experiment of
their efficacy? Could we not pay our friend the
compliment of truth, of silence, of forbearing?
Need we be so eager to seek him? If we are related, we shall meet. It was a tradition of the ancient world that no metamorphosis could hide a
god from a god; and there is a Greek verse which
runs, —

> " The Gods are to each other not unknown."

Friends also follow the laws of divine necessity;
they gravitate to each other, and cannot otherwise : —

> When each the other shall avoid,
> Shall each by each be most enjoyed.

Their relation is not made, but allowed. The gods
must seat themselves without seneschal in our Olympus, and as they can instal themselves by seniority
divine. Society is spoiled if pains are taken, if the
associates are brought a mile to meet. And if it
be not society, it is a mischievous, low, degrading
jangle, though made up of the best. All the greatness of each is kept back and every foible in painful activity, as if the Olympians should meet to ex
change snuff-boxes.

Life goes headlong. We chase some flying
scheme, or we are hunted by some fear or command behind us. But if suddenly we encounter a

friend, we pause ; our heat and hurry look foolish enough ; now pause, now possession is required, and the power to swell the moment from the resources of the heart. The moment is all, in all noble rela-tions.

A divine person is the prophecy of the mind; a friend is the hope of the heart. Our beatitude waits for the fulfilment of these two in one. The ages are opening this moral force. All force is the shadow or symbol of that. Poetry is joyful and strong as it draws its inspiration thence. Men write their names on the world as they are filled with this. History has been mean ; our nations have been mobs; we have never seen a man : that divine form we do not yet know, but only the dream and prophecy of such : we do not know the majestic manners which belong to him, which appease and exalt the beholder. We shall one day see that the most private is the most public energy, that quality atones for quantity, and grandeur of character acts in the dark, and succors them who never saw it. What greatness has yet appeared is beginnings and encouragements to us in this direction. The history of those gods and saints which the world has writ-ten and then worshipped, are documents of charac-ter. The ages have exulted in the manners of a youth who owed nothing to fortune, and who was hanged at the Tyburn of his nation, who, by the pure quality of his nature, shed an epic splendor around the facts of his death which has transfigured every particular into an universal symbol for the eyes of mankind. This great defeat is hitherto our highest fact. But the mind requires a victory to the senses; a force of character which will convert judge, jury, soldier, and king ; which will rule animal and mineral virtues, and blend with the courses of sap, of rivers, of winds, of stars, and of moral agents.

If we cannot attain at a bound to these grandeurs, at least let us do them homage. In society, high advantages are set down to the possessor as disadvantages. It requires the more wariness in our private estimates. I do not forgive in my friends the failure to know a fine character and to entertain it with thankful hospitality. When at last that which we have always longed for is arrived and shines on us with glad rays out of that far celestial land, then to be coarse, then to be critical and treat such a visitant with the jabber and suspicion of the streets, argues a vulgarity that seems to shut the doors of heaven. This is confusion, this the right insanity, when the soul no longer knows its own, nor where its allegiance, its religion, are due. Is there any religion but this, to know that wherever in the wide desert of being the holy sentiment we cherish has opened into a flower, it blooms for me? if none sees it, I see it; I am aware, if I alone, of the greatness of the fact. Whilst it blooms, I will keep sabbath or holy time, and suspend my gloom and my folly and jokes. Nature is indulged by the presence of this guest. There are many eyes that can detect and honor the prudent and household virtues; there are many that can discern Genius on his starry track, though the mob is incapable; but when that love which is all-suffering, all-abstaining, all-aspiring, which has vowed to itself that it will be a wretch and also a fool in this world sooner than soil its white hands by any compliances, comes into our streets and houses, — only the pure and aspiring can know its face, and the only compliment they can pay it is to own it.

MANNERS.

—◆—

'**How** near to good is what is fair?
Which we no sooner see,
But with the lines and outward air
Our senses taken be.

Again yourselves compose,
And now put all the aptness on
Of Figure, that Proportion
Or Color can disclose;
That if those silent arts were lost,
Design and Picture, they might boast
From you a newer ground,
Instructed by the heightening sense
Of dignity and reverence
In their true motions found."

BEN JONSON

IV.

MANNERS.

———◆———

HALF the world, it is said, knows not how the other half live. Our Exploring Expedition saw the Feejee islanders getting their dinner off human bones; and they are said to eat their own wives and children. The husbandry of the modern inhabitants of Gournou (west of old Thebes) is philosophical to a fault. To set up their house-keeping nothing is requisite but two or three earthen pots, a stone to grind meal, and a mat which is the bed. The house, namely a tomb, is ready without rent or taxes. No rain can pass through the roof, and there is no door, for there is no want of one, as there is nothing to lose. If the house do not please them, they walk out and enter another, as there are several hundreds at their command. "It is somewhat singular," adds Belzoni, to whom we owe this account, "to talk of happiness among people who live in sepulchres, among the corpses and rags of an ancient nation which they know nothing of." In the deserts of

Borgoo the rock-Tibboos still dwell in caves, like
cliff-swallows, and the language of these negroes is
compared by their neighbors to the shrieking of
bats and to the whistling of birds. Again, the Bor-
noos have no proper names; individuals are called
after their height, thickness, or other accidental
quality, and have nicknames merely. But the salt,
the dates, the ivory, and the gold, for which these
horrible regions are visited, find their way into
countries where the purchaser and consumer can
hardly be ranked in one race with these cannibals
and man-stealers; countries where man serves himself with metals, wood, stone, glass, gum, cotton,
silk, and wool; honors himself with architecture;
writes laws, and contrives to execute his will
through the hands of many nations; and, especially, establishes a select society, running through
all the countries of intelligent men, a self-consti-
tuted aristocracy, or fraternity of the best, which,
without written law or exact usage of any kind,
perpetuates itself, colonizes every new-planted isl-
and and adopts and makes its own whatever personal beauty or extraordinary native endowment
anywhere appears.

What fact more conspicuous in modern history
than the creation of the gentleman? Chivalry is
that, and loyalty is that, and, in English literature
half the drama, and all the novels, from Sir Philip

Sidney to Sir Walter Scott, paint this figure. The word *gentleman*, which, like the word Christian, must hereafter characterize the present and the few preceding centuries by the importance attached to it, is a homage to personal and incommunicable properties. Frivolous and fantastic additions have got associated with the name, but the steady interest of mankind in it must be attributed to the valuable properties which it designates. An element which unites all the most forcible persons of every country, makes them intelligible and agreeable to each other, and is somewhat so precise that it is at once felt if an individual lack the masonic sign, — cannot be any casual product, but must be an average result of the character and faculties universally found in men. It seems a certain permanent average; as the atmosphere is a permanent composition, whilst so many gases are combined only to be decompounded. *Comme il faut*, is the Frenchman's description of good society : *as we must be.* It is a spontaneous fruit of talents and feelings of precisely that class who have most vigor, who take the lead in the world of this hour, and though far from pure, far from constituting the gladdest and highest tone of human feeling, it is as good as the whole society permits it to be. It is made of the spirit, more than of the talent of men, and is a compound result into which every great force en ters as an ingredient, namely virtue, wit, beauty, wealth, and power.

There is something equivocal in all the words in use to express the excellence of manners and social cultivation, because the quantities are fluxional, and the last effect is assumed by the senses as the cause. The word *gentleman* has not any correlative abstract to express the quality. *Gentility* is mean, and *gentilesse* is obsolete. But we must keep alive in the vernacular the distinction between *fashion*, a word of narrow and often sinister meaning, and the heroic character which *the gentleman* imports. The usual words, however, must be respected; they will be found to contain the root of the matter. The point of distinction in all this class of names, as courtesy, chivalry, fashion, and the like, is that the flower and fruit, not the grain of the tree, are contemplated. It is beauty which is the aim this time, and not worth. The result is now in question, although our words intimate well enough the popular feeling that the appearance supposes a substance. The gentleman is a man of truth, lord of his own actions, and expressing that lordship in his behavior; not in any manner dependent and servile, either on persons, or opinions, or possessions. Beyond this fact of truth and real force, the word denotes good-nature or benevolence: manhood first, and then gentleness. The

popular notion certainly adds a condition of ease
and fortune ; but that is a natural result of personal force and love, that they should possess and
dispense the goods of the world. In times of
violence, every eminent person must fall in with
many opportunities to approve his stoutness and
worth ; therefore every man's name that emerged
at all from the mass in the feudal ages, rattles in
our ear like a flourish of trumpets. But personal
force never goes out of fashion. That is still paramount to-day, and in the moving crowd of good
society the men of valor and reality are known
and rise to their natural place. The competition
is transferred from war to politics and trade, but
the personal force appears readily enough in these
new arenas.

Power first, or no leading class. In politics and
in trade, bruisers and pirates are of better promise
than talkers and clerks. God knows that all sorts
of gentlemen knock at the door ; but whenever
used in strictness and with any emphasis, the name
will be found to point at original energy. It describes a man standing in his own right and working after untaught methods. In a good lord there
must first be a good animal, at least to the extent
of yielding the incomparable advantage of animal
spirits. The ruling class must have more, but
they must have these, giving in every company the

sense of power, which makes things easy to be
done which daunt the wise.   The society of the energetic class, in their friendly and festive meetings,
is full of courage and of attempts which intimidate
the pale scholar.   The courage which girls exhibit
is like a battle of Lundy's Lane, or a sea-fight
The intellect relies on memory to make some sup-
plies to face these extemporaneous squadrons.   But
memory is a base mendicant with basket and
badge, in the presence of these sudden masters.
The rulers of society must be up to the work of the
world, and equal to their versatile office : men of
the right Cæsarian pattern, who have great range of
affinity.   I am far from believing the timid maxim
of Lord Falkland ("that for ceremony there must
go two to it ; since a bold fellow will go through
the cunningest forms "), and am of opinion that
the gentleman is the bold fellow whose forms are
not to be broken through ; and only that plenteous
nature is rightful master which is the complement
of whatever person it converses with.   My gentleman gives the law where he is ; he will outpray
saints in chapel, outgeneral veterans in the field,
and outshine all courtesy in the hall.   He is good
company for pirates and good with academicians ;
so that it is useless to fortify yourself against him ;
he has the private entrance to all minds, and I
could as easily exclude myself, as him.   The fa-

 nous gentlemen of Asia and Europe have been of this strong type; Saladin, Sapor, the Cid, Julius Cæsar, Scipio, Alexander, Pericles, and the lordliest personages. They sat very carelessly in their chairs, and were too excellent themselves, to value any condition at a high rate.

A plentiful fortune is reckoned necessary, in the popular judgment, to the completion of this man of the world; and it is a material deputy which walks through the dance which the first has led. Money is not essential, but this wide affinity is, which transcends the habits of clique and caste and makes itself felt by men of all classes. If the aristocrat is only valid in fashionable circles and not with truckmen, he will never be a leader in fashion; and if the man of the people cannot speak on equal terms with the gentleman, so that the gentleman shall perceive that he is already really of his own order, he is not to be feared. Diogenes, Socrates, and Epaminondas, are gentlemen of the best blood who have chosen the condition of poverty when that of wealth was equally open to them. I use these old names, but the men I speak of are my contemporaries. Fortune will not supply to every generation one of these well-appointed knights, but every collection of men furnishes some example of the class; and the politics of this country, and the trade of every town, are controlled by these

hardy and irresponsible doers, who have invention
to take the lead, and a broad sympathy which puts
them in fellowship with crowds, and makes their
action popular.

The manners of this class are observed and
caught with devotion by men of taste. The association of these masters with each other and with
men intelligent of their merits, is mutually agreeable and stimulating. The good forms, the happiest
expressions of each, are repeated and adopted. By
swift consent everything superfluous is dropped,
everything graceful is renewed. Fine manners
show themselves formidable to the uncultivated
man. They are a subtler science of defence to
parry and intimidate; but once matched by the
skill of the other party, they drop the point of the
sword, — points and fences disappear, and the youth
finds himself in a more transparent atmosphere,
wherein life is a less troublesome game, and not a
misunderstanding rises between the players. Manners aim to facilitate life, to get rid of impediments
and bring the man pure to energize. They aid our
dealing and conversation as a railway aids travelling, by getting rid of all avoidable obstructions of
the road and leaving nothing to be conquered but
pure space. These forms very soon become fixed,
and a fine sense of propriety is cultivated with the
more heed that it becomes a badge of social and

civil distinctions. Thus grows up Fashion, an equivocal semblance, the most puissant, the most fantastic and frivolous, the most feared and followed, and which morals and violence assault in vain.

There exists a strict relation between the class of power and the exclusive and polished circles. The last are always filled or filling from the first. The strong men usually give some allowance even to the petulances of fashion, for that affinity they find in it. Napoleon, child of the revolution, destroyer of the old noblesse, never ceased to court the Faubourg St. Germain ; doubtless with the feeling that fashion is a homage to men of his stamp. Fashion, though in a strange way, represents all manly virtue. It is virtue gone to seed : it is a kind of posthumous honor. It does not often caress the great, but the children of the great : it is a hall of the Past. It usually sets its face against the great of this hour. Great men are not commonly in its halls ; they are absent in the field : they are working, not triumphing. Fashion is made up of their children ; of those who through the value and virtue of somebody, have acquired lustre to their name, marks of distinction, means of cultivation and generosity, and in their physical organization a certain health and excellence which secure to them, if not **the highest power to work, yet high power to enjoy.**

The class of power, the working heroes, the Cortez the Nelson, the Napoleon, see that this is the festivity and permanent celebration of such as they; that fashion is funded talent; is Mexico, Marengo, and Trafalgar beaten out thin ; that the brilliant names of fashion run back to just such busy names as their own, fifty or sixty years ago. They are the sowers, their sons shall be the reapers, and *their* sons, in the ordinary course of things, must yield the possession of the harvest to new competitors with keener eyes and stronger frames. The city is recruited from the country. In the year 1805, it is said, every legitimate monarch in Europe was imbecile. The city would have died out, rotted, and exploded, long ago, but that it was reinforced from the fields. It is only country which came to town day before yesterday that is city and court to-day.

Aristocracy and fashion are certain inevitable results. These mutual selections are indestructible. If they provoke anger in the least favored class, and the excluded majority revenge themselves on the excluding minority by the strong hand and kill them, at once a new class finds itself at the top, as certainly as cream rises in a bowl of milk : and if the people should destroy class after class, until two men only were left, one of these would be the leader and would be involuntarily served and copied by the other. You may keep this minority out of sight and out of mind, but it is tenacious of life, and is one of the estates of the realm. I am the more struck with this tenacity, when I see its work. It respects the administration of such unimportant matters, that we should not look for any durability in its rule. We sometimes meet men under some strong moral influence, as a patriotic, a literary, a religious movement, and feel that the moral sentiment rules man and nature. We think all other distinctions and ties will be slight and fugitive, this of caste or fashion for example ; yet come from year to year and see how permanent that is, in this Boston or New York life of man, where too it has not the least countenance from the law of the land. Not in Egypt or in India a firmer or more impassable line. Here are associations whose ties go over and under and through it, a meeting of merchants, a military corps, a college class, a fire-club, a professional association, a political, a religious convention ; — the persons seem to draw inseparably near; yet, that assembly once dispersed, its members will not in the year meet again. Each returns to his degree in the scale of good society, porcelain remains porcelain, and earthen earthen. The objects of fashion may be frivolous, or fashion may be objectless, but the nature of this union and selection can be neither frivolous nor accidental. Each man's rank in that perfect graduation depends on some symmetry in his structure or some agreement in his structure to the symmetry of society. Its doors unbar instantaneously to a natural claim of their own kind. A natural gentleman finds his way in, and will keep the oldest patrician out who has lost his intrinsic rank. Fashion understands itself; good-breeding and personal superiority of whatever country readily fraternize with those of every other. The chiefs of savage tribes have distinguished themselves in London and Paris by the purity of their tournure.

To say what good of fashion we can, it rests on reality, and hates nothing so much as pretenders; to exclude and mystify pretenders and send them into everlasting 'Coventry,' is its delight. We contemn in turn every other gift of men of the world; but the habit even in little and the least matters of not appealing to any but our own sense of propriety, constitutes the foundation of all chivalry. There is almost no kind of self-reliance, so it be sane and proportioned, which fashion does not occasionally adopt and give it the freedom of its saloons. A sainted soul is always elegant, and, if it will, passes unchallenged into the most guarded ring. But so will Jock the teamster pass, in some crisis that brings him thither, and find favor, as long as his head is not giddy with the new circumstance, and the iron shoes do not wish to dance in

waltzes and cotillons. For there is nothing settled
in manners, but the laws of behavior yield to the
energy of the individual. The maiden at her first
ball, the countryman at a city dinner, believes that
there is a ritual according to which every act and
compliment must be performed, or the failing party
must be cast out of this presence. Later they learn
that good sense and character make their own forms
every moment, and speak or abstain, take wine or
refuse it, stay or go, sit in a chair or sprawl with
children on the floor, or stand on their head, or
what else soever, in a new and aboriginal way; and
that strong will is always in fashion, let who will
be unfashionable. All that fashion demands is
composure and self-content. A circle of men per-
fectly well-bred would be a company of sensible
persons in which every man's native manners and
character appeared. If the fashionist have not this
quality, he is nothing. We are such lovers of self-
reliance that we excuse in a man many sins if he
will show us a complete satisfaction in his position,
which asks no leave to be, of mine, or any man's
good opinion. But any deference to some eminent
man or woman of the world, forfeits all privilege
of nobility. He is an underling: I have nothing
to do with him; I will speak with his master. A
man should not go where he cannot carry his whole
sphere or society with him, — not bodily, the whole

circle of his friends, but atmospherically. He
should preserve in a new company the same attitude of mind and reality of relation which his daily
associates draw him to, else he is shorn of his best
beams, and will be an orphan in the merriest club.
" If you could see Vich Ian Vohr with his tail on !
——— " But Vich Ian Vohr must always carry his
belongings in some fashion, if not added as honor,
then severed as disgrace.

There will always be in society certain persons
who are mercuries of its approbation, and whose
glance will at any time determine for the curious
their standing in the world. These are the cham-
berlains of the lesser gods. Accept their coldness
as an omen of grace with the loftier deities, and
allow them all their privilege. They are clear in
their office, nor could they be thus formidable without their own merits. But do not measure the importance of this class by their pretension, or imagine that a fop can be the dispenser of honor and
shame. They pass also at their just rate ; for how
can they otherwise, in circles which exist as a sort
of herald's office for the sifting of character ?

As the first thing man requires of man is reality,
so that appears in all the forms of society. We
pointedly, and by name, introduce the parties to
each other. Know you before all heaven and earth,
that this is Andrew, and this is Gregory, — they

look each other in the eye ; they grasp each other's hand, to identify and signalize each other. It is a great satisfaction. A gentleman never dodges; his eyes look straight forward, and he assures the other party, first of all, that he has been met. For what is it that we seek, in so many visits and hospitali· ties ? Is it your draperies, pictures, and decora· tions? Or do we not insatiably ask, Was a man in the house ? I may easily go into a great house· hold where there is much substance, excellent pro· vision for comfort, luxury, and taste, and yet not encounter there any Amphitryon who shall subor· dinate these appendages. I may go into a cottage, and find a farmer who feels that he is the man I have come to see, and fronts me accordingly. It was therefore a very natural point of old feudal etiquette that a gentleman who received a visit, though it were of his sovereign, should not leave his roof, but should wait his arrival at the door of his house. No house, though it were the Tuileries or the Escurial, is good for anything without a master. And yet we are not often gratified by this hospitality. Every body we know surrounds him· self with a fine house, fine books, conservatory, gar· dens, equipage and all manner of toys, as screens to interpose between himself and his guest. Does It not seem as if man was of a very sly, elusive na· ture, and dreaded nothing so much as a full reu

contre front to front with his fellow? It were un-
merciful, I know, quite to abolish the use of these
screens, which are of eminent convenience, whether
the guest is too great or too little. We call together many friends who keep each other in play,
or by luxuries and ornaments we amuse the young
people, and guard our retirement. Or if perchance
a searching realist comes to our gate, before whose
eye we have no care to stand, then again we run
to our curtain, and hide ourselves as Adam at the
voice of the Lord God in the garden. Cardinal
Caprara, the Pope's legate at Paris, defended himself from the glances of Napoleon by an immense
pair of green spectacles. Napoleon remarked them,
and speedily managed to rally them off: and yet
Napoleon, in his turn, was not great enough, with
eight hundred thousand troops at his back, to face
a pair of freeborn eyes, but fenced himself with etiquette and within triple barriers of reserve; and,
as all the world knows from Madame de Staël, was
wont, when he found himself observed, to discharge
his face of all expression. But emperors and rich
men are by no means the most skilful masters of
good manners. No rentroll nor army-list can dignify skulking and dissimulation; and the first point
of courtesy must always be truth, as really all the
forms of good breeding point that way.

I have just been reading, in Mr. Hazlitt's translation, Montaigne's account of his journey into Italy, and am struck with nothing more agreeably than the self-respecting fashions of the time. His arrival in each place, the arrival of a gentleman of France, is an event of some consequence. Wherever he goes he pays a visit to whatever prince or gentleman of note resides upon his road, as a duty to himself and to civilization. When he leaves any house in which he has lodged for a few weeks, he causes his arms to be painted and hung up as a perpetual sign to the house, as was the custom of gentlemen.

The complement of this graceful self-respect, and that of all the points of good breeding I most require and insist upon, is deference. I like that every chair should be a throne, and hold a king. I prefer a tendency to stateliness to an excess of fellowship. Let the incommunicable objects of nature and the metaphysical isolation of man teach us independence. Let us not be too much acquainted. I would have a man enter his house through a hall filled with heroic and sacred sculptures, that he might not want the hint of tranquillity and self-poise. We should meet each morning as from foreign countries, and, spending the day together, should depart at night, as into foreign countries. In all things I would have the island of a man inviolate. Let us sit apart as the gods, talking from peak to peak all round Olympus. No degree ot affection need invade this religion. This is myrrh and rosemary to keep the other sweet. Lovers should guard their strangeness. If they forgive too much, all slides into confusion and meanness. It is easy to push this deference to a Chinese etiquette ; but coolness and absence of heat and haste indicate fine qualities. A gentleman makes no noise; a lady is serene. Proportionate is our disgust at those invaders who fill a studious house with blast and running, to secure some paltry convenience. Not less I dislike a low sympathy of each with his neighbor's needs. Must we have a good understanding with one another's palates? as foolish people who have lived long together know when each wants salt or sugar. I pray my companion, if he wishes for bread, to ask me for bread, and if he wishes for sassafras or arsenic, to ask me for them, and not to hold out his plate as if I knew already. Every natural function can be dignified by deliberation and privacy. Let us leave hurry to slaves. The compliments and ceremonies of our breeding should recall, however remotely, the grandeur of our destiny.

The flower of courtesy does not very well bide handling, but if we dare to open another leaf and explore what parts go to its conformation, we shall find also an intellectual quality. To the leaders of men, the brain as well as the flesh and the heart must furnish a proportion. Defect in manners is usually the defect of fine perceptions. Men are too coarsely made for the delicacy of beautiful carriage and customs. It is not quite sufficient to good-breeding, a union of kindness and independence. We imperatively require a perception of, and a homage to beauty in our companions. Other virtues are in request in the field and workyard, but a certain degree of taste is not to be spared in those we sit with. I could better eat with one who did not respect the truth or the laws than with a sloven and unpresentable person. Moral qualities rule the world, but at short distances the senses are despotic. The same discrimination of fit and fair runs out, if with less rigor, into all parts of life. The average spirit of the energetic class is good sense, acting under certain limitations and to certain ends. It entertains every natural gift. Social in its nature, it respects everything which tends to unite men. It delights in measure. The love of beauty is mainly the love of measure or proportion. The person who screams, or uses the superlative degree, or converses with heat, puts whole drawing-rooms to flight. If you wish to be loved, love measure. You must have genius or a prodigious usefulness if you will hide the want of measure. This perception comes in to polish and perfect the parts of the social instrument. Society will pardon much to genius and special gifts, but, being in its nature a convention, it loves what is conventional, or what belongs to coming together. That makes the good and bad of manners, namely what helps or hinders fellowship. For fashion is not good sense absolute, but relative; not good sense private, but good sense entertaining company. It hates corners and sharp points of character, hates quarrelsome, egotistical, solitary, and gloomy people; hates whatever can interfere with total blending of parties; whilst it values all peculiarities as in the highest degree refreshing, which can consist with good fellowship. And besides the general infusion of wit to heighten civility, the direct splendor of intellectual power is ever welcome in fine society as the costliest addition to its rule and its credit.

The dry light must shine in to adorn our festival, but it must be tempered and shaded, or that will also offend. Accuracy is essential to beauty, and quick perceptions to politeness, but not too quick perceptions. One may be too punctual and too precise. He must leave the omniscience of business at the door, when he comes into the palace of beauty. Society loves creole natures, and sleepy languishing manners, so that they cover sense, grace and good-will: the air of drowsy strength, which disarms criticism; perhaps because such a person seems to reserve himself for the best of the game, and not spend himself on surfaces; an ignoring eye, which does not see the annoyances, shifts, and inconveniences that cloud the brow and smother the voice of the sensitive.

Therefore besides personal force and so much perception as constitutes unerring taste, society demands in its patrician class another element already intimated, which it significantly terms good-nature, — expressing all degrees of generosity, from the lowest willingness and faculty to oblige, up to the heights of magnanimity and love. Insight we must have, or we shall run against one another and miss the way to our food ; but intellect is selfish and barren. The secret of success in society is a certain heartiness and sympathy. A man who is not happy in the company cannot find any word in his memory that will fit the occasion. All his information is a little impertinent. A man who is happy there, finds in every turn of the conversation equally lucky occasions for the introduction of that which he has to say. The favorites of society, and what it calls *whole souls*, are able men and of more spirit than wit, who have no uncomfortable egotism, but who exactly fill the hour and the company ; contented and contenting, at a marriage or a funeral, a ball or a jury, a water-party or a shooting-match. England, which is rich in gentlemen, furnished, in the beginning of the present century, a good model of that genius which the world loves, in Mr. Fox, who added to his great abilities the most social disposition and real love of men. Parliamentary history has few better passages than the debate in which Burke and Fox separated in the House of Commons; when Fox urged on his old friend the claims of old friendship with such tenderness that the house was moved to tears. Another anecdote is so close to my matter, that I must hazard the story. A tradesman who had long dunned him for a note of three hundred guineas, found him one day counting gold, and demanded payment: — " No," said Fox, " I owe this money to Sheridan ; it is a debt of honor ; if an accident should happen to me, he has nothing to show." " Then," said the creditor, " I change my debt into a debt of honor," and tore the note in pieces. Fox thanked the man for his confidence and paid him, saying, " his debt was of older standing, and Sheridan must wait." Lover of liberty, friend of the Hindoo, friend of the African slave, he possessed a great personal popularity; and Napoleon said of him on the occasion of his visit to Paris, in 1805, " Mr. Fox will always hold the first place in an assembly at the Tuileries."

We may easily seem ridiculous in our eulogy of courtesy, whenever we insist on benevolence as its foundation. The painted phantasm Fashion rises to

aast a species of derision on what we say. But I
will neither be driven from some allowance to Fashion as a symbolic institution, nor from the belief
that love is the basis of courtesy. We must obtain
that, if we can; but by all means we must affirm
this. Life owes much of its spirit to these sharp
ontrasts. Fashion, which affects to be honor, is
often, in all men's experience, only a ballroom-code.
Yet so long as it is the highest circle in the imagination of the best heads on the planet, there is
something necessary and excellent in it; for it is
not to be supposed that men have agreed to be the
dupes of anything preposterous ; and the respect
which these mysteries inspire in the most rude and
sylvan characters, and the curiosity with which details of high life are read, betray the universality
of the love of cultivated manners. I know that a
comic disparity would be felt, if we should enter
the acknowledged ' first circles ' and apply these
terrific standards of justice, beauty, and benefit to
the individuals actually found there. Monarchs
and heroes, sages and lovers, these gallants are not.
Fashion has many classes and many rules of probation and admission, and not the best alone. There
is not only the right of conquest, which genius pretends, — the individual demonstrating his natural
aristocracy best of the best ; — but less claims will
pass for the time; for Fashion loves lions, and

points like Circe to her horned company. This
gentleman is this afternoon arrived from Denmark;
and that is my Lord Ride, who came yesterday
from Bagdat; here is Captain Friese, from Cape
Turnagain; and Captain Symmes, from the interior of the earth; and Monsieur Jovaire, who came
down this morning in a balloon; Mr. Hobnail, the
reformer; and Reverend Jul Bat, who has con-
verted the whole torrid zone in his Sunday school;
and Signor Torre del Greco, who extinguished Ve-
suvius by pouring into it the Bay of Naples; Spahi,
the Persian ambassador; and Tul Wil Shan, the
exiled nabob of Nepaul, whose saddle is the new
moon. — But these are monsters of one day, and
to-morrow will be dismissed to their holes and
dens; for in these rooms every chair is waited for.
The artist, the scholar, and, in general, the clerisy,
win their way up into these places and get represented here, somewhat on this footing of conquest.
Another mode is to pass through all the degrees,
spending a year and a day in St. Michael's Square,
being steeped in Cologne water, and perfumed, and
dined, and introduced, and properly grounded in
all the biography and politics and anecdotes of the
boudoirs.

Yet these fineries may have grace and wit. Let
there be grotesque sculpture about the gates and
offices of temples. Let the creed and command-

ments even have the saucy homage of parody. The forms of politeness universally express benevolence in superlative degrees. What if they are in the mouths of selfish men, and used as means of selfishness? What if the false gentleman almost bows the true out of the world? What if the false gentleman contrives so to address his companion as civilly to exclude all others from his discourse, and also to make them feel excluded? Real service will not lose its nobleness. All generosity is not merely French and sentimental; nor is it to be concealed that living blood and a passion of kindness does at last distinguish God's gentleman from Fashion's. The epitaph of Sir Jenkin Grout is not wholly unintelligible to the present age: " Here lies Sir Jenkin Grout, who loved his friend and persuaded his enemy : what his mouth ate, his hand paid for : what his servants robbed, he restored : if a woman gave him pleasure, he supported her in pain : he never forgot his children; and whoso touched his finger, drew after it his whole body." Even the line of heroes is not utterly extinct. There is still ever some admirable person in plain clothes, standing on the wharf, who jumps in to rescue a drowning man ; there is still some absurd inventor of charities ; some guide and comforter of runaway slaves ; some friend of Poland ; some Philhellene ; some fanatic who plants

shade-trees for the second and third generation,
and orchards when he is grown old; some well-con-
cealed piety; some just man happy in an ill fame;
some youth ashamed of the favors of fortune and
impatiently casting them on other shoulders. And
these are the centres of society, on which it returns
for fresh impulses. These are the creators of
Fashion, which is an attempt to organize beauty
of behavior. The beautiful and the generous are,
in the theory, the doctors and apostles of this
church: Scipio, and the Cid, and Sir Philip Sidney, and Washington, and every pure and valiant
heart who worshipped Beauty by word and by
deed. The persons who constitute the natural
aristocracy are not found in the actual aristocracy,
or only on its edge; as the chemical energy of the
spectrum is found to be greatest just outside of the
spectrum. Yet that is the infirmity of the senes-
chals, who do not know their sovereign when he
appears. The theory of society supposes the existence and sovereignty of these. It divines afar off
their coming. It says with the elder gods, —

" As Heaven and Earth are fairer far
  Than Chaos and blank Darkness, though once chiefs;
  And as we show beyond that Heaven and Earth,
  In form and shape compact and beautiful:
  So, on our heels a fresh perfection treads;
  A power, more strong in beauty, born of us.

And fated to excel us, as we pass
In glory that old Darkness:
———————— for, 't is the eternal law,
That first in beauty shall be first in might."

Therefore, within the ethnical circle of good so
ety there is a narrower and higher circle, concen
tration of its light, and flower of courtesy, to which
there is always a tacit appeal of pride and refer
ence, as to its inner and imperial court; the parliament of love and chivalry. And this is constituted
of those persons in whom heroic dispositions are
native; with the love of beauty, the delight in so
ciety, and the power to embellish the passing day.
If the individuals who compose the purest circles of
aristocracy in Europe, the guarded blood of centuries, should pass in review, in such manner as
that we could at leisure and critically inspect their
behavior, we might find no gentleman and no lady;
for although excellent specimens of courtesy and
high-breeding would gratify us in the assemblage,
in the particulars we should detect offence. Because elegance comes of no breeding, but of birth.
There must be romance of character, or the most
fastidious exclusion of impertinencies will not avail.
It must be genius which takes that direction: it
must be not courteous, but courtesy. High behavior is as rare in fiction as it is in fact. Scott is
praised for the fidelity with which he painted the

demeanor and conversation of the superior classes.
Certainly, kings and queens, nobles and great ladies, had some right to complain of the absurdity
that had been put in their mouths before the days
of Waverley; but neither does Scott's dialogue
bear criticism. His lords brave each other in
smart epigrammatic speeches, but the dialogue is
in costume, and does not please on the second
reading : it is not warm with life. In Shakspeare
alone the speakers do not strut and bridle, the dialogue is easily great, and he adds to so many titles
that of being the best-bred man in England and
in Christendom. Once or twice in a lifetime we
are permitted to enjoy the charm of noble manners,
in the presence of a man or woman who have no
bar in their nature, but whose character emanates
freely in their word and gesture. A beautiful
form is better than a beautiful face; a beautiful
behavior is better than a beautiful form : it gives
a higher pleasure than statues or pictures ; it is the
finest of the fine arts. A man is but a little thing
in the midst of the objects of nature, yet, by the
moral quality radiating from his countenance he
may abolish all considerations of magnitude, and
in his manners equal the majesty of the world. I
have seen an individual whose manners, though
wholly within the conventions of elegant society,
were never learned there, but were original and

commanding and held out protection and prosperity; one who did not need the aid of a court-suit,
but carried the holiday in his eye; who exhilarated
the fancy by flinging wide the doors of new modes
of existence; who shook off the captivity of etiquette, with happy, spirited bearing, good-natured
and free as Robin Hood; yet with the port of an
emperor, if need be,—calm, serious, and fit to
stand the gaze of millions.

The open air and the fields, the street and public chambers are the places where Man executes his
will; let him yield or divide the sceptre at the door
of the house.   Woman, with her instinct of behavior, instantly detects in man a love of trifles, any
coldness or imbecility, or, in short, any want of
that large, flowing, and magnanimous deportment
which is indispensable as an exterior in the hall.
Our American institutions have been friendly to
her, and at this moment I esteem it a chief felicity
of this country, that it excels in women.   A certain awkward consciousness of inferiority in the
men may give rise to the new chivalry in behalf of
Woman's Rights.   Certainly let her be as much
better placed in the laws and in social forms as the
most zealous reformer can ask, but I confide so entirely in her inspiring and musical nature, that I
believe only herself can show us how she shall be
served.   The wonderful generosity of her senti

ments raises her at times into heroical and godlike
regions, and verifies the pictures of Minerva, Juno,
or Polymnia; and by the firmness with which she
treads her upward path, she convinces the coarsest
calculators that another road exists than that which
their feet know.   But besides those who make
good in our imagination the place of muses and of
Delphic Sibyls, are there not women who fill our
vase with wine and roses to the brim, so that the
wine runs over and fills the house with perfume;
who inspire us with courtesy; who unloose our
tongues and we speak; who anoint our eyes and
we see?   We say things we never thought to have
said; for once, our walls of habitual reserve van-
ished and left us at large; we were children playing with children in a wide field of flowers.   Steep
us, we cried, in these influences, for days, for
weeks, and we shall be sunny poets and will write
out in many-colored words the romance that you
are.   Was it Hafiz or Firdousi that said of his
Persian Lilla, She was an elemental force, and as
tonished me by her amount of life, when I saw her
day after day radiating, every instant, redundant
joy and grace on all around her?   She was a solvent powerful to reconcile all heterogeneous persons into one society: like air or water, an element
of such a great range of affinities that it combines
readily with a thousand substances.   Where she is

present all others will be more than they are wont.
She was a unit and whole, so that whatsoever she
did, became her. She had too much sympathy and
desire to please, than that you could say her manners were marked with dignity, yet no princess
could surpass her clear and erect demeanor on each
occasion. She did not study the Persian grammar,
nor the books of the seven poets, but all the poems
of the seven seemed to be written upon her. For
though the bias of her nature was not to thought,
but to sympathy, yet was she so perfect in her own
nature as to meet intellectual persons by the fulness of her heart, warming them by her sentiments;
believing, as she did, that by dealing nobly with
all, all would show themselves noble.

I know that this Byzantine pile of chivalry or
Fashion, which seems so fair and picturesque to
those who look at the contemporary facts for science or for entertainment, is not equally pleasant
to all spectators. The constitution of our society
makes it a giant's castle to the ambitious youth
who have not found their names enrolled in its
Golden Book, and whom it has excluded from its
coveted honors and privileges. They have yet to
learn that its seeming grandeur is shadowy and relative: it is great by their allowance; its proudest
gates will fly open at the approach of their courage

and virtue. For the present distress, however, of those who are predisposed to suffer from the tyrannies of this caprice, there are easy remedies. To remove your residence a couple of miles, or at most four, will commonly relieve the most extreme susceptibility. For the advantages which fashion values are plants which thrive in very confined localities, in a few streets namely. Out of this precinct they go for nothing; are of no use in the farm, in the forest, in the market, in war, in the nuptial society, in the literary or scientific circle, at sea, in friendship, in the heaven of thought or virtue.

But we have lingered long enough in these painted courts. The worth of the thing signified must vindicate our taste for the emblem. Everything that is called fashion and courtesy humbles itself before the cause and fountain of honor, creator of titles and dignities, namely the heart of love. This is the royal blood, this the fire, which, in all countries and contingencies, will work after its kind and conquer and expand all that approaches it. This gives new meanings to every fact. This impoverishes the rich, suffering no grandeur but its own. What *is* rich? Are you rich enough to help anybody? to succor the unfashionable and the eccentric? rich enough to make the Canadian in his wagon, the itinerant with his consul's paper which commends him " To the chari

table," the swarthy Italian with his few broken
words of English, the lame pauper hunted by over-
seers from town to town, even the poor insane or
besotted wreck of man or woman, feel the noble exception of your presence and your house from the
general bleakness and stoniness; to make such feel
that they were greeted with a voice which made
them both remember and hope? What is vulgar
but to refuse the claim on acute and conclusive
reasons? What is gentle, but to allow it, and give
their heart and yours one holiday from the national
caution? Without the rich heart, wealth is an
ugly beggar. The king of Schiraz could not afford
to be so bountiful as the poor Osman who dwelt
at his gate. Osman had a humanity so broad and
deep that although his speech was so bold and free
with the Koran as to disgust all the dervishes, yet
was there never a poor outcast, eccentric, or insane
man, some fool who had cut off his beard, or who
had been mutilated under a vow, or had a pet madness in his brain, but fled at once to him; that great
heart lay there so sunny and hospitable in the centre of the country, that it seemed as if the instinct
of all sufferers drew them to his side. And the
madness which he harbored he did not share. Is
not this to be rich? this only to be rightly rich?

But I shall hear without pain that I play the
courtier very ill, and talk of that which I do not

well understand. It is easy to see that what i
called by distinction society and fashion has goo'
laws as well as bad, has much that is necessary,
and much that is absurd. Too good for banning,
and too bad for blessing, it reminds us of a tra
dition of the pagan mythology, in any attempt to
settle its character. ' I overheard Jove, one day,'
said Silenus, ' talking of destroying the earth; he
said it had failed ; they were all rogues and vixens,
who went from bad to worse, as fast as the days
succeeded each other. Minerva said she hoped not;
they were only ridiculous little creatures, with this
odd circumstance, that they had a blur, or indeter-
minate aspect, seen far or seen near; if you called
them bad, they would appear so; if you called
them good, they would appear so ; and there was
no one person or action among them which would
not puzzle her owl, much more all Olympus, to
know whether it was fundamentally bad or good.'

GIFTS.

———◆———

Gifts of one who loved me,
'T was high time they came;
When he ceased to love me,
Time they stopped for shame.

GIFTS.

———◆——

IT is said that the world is in a state of bank‹
ruptcy; that the world owes the world more than
the world can pay, and ought to go into chancery
and be sold. I do not think this general insolvency,
which involves in some sort all the population, to
be the reason of the difficulty experienced at Christ-
mas and New Year and other times, in bestowing
gifts; since it is always so pleasant to be generous,
though very vexatious to pay debts. But the impediment lies in the choosing. If at any time it
comes into my head that a present is due from me
to somebody, I am puzzled what to give, until the
opportunity is gone. Flowers and fruits are always fit presents; flowers, because they are a proud
assertion that a ray of beauty outvalues all the
utilities of the world. These gay natures contrast
with the somewhat stern countenance of ordinary
nature: they are like music heard out of a work‹
house. Nature does not cocker us; we are chil‹
dren, not pets; she is not fond; everything is

dealt to us without fear or favor, after severe universal laws. Yet these delicate flowers look like
the frolic and interference of love and beauty.
Men use to tell us that we love flattery even though
we are not deceived by it, because it shows that
we are of importance enough to be courted. Something like that pleasure, the flowers give us : what
am I to whom these sweet hints are addressed ?
Fruits are acceptable gifts, because they are the
flower of commodities, and admit of fantastic values being attached to them. If a man should send
to me to come a hundred miles to visit him and
should set before me a basket of fine summer-fruit,
I should think there was some proportion between
the labor and the reward.

For common gifts, necessity makes pertinences
and beauty every day, and one is glad when an im-
perative leaves him no option ; since if the man at
the door have no shoes, you have not to consider
whether you could procure him a paint-box. And
as it is always pleasing to see a man eat bread, or
drink water, in the house or out of doors, so it
is always a great satisfaction to supply these first
wants. Necessity does everything well. In our condition of universal dependence it seems heroic to
let the petitioner be the judge of his necessity, and
to give all that is asked, though at great inconvenience. If it be a fantastic desire, it is better to

leave to others the office of punishing him. I can
think of many parts I should prefer playing to that
of the Furies. Next to things of necessity, the
rule for a gift, which one of my friends prescribed,
is that we might convey to some person that which
properly belonged to his character, and was easily
associated with him in thought. But our tokens
of compliment and love are for the most part barbarous. Rings and other jewels are not gifts, but
apologies for gifts. The only gift is a portion of
thyself. Thou must bleed for me. Therefore the
poet brings his poem; the shepherd, his lamb; the
farmer, corn; the miner, a gem; the sailor, coral
and shells; the painter, his picture; the girl, a
handkerchief of her own sewing. This is right and
pleasing, for it restores society in so far to the primary basis, when a man's biography is conveyed
in his gift, and every man's wealth is an index of
his merit. But it is a cold lifeless business when
you go to the shops to buy me something which
does not represent your life and talent, but a gold-
smith's. This is fit for kings, and rich men who
represent kings, and a false state of property, to
make presents of gold and silver stuffs, as a kind
of symbolical sin-offering, or payment of black-
mail.

The law of benefits is a difficult channel, which
requires careful sailing, or rude boats. It is not

the office of a man to receive gifts. How dare you
give them? We wish to be self-sustained. We do
not quite forgive a giver. The hand that feeds us
is in some danger of being bitten. We can receive
anything from love, for that is a way of receiving
it from ourselves; but not from any one who assumes to bestow. We sometimes hate the meat
which we eat, because there seems something of
degrading dependence in living by it: —

> " Brother, if Jove to thee a present make,
>   Take heed that from his hands thou nothing take."

We ask the whole. Nothing less will content us.
We arraign society if it do not give us, besides
earth and fire and water, opportunity, love, reverence, and objects of veneration.

He is a good man who can receive a gift well.
We are either glad or sorry at a gift, and both
emotions are unbecoming. Some violence I think
is done, some degradation borne, when I rejoice or
grieve at a gift. I am sorry when my independence
is invaded, or when a gift comes from such as do
not know my spirit, and so the act is not supported;
and if the gift pleases me overmuch, then I should
be ashamed that the donor should read my heart,
and see that I love his commodity, and not him.
The gift, to be true, must be the flowing of the
giver unto me, correspondent to my flowing unto

him. When the waters are at level, then my goods pass to him, and his to me. All his are mine, all mine his. I say to him, How can you give me this pot of oil or this flagon of wine when all your oil and wine is mine, which belief of mine this gift seems to deny? Hence the fitness of beautiful, not useful things, for gifts. This giving is flat usurpation, and therefore when the beneficiary is ungrateful, as all beneficiaries hate all Timons, not at all considering the value of the gift but looking back to the greater store it was taken from, — I rather sympathize with the beneficiary than with the anger of my lord Timon. For the expectation of gratitude is mean, and is continually punished by the total insensibility of the obliged person. It is a great happiness to get off without injury and heart-burning from one who has had the ill-luck to be served by you. It is a very onerous business, this of being served, and the debtor naturally wishes to give you a slap. A golden text for these gentlemen is that which I so admire in the Buddhist, who never thanks, and who says, " Do not flatter your bene-factors."

The reason of these discords I conceive to be that there is no commensurability between a man and any gift. You cannot give anything to a magnanimous person. After you have served him he at once puts you in debt by his magnanimity. The

service a man renders his friend is trivial and selfish compared with the service he knows his friend
stood in readiness to yield him, alike before he had
begun to serve his friend, and now also. Compared
with that good-will I bear my friend, the benefit it is
in my power to render him seems small. Besides
our action on each other, good as well as evil, is so
incidental and at random that we can seldom hear
the acknowledgments of any person who would
thank us for a benefit, without some shame and
humiliation. We can rarely strike a direct stroke,
but must be content with an oblique one; we seldom have the satisfaction of yielding a direct benefit which is directly received. But rectitude scatters favors on every side without knowing it, and
receives with wonder the thanks of all people.

I fear to breathe any treason against the majesty
of love, which is the genius and god of gifts, and to
whom we must not affect to prescribe. Let him
give kingdoms or flower-leaves indifferently. There
are persons from whom we always expect fairy-
tokens; let us not cease to expect them. This is
prerogative, and not to be limited by our municipal
rules. For the rest, I like to see that we cannot be
bought and sold. The best of hospitality and of
generosity is also not in the will, but in fate. I find
that I am not much to you; you do not need me;
you do not feel me; then am I thrust out of doors.

though you proffer me house and lands. No services are of any value, but only likeness. When I have attempted to join myself to others by services, it proved an intellectual trick, — no more. They eat your service like apples, and leave you out. But love them, and they feel you and delight in you all the time.

NATURE.

The rounded world is fair to see,
Nine times folded in mystery:
Though baffled seers cannot impart
The secret of its laboring heart,
Throb thine with Nature's throbbing breast,
And all is clear from east to west.
Spirit that lurks each form within
Beckons to spirit of its kin;
Self-kindled every atom glows,
And hints the future which it owes.

VI.

NATURE.

————•————

THERE are days which occur in this climate, at almost any season of the year, wherein the world reaches its perfection; when the air, the heavenly bodies and the earth, make a harmony, as if nature would indulge her offspring; when, in these bleak upper sides of the planet, nothing is to desire that we have heard of the happiest latitudes, and we bask in the shining hours of Florida and Cuba; when everything that has life gives sign of satisfaction, and the cattle that lie on the ground seem to have great and tranquil thoughts. These halcyons may be looked for with a little more assurance in that pure October weather which we distinguish by the name of the Indian summer. The day, immeasurably long, sleeps over the broad hills and warm wide fields. To have lived through all its sunny hours, seems longevity enough. The solitary places do not seem quite lonely. At the gates of the forest, the surprised man of the world is forced to leave his city estimates of great and

small, wise and foolish.   The knapsack of custom
falls off his back with the first step he takes into
these precincts.   Here is sanctity which shames
our religions, and reality which discredits our heroes.   Here we find Nature to be the circumstance
which dwarfs every other circumstance, and judges
like a god all men that come to her.   We have
crept out of our close and crowded houses into
the night and morning, and we see what majestic beauties daily wrap us in their bosom.   How
willingly we would escape the barriers which render them comparatively impotent, escape the so-
phistication and second thought, and suffer nature
to intrance us.   The tempered light of the woods
is like a perpetual morning, and is stimulating and
heroic.   The anciently - reported spells of these
places creep on us.   The stems of pines, hemlocks,
and oaks almost gleam like iron on the excited eye.
The incommunicable trees begin to persuade us to
live with them, and quit our life of solemn trifles.
Here no history, or church, or state, is interpolated
on the divine sky and the immortal year.   How
easily we might walk onward into the opening landscape, absorbed by new pictures and by thoughts
fast succeeding each other, until by degrees the recollection of home was crowded out of the mind, all
memory obliterated by the tyranny of the present,
and we were led in triumph by nature.

These enchantments are medicinal, they sober
and heal us. These are plain pleasures, kindly and
native to us. We come to our own, and make
friends with matter, which the ambitious chatter
of the schools would persuade us to despise. We
never can part with it; the mind loves its old home;
as water to our thirst, so is the rock, the ground, to
our eyes and hands and feet. It is firm water; it
is cold flame; what health, what affinity! Ever
an old friend, ever like a dear friend and brother
when we chat affectedly with strangers, comes in
this honest face, and takes a grave liberty with us,
and shames us out of our nonsense. Cities give
not the human senses room enough. We go out
daily and nightly to feed the eyes on the horizon,
and require so much scope, just as we need water
for our bath. There are all degrees of natural influence, from these quarantine powers of nature, up
to her dearest and gravest ministrations to the imagination and the soul. There is the bucket of
cold water from the spring, the wood-fire to which
the chilled traveller rushes for safety, — and there
is the sublime moral of autumn and of noon. We
nestle in nature, and draw our living as parasites
from her roots and grains, and we receive glances
from the heavenly bodies, which call us to solitude
and foretell the remotest future. The blue zenith
is the point in which romance and reality meet. I

think if we should be rapt away into all that we dream of heaven, and should converse with Gabriel and Uriel, the upper sky would be all that would remain of our furniture.

It seems as if the day was not wholly profane in which we have given heed to some natural object. The fall of snowflakes in a still air, preserving to each crystal its perfect form; the blowing of sleet over a wide sheet of water, and over plains; the waving ryefield; the mimic waving of acres of houstonia, whose innumerable florets whiten and ripple before the eye; the reflections of trees and flowers in glassy lakes; the musical steaming odorous south wind, which converts all trees to windharps; the crackling and spurting of hemlock in the flames, or of pine logs, which yield glory to the walls and faces in the sittingroom, — these are the music and pictures of the most ancient religion. My house stands in low land, with limited outlook, and on the skirt of the village. But I go with my friend to the shore of our little river, and with one stroke of the paddle I leave the village politics and personalities, yes, and the world of villages and personalities, behind, and pass into a delicate realm of sunset and moonlight, too bright almost for spotted man to enter without novitiate and probation. We penetrate bodily this incredible beauty; we dip our hands in this painted element; our eyes

are bathed in these lights and forms. A holiday, a villeggiatura, a royal revel, the proudest,
most heart-rejoicing festival that valor and beauty,
power and taste, ever decked and enjoyed, establishes itself on the instant. These sunset clouds,
these delicately emerging stars, with their private
and ineffable glances, signify it and proffer it. I
am taught the poorness of our invention, the ugliness of towns and palaces. Art and luxury have
early learned that they must work as enhancement
and sequel to this original beauty. I am overin-
structed for my return. Henceforth I shall be
hard to please. I cannot go back to toys. I am
grown expensive and sophisticated. I can no
longer live without elegance, but a countryman
shall be my master of revels. He who knows the
most; he who knows what sweets and virtues are
in the ground, the waters, the plants, the heavens,
and how to come at these enchantments, — is the
rich and royal man. Only as far as the masters of
the world have called in nature to their aid, can
they reach the height of magnificence. This is the
meaning of their hanging-gardens, villas, garden-
houses, islands, parks and preserves, to back their
faulty personality with these strong accessories. I
do not wonder that the landed interest should be
invincible in the State with these dangerous auxiliaries. These bribe and invite; not kings, not pal

aces, not men, not women, but these tender and
poetic stars, eloquent of secret promises. We heard
what the rich man said, we knew of his villa, his
grove, his wine and his company, but the provoca-
tion and point of the invitation came out of these
beguiling stars. In their soft glances I see what
men strove to realize in some Versailles, or Paphos,
or Ctesiphon. Indeed, it is the magical lights of
the horizon and the blue sky for the background
which save all our works of art, which were otherwise bawbles. When the rich tax the poor with ser-
vility and obsequiousness, they should consider the
effect of men reputed to be the possessors of nature,
on imaginative minds. Ah! if the rich were rich
as the poor fancy riches! A boy hears a military
band play on the field at night, and he has kings
and queens and famous chivalry palpably before
him. He hears the echoes of a horn in a hill country, in the Notch Mountains, for example, which
converts the mountains into an Æolian harp, —
and this supernatural *tiralira* restores to him the
Dorian mythology, Apollo, Diana, and all divine
hunters and huntresses. Can a musical note be so
lofty, so haughtily beautiful! To the poor young
poet, thus fabulous is his picture of society; he is
loyal; he respects the rich; they are rich for the
sake of his imagination; how poor his fancy would
be, if they were not rich! That they have some

high-fenced grove which they call a park ; that
they live in larger and better-garnished saloons
than he has visited, and go in coaches, keeping only
the society of the elegant, to watering-places and to
distant cities, — these make the groundwork from
which he has delineated estates of romance, compared with which their actual possessions are shan-
ties and paddocks. The muse herself betrays her
son, and enhances the gifts of wealth and well-born
beauty by a radiation out of the air, and clouds,
and forests that skirt the road, — a certain haughty
favor, as if from patrician genii to patricians, a
kind of aristocracy in nature, a prince of the power
of the air.

The moral sensibility which makes Edens and
Tempes so easily, may not be always found, but the
material landscape is never far off. We can find
these enchantments without visiting the Como Lake,
or the Madeira Islands. We exaggerate the praises
of local scenery. In every landscape the point of
astonishment is the meeting of the sky and the
earth, and that is seen from the first hillock
as well as from the top of the Alleghanies. The
stars at night stoop down over the brownest, home-
liest common with all the spiritual magnificence
which they shed on the Campagna, or on the marble deserts of Egypt. The uprolled clouds and the
colors of morning and evening will transfigure

maples and alders. The difference between landscape and landscape is small, but there is great
difference in the beholders. There is nothing so
wonderful in any particular landscape as the necessity of being beautiful under which every landscape
lies. Nature cannot be surprised in undress. Beauty breaks in everywhere.

But it is very easy to outrun the sympathy of
readers on this topic, which schoolmen called *natura
naturata*, or nature passive. One can hardly speak
directly of it without excess. It is as easy to broach
in mixed companies what is called " the subject of
religion." A susceptible person does not like to indulge his tastes in this kind without the apology of
some trivial necessity: he goes to see a wood-lot, or
to look at the crops, or to fetch a plant or a mineral
from a remote locality, or he carries a fowling-piece
or a fishing-rod. I suppose this shame must have
a good reason. A dilettantism in nature is barren
and unworthy. The fop of fields is no better than
his brother of Broadway. Men are naturally hunters and inquisitive of wood-craft, and I suppose
that such a gazetteer as wood-cutters and Indians
should furnish facts for, would take place in the
most sumptuous drawing-rooms of all the "Wreaths"
and " Flora's chaplets " of the bookshops; yet ordinarily, whether we are too clumsy for so subtle a
topic, or from whatever cause, as soon as men begin

to write on nature, they fall into euphuism. **Frivolity** is a most unfit tribute to Pan, who ought **to** be represented in the mythology as the most continent of gods. I would not be frivolous before the admirable reserve and prudence of time, yet I cannot renounce the right of returning often to this old topic. The multitude of false churches accredits the true religion. Literature, poetry, science are the homage of man to this unfathomed secret, concerning which no sane man can affect an indifference or incuriosity. Nature is loved by what is best in us. It is loved as the city of God, although, or rather because there is no citizen. The sunset is unlike anything that is underneath it: it wants men. And the beauty of nature must always seem unreal and mocking, until the landscape has human figures that are as good as itself. If there were good men, there would never be this rapture in nature. If the king is in the palace, nobody looks at the walls. It is when he is gone, and the house is filled with grooms and gazers, that we turn from the people to find relief in the majestic men that are suggested by the pictures and the architecture. The critics who complain of the sickly separation of the beauty of nature from the thing to be done, must consider that our hunting of the picturesque is inseparable from our protest against false society. Man is fallen; nature is erect, and serves as a differential thermometer, detecting the presence or absence of the divine sentiment in man. By fault of our dulness and selfishness we are looking up to nature, but when we are convalescent, nature will look up to us. We see the foaming brook with compunction : if our own life flowed with the right energy, we should shame the brook. The stream of zeal sparkles with real fire, and not with reflex rays of sun and moon. Nature may be as selfishly studied as trade. Astronomy to the selfish becomes astrology; psychology, mesmerism (with intent to show where our spoons are gone); and anatomy and physiology become phrenology and palmistry.

But taking timely warning, and leaving many things unsaid on this topic, let us not longer omit our homage to the Efficient Nature, *natura natu-rans*, the quick cause before which all forms flee as the driven snows; itself secret, its works driven before it in flocks and multitudes, (as the ancients represented nature by Proteus, a shepherd,) and in undescribable variety. It publishes itself in crea-tures, reaching from particles and spiculæ through transformation on transformation to the highest symmetries, arriving at consummate results without a shock or a leap. A little heat, that is a little mo-tion, is all that differences the bald, dazzling white and deadly cold poles of the earth from the prolific tropical climates. All changes pass without vio-

lence, by reason of the two cardinal conditions of
boundless space and boundless time. Geology has
initiated us into the secularity of nature, and taught
us to disuse our dame-school measures, and exchange
our Mosaic and Ptolemaic schemes for her large
style. We knew nothing rightly, for want of perspective. Now we learn what patient periods must
round themselves before the rock is formed; then
before the rock is broken, and the first lichen race
has disintegrated the thinnest external plate into
soil, and opened the door for the remote Flora,
Fauna, Ceres, and Pomona to come in. How far
off yet is the trilobite! how far the quadruped!
how inconceivably remote is man! All duly arrive,
and then race after race of men. It is a long way
from granite to the oyster; farther yet to Plato and
the preaching of the immortality of the soul. Yet
all must come, as surely as the first atom has two
sides.

Motion or change and identity or rest are the
first and second secrets of nature : — Motion and
Rest. The whole code of her laws may be written
on the thumbnail, or the signet of a ring. The
whirling bubble on the surface of a brook admits
us to the secret of the mechanics of the sky. Every
shell on the beach is a key to it. A little water
made to rotate in a cup explains the formation of
the simpler shells; the addition of matter from

year to year arrives at last at the most complex forms; and yet so poor is nature with all her craft, that from the beginning to the end of the universe she has but one stuff, — but one stuff with its two ends, to serve up all her dream-like variety. Compound it how she will, star, sand, fire, water, tree, man, it is still one stuff, and betrays the same properties.

Nature is always consistent, though she feigns to contravene her own laws. She keeps her laws, and seems to transcend them. She arms and equips an animal to find its place and living in the earth, and at the same time she arms and equips another animal to destroy it. Space exists to divide creatures; but by clothing the sides of a bird with a few feathers she gives him a petty omnipresence. The direction is forever onward, but the artist still goes back for materials and begins again with the first elements on the most advanced stage : otherwise all goes to ruin. If we look at her work, we seem to catch a glance of a system in transition. Plants are the young of the world, vessels of health and vigor; but they grope ever upward towards consciousness; the trees are imperfect men, and seem to bemoan their imprisonment, rooted in the ground. The animal is the novice and probationer of a more advanced order. The men, though young, having tasted the first drop from the cup of thought, are already dissipated : the maples and ferns are still uncorrupt ; yet no doubt when they come to consciousness they too will curse and swear. Flowers so strictly belong to youth that we adult men soon come to feel that their beautiful generations con cern not us : we have had our day ; now let the children have theirs. The flowers jilt us, and we are old bachelors with our ridiculous tenderness.

Things are so strictly related, that according to the skill of the eye, from any one object the parts and properties of any other may be predicted. If we had eyes to see it, a bit of stone from the city wall would certify us of the necessity that man must exist, as readily as the city. That identity makes us all one, and reduces to nothing great intervals on our customary scale. We talk of deviations from natural life, as if artificial life were not also natural. The smoothest curled courtier in the boudoirs of a palace has an animal nature, rude and aboriginal as a white bear, omnipotent to its own ends, and is directly related, there amid essences and billetsdoux, to Himmaleh mountain chains and the axis of the globe. If we consider how much we are nature's, we need not be superstitious about towns, as if that terrific or benefic force did not find us there also, and fashion cities. Nature, who made the mason, made the house. We may easily hear too much of rural influences. The

cool disengaged air of natural objects makes them
enviable to us, chafed and irritable creatures with
red faces, and we think we shall be as grand as
they if we camp out and eat roots ; but let us be
men instead of woodchucks and the oak and the
elm shall gladly serve us, though we sit in chairs
of ivory on carpets of silk.

This guiding identity runs through all the surprises and contrasts of the piece, and characterizes
every law. Man carries the world in his head, the
whole astronomy and chemistry suspended in a
thought. Because the history of nature is charac-
tered in his brain, therefore is he the prophet and
discoverer of her secrets. Every known fact in
natural science was divined by the presentiment of
somebody, before it was actually verified. A man
does not tie his shoe without recognizing laws which
bind the farthest regions of nature : moon, plant,
gas, crystal, are concrete geometry and numbers.
Common sense knows its own, and recognizes the
fact at first sight in chemical experiment. The
common sense of Franklin, Dalton, Davy and
Black, is the same common sense which made the
arrangements which now it discovers.

If the identity expresses organized rest, the counter action runs also into organization. The astronomers said, ' Give us matter and a little motion and
we will construct the universe. It is not enough

that we should have matter, we must also have
a single impulse, one shove to launch the mass and
generate the harmony of the centrifugal and centripetal forces. Once heave the ball from the hand,
and we can show how all this mighty order grew.'
— ' A very unreasonable postulate,' said the meta-
physicians, 'and a plain begging of the question.
Could you not prevail to know the genesis of pro-
jection, as well as the continuation of it?' Nature,
meanwhile, had not waited for the discussion, but,
right or wrong, bestowed the impulse, and the balls
rolled. It was no great affair, a mere push, but the
astronomers were right in making much of it, for
there is no end to the consequences of the act. That
famous aboriginal push propagates itself through
all the balls of the system, and through every atom
of every ball; through all the races of creatures,
and through the history and performances of every
individual. Exaggeration is in the course of things.
Nature sends no creature, no man into the world
without adding a small excess of his proper quality.
Given the planet, it is still necessary to add the
impulse; so to every creature nature added a little
violence of direction in its proper path, a shove to
put it on its way; in every instance a slight generosity, a drop too much. Without electricity the
air would rot, and without this violence of direction which men and women have, without a spice of

bigot and fanatic, no excitement, no efficiency. We
aim above the mark to hit the mark. Every act
hath some falsehood of exaggeration in it. And
when now and then comes along some sad, sharp-
eyed man, who sees how paltry a game is played,
and refuses to play but blabs the secret; — how
then? Is the bird flown? O no, the wary Nature sends a new troop of fairer forms, of lordlier
youths, with a little more excess of direction to hold
them fast to their several aim; makes them a little
wrong-headed in that direction in which they are
rightest, and on goes the game again with new whirl,
for a generation or two more. The child with his
sweet pranks, the fool of his senses, commanded by
every sight and sound, without any power to compare and rank his sensations, abandoned to a whistle
or a painted chip, to a lead dragoon or a ginger-
bread-dog, individualizing everything, generalizing
nothing, delighted with every new thing, lies down
at night overpowered by the fatigue which this day
of continual pretty madness has incurred. But Nature has answered her purpose with the curly, dim-
pled lunatic. She has tasked every faculty, and has
secured the symmetrical growth of the bodily frame
by all these attitudes and exertions, — an end of the
first importance, which could not be trusted to any
care less perfect than her own. This glitter, this
opaline lustre plays round the top of every toy to

his eye to insure his fidelity, and he is deceived to his good. We are made alive and kept alive by the same arts. Let the stoics say what they please, we do not eat for the good of living, but because the meat is savory and the appetite is keen. The vegetable life does not content itself with casting from the flower or the tree a single seed, but it fills the air and earth with a prodigality of seeds, that, if thousands perish, thousands may plant themselves; that hundreds may come up, that tens may live to maturity; that at least one may replace the parent. All things betray the same calculated profusion. The excess of fear with which the animal frame is hedged round, shrinking from cold, starting at sight of a snake or at a sudden noise, protects us, through a multitude of groundless alarms, from some one real danger at last. The lover seeks in marriage his private felicity and perfection, with no prospective end; and nature hides in his happiness her own end, namely progeny, or the perpetuity of the race.

But the craft with which the world is made, runs also into the mind and character of men. No man is quite sane; each has a vein of folly in his composition, a slight determination of blood to the head, to make sure of holding him hard to some one point which nature had taken to heart. Great causes are never tried on their merits; but the cause is re-

duced to particulars to suit the size of the partisans,
and the contention is ever hottest on minor matters.
Not less remarkable is the overfaith of each man in
the importance of what he has to do or say.   The
poet, the prophet, has a higher value for what he
utters than any hearer, and therefore it gets spoken.
The strong, self-complacent Luther declares with
an emphasis not to be mistaken, that " God himself cannot do without wise men."   Jacob Behmen
and George Fox betray their egotism in the perti-
nacity of their controversial tracts, and James Nay-
lor once suffered himself to be worshipped as the
Christ.   Each prophet comes presently to identify
himself with his thought, and to esteem his hat and
shoes sacred.   However this may discredit such persons with the judicious, it helps them with the people, as it gives heat, pungency, and publicity to
their words.   A similar experience is not infrequent
in private life.   Each young and ardent person
writes a diary, in which, when the hours of prayer
and penitence arrive, he inscribes his soul.   The
pages thus written are to him burning and fragrant ;
he reads them on his knees by midnight and by the
morning star ; he wets them with his tears ; they
are sacred ; too good for the world, and hardly yet
to be shown to the dearest friend.   This is the man-
child that is born to the soul, and her life still cir-
culates in the babe.   The umbilical cord has not yet

been cut. After some time has elapsed, he begins to wish to admit his friend to this hallowed experience, and with hesitation, yet with firmness, exposes the pages to his eye. Will they not burn his eyes? The friend coldly turns them over, and passes from the writing to conversation, with easy transition, which strikes the other party with astonishment and vexation. He cannot suspect the writing itself. Days and nights of fervid life, of communion with angels of darkness and of light have engraved their shadowy characters on that tear-stained book. He suspects the intelligence or the heart of his friend. Is there then no friend? He cannot yet credit that one may have impressive experience and yet may not know how to put his private fact into literature: and perhaps the discovery that wisdom has other tongues and ministers than we, that though we should hold our peace the truth would not the less be spoken, might check injuriously the flames of our zeal. A man can only speak so long as he does not feel his speech to be partial and inadequate. It is partial, but he does not see it to be so whilst he utters it. As soon as he is released from the instinctive and particular and sees its partiality, he shuts his mouth in disgust. For no man can write anything who does not think that what he writes is for the time the history of the world; or do anything well who does not esteem his work to be of

importance. My work may be of none, but I must
not think it of none, or I shall not do it with im-
punity.

In like manner, there is throughout nature something mocking, something that leads us on and on,
but arrives nowhere; keeps no faith with us. All
promise outruns the performance. We live in a
system of approximations. Every end is prospective of some other end, which is also temporary;
a round and final success nowhere. We are en-
camped in nature, not domesticated. Hunger and
thirst lead us on to eat and to drink; but bread and
wine, mix and cook them how you will, leave us
hungry and thirsty, after the stomach is full. It is
the same with all our arts and performances. Our
music, our poetry, our language itself are not satisfactions, but suggestions. The hunger for wealth,
which reduces the planet to a garden, fools the
eager pursuer. What is the end sought? Plainly
to secure the ends of good sense and beauty from
the intrusion of deformity or vulgarity of any kind.
But what an operose method! What a train of
means to secure a little conversation! This palace
of brick and stone, these servants, this kitchen,
these stables, horses and equipage, this bank-stock
and file of mortgages; trade to all the world, coun-
try-house and cottage by the waterside, all for a
little conversation, high, clear, and spiritual! Could

it not be had as well by beggars on the highway? No, all these things came from successive
efforts of these beggars to remove friction from the
wheels of life, and give opportunity. Conversation, character, were the avowed ends; wealth was
good as it appeased the animal cravings, cured the
smoky chimney, silenced the creaking door, brought
friends together in a warm and quiet room, and
kept the children and the dinner-table in a different apartment. Thought, virtue, beauty, were the
ends; but it was known that men of thought and
virtue sometimes had the headache, or wet feet, or
could lose good time whilst the room was getting
warm in winter days. Unluckily, in the exertions
necessary to remove these inconveniences, the main
attention has been diverted to this object; the
old aims have been lost sight of, and to remove
friction has come to be the end. That is the ridicule of rich men; and Boston, London, Vienna, and
now the governments generally of the world are
cities and governments of the rich; and the masses
are not men, but *poor men*, that is, men who would
be rich; this is the ridicule of the class, that they
arrive with pains and sweat and fury nowhere;
when all is done, it is for nothing. They are like
one who has interrupted the conversation of a
company to make his speech, and now has forgotten what he went to say. The appearance strikes

the eye everywhere of an aimless society, of aimless nations. Were the ends of nature so great
and cogent as to exact this immense sacrifice of
men?

Quite analogous to the deceits in life, there is,
as might be expected, a similar effect on the eye
from the face of external nature. There is in
woods and waters a certain enticement and flattery, together with a failure to yield a present satisfaction. This disappointment is felt in every
landscape. I have seen the softness and beauty
of the summer clouds floating feathery overhead,
enjoying, as it seemed, their height and privilege
of motion, whilst yet they appeared not so much
the drapery of this place and hour, as forelooking
to some pavilions and gardens of festivity beyond.
It is an odd jealousy, but the poet finds himself
not near enough to his object. The pine-tree, the
river, the bank of flowers before him does not seem
to be nature. Nature is still elsewhere. This or
this is but outskirt and far-off reflection and echo
of the triumph that has passed by and is now at
its glancing splendor and heyday, perchance in the
neighboring fields, or, if you stand in the field,
then in the adjacent woods. The present object
shall give you this sense of stillness that follows a
pageant which has just gone by. What splendid
distance, what recesses of ineffable pomp and love

finess in the sunset! But who can go where they are, or lay his hand or plant his foot thereon? Off they fall from the round world forever and ever. It is the same among the men and women as among the silent trees; always a referred existence, an absence, never a presence and satisfaction. Is it that beauty can never be grasped? in persons and in landscape is equally inaccessible? The accepted and betrothed lover has lost the wildest charm of his maiden in her acceptance of him. She was heaven whilst he pursued her as a star: she cannot be heaven if she stoops to such a one as he.

What shall we say of this omnipresent appearance of that first projectile impulse, of this flattery and balking of so many well-meaning creatures? Must we not suppose somewhere in the universe a slight treachery and derision? Are we not engaged to a serious resentment of this use that is made of us? Are we tickled trout, and fools of nature? One look at the face of heaven and earth lays all petulance at rest, and soothes us to wiser convictions. To the intelligent, nature converts itself into a vast promise, and will not be rashly explained. Her secret is untold. Many and many an Œdipus arrives; he has the whole mystery teeming in his brain. Alas! the same sorcery has spoiled his skill; no syllable can he shape on his lips. Her mighty orbit vaults like the fresh rainbow into the deep, but no archangel's wing was yet strong enough to follow it and report of the return of the curve. But it also appears that our actions are seconded and disposed to greater conclusions than we designed. We are escorted on every hand through life by spiritual agents, and a beneficent purpose lies in wai' for us. We cannot bandy words with Nature, or deal with her as we deal with persons. If we measure our individual forces against hers we may easily feel as if we were the sport of an insuperable destiny. But if, instead of identifying ourselves with the work, we feel that the soul of the workman streams through us, we shall find the peace of the morning dwelling first in our hearts, and the fathomless powers of gravity and chemistry, and, over them, of life, preëxisting within us in their highest form.

The uneasiness which the thought of our helplessness in the chain of causes occasions us, results from looking too much at one condition of nature, namely, Motion. But the drag is never taken from the wheel. Wherever the impulse exceeds, the Rest or Identity insinuates its compensation. All over the wide fields of earth grows the prunella or self-heal. After every foolish day we sleep off the fumes and furies of its hours; and though we are always engaged with particulars, and often enslaved

to them, we bring with us to every experiment the
innate universal laws.   These, while they exist in
the mind as ideas, stand around us in nature forever embodied, a present sanity to expose and cure
the insanity of men.   Our servitude to particulars betrays us into a hundred foolish expectations.
We anticipate a new era from the invention of a
locomotive, or a balloon; the new engine brings
with it the old checks.   They say that by electro-
magnetism your salad shall be grown from the seed
whilst your fowl is roasting for dinner; it is a symbol of our modern aims and endeavors, of our con-
densation and acceleration of objects; — but nothing is gained; nature cannot be cheated; man's life
is but seventy salads long, grow they swift or grow
they slow.   In these checks and impossibilities however we find our advantage, not less than in the impulses.   Let the victory fall where it will, we are
on that side.   And the knowledge that we traverse
the whole scale of being, from the centre to the
poles of nature, and have some stake in every possibility, lends that sublime lustre to death, which
philosophy and religion have too outwardly and lit-
erally striven to express in the popular doctrine of
the immortality of the soul.   The reality is more
excellent than the report.   Here is no ruin, no dis-
continuity, no spent ball.   The divine circulations
never rest nor linger.   Nature is the incarnation of

a thought, and turns to a thought again, as ice becomes water and gas. The world is mind precipi-
tated, and the volatile essence is forever escaping
again into the state of free thought. Hence the virtue and pungency of the influence on the mind
of natural objects, whether inorganic or organized.
Man imprisoned, man crystallized, man vegetative,
speaks to man impersonated. That power which
does not respect quantity, which makes the whole
and the particle its equal channel, delegates its smile
to the morning, and distils its essence into every
drop of rain. Every moment instructs, and every
object; for wisdom is infused into every form. It
has been poured into us as blood; it convulsed us
as pain; it slid into us as pleasure; it enveloped us
in dull, melancholy days, or in days of cheerful labor; we did not guess its essence until after a long
time.

POLITICS.

Gold and iron are good
To buy iron and gold;
All earth's fleece and food
For their like are sold.
Boded Merlin wise,
Proved Napoleon great, —
Nor kind nor coinage buys
Aught above its rate.
Fear, Craft, and Avarice
Cannot rear a State.
Out of dust to build
What is more than dust, —
Walls Amphion piled
Phœbus stablish must.
When the Muses nine
With the Virtues meet,
Find to their design
An Atlantic seat,
By green orchard boughs
Fended from the heat,
Where the statesman ploughs
Furrow for the wheat;
When the Church is social worth,
When the state-house is the hearth,
Then the perfect State is come,
The republican at home.

POLITICS.

———◆———

In dealing with the State we ought to remember
that its institutions are not aboriginal, though they
existed before we were born ; that they are not superior to the citizen ; that every one of them was
once the act of a single man ; every law and usage
was a man's expedient to meet a particular case ;
that they all are imitable, all alterable ; we may
make as good, we may make better. Society is an
illusion to the young citizen. It lies before him in
rigid repose, with certain names, men and institutions rooted like oak-trees to the centre, round
which all arrange themselves the best they can.
But the old statesman knows that society is fluid ;
there are no such roots and centres, but any particle may suddenly become the centre of the movement and compel the system to gyrate round it ; as
every man of strong will, like Pisistratus or Cromwell, does for a time, and every man of truth, like
Plato or Paul, does forever. But politics rest on
necessary foundations, and cannot be treated with

levity. Republics abound in young civilians who believe that the laws make the city, that grave modifications of the policy and modes of living and employments of the population, that commerce, education, and religion, may be voted in or out ; and that any measure, though it were absurd, may be imposed on a people if only you can get sufficient voices to make it a law. But the wise know that foolish legislation is a rope of sand which perishes in the twisting ; that the State must follow and not lead the character and progress of the citizen ; the strongest usurper is quickly got rid of ; and they only who build on Ideas, build for eternity ; and that the form of government which prevails is the expression of what cultivation exists in the population which permits it. The law is only a memorandum. We are superstitious, and esteem the statute somewhat : so much life as it has in the character of living men is its force. The statute stands there to say, Yesterday we agreed so and so, but how feel ye this article to-day ? Our statute is a currency which we stamp with our own portrait : it soon becomes unrecognizable, and in process of time will return to the mint. Nature is not democratic, nor limited-monarchical, but despotic, and will not be fooled or abated of any jot of her authority by the pertest of her sons ; and as fast as the public mind is opened to more intelligence, the

code is seen to be brute and stammering. It speaks
not articulately, and must be made to. Meantime
the education of the general mind never stops
The reveries of the true and simple are prophetic.
What the tender poetic youth dreams, and prays,
and paints to-day, but shuns the ridicule of saying
aloud, shall presently be the resolutions of public
bodies ; then shall be carried as grievance and bill
of rights through conflict and war, and then shall
be triumphant law and establishment for a hundred years, until it gives place in turn to new prayers and pictures. The history of the State sketches
in coarse outline the progress of thought, and follows at a distance the delicacy of culture and of aspiration.

The theory of politics which has possessed the
mind of men, and which they have expressed the
best they could in their laws and in their revolutions, considers persons and property as the two objects for whose protection government exists. Of
persons, all have equal rights, in virtue of being
identical in nature. This interest of course with
its whole power demands a democracy. Whilst the
rights of all as persons are equal, in virtue of their
access to reason, their rights in property are very
unequal. One man owns his clothes, and another
owns a county. This accident, depending primarily on the skill and virtue of the parties, of which

there is every degree, and secondarily on patrimo‹
ny, falls unequally, and its rights of course are
unequal.   Personal rights, universally the same,
demand a government framed on the ratio of the
census ; property demands a government framed
on the ratio of owners and of owning.   Laban, who
has flocks and herds, wishes them looked after by
an officer on the frontiers, lest the Midianites shall
drive them off ; and pays a tax to that end.   Jacob
has no flocks or herds and no fear of the Midianites, and pays no tax to the officer.   It seemed fit
that Laban and Jacob should have equal rights to
elect the officer who is to defend their persons, but
that Laban and not Jacob should elect the officer
who is to guard the sheep and cattle.   And if question arise whether additional officers or watch-tow-
ers should be provided, must not Laban and Isaac,
and those who must sell part of their herds to buy
protection for the rest, judge better of this, and with
more right, than Jacob, who, because he is a youth
and a traveller, eats their bread and not his own ?

In the earliest society the proprietors made their
own wealth, and so long as it comes to the owners
in the direct way, no other opinion would arise in
any equitable community than that property should
make the law for property, and persons the law for
persons.

But property passes through donation or inherit

ence to those who do not create it. Gift, in one case, makes it as really the new owner's, as labor made it the first owner's: in the other case, of patrimony, the law makes an ownership which will be valid in each man's view according to the estimate which he sets on the public tranquillity.

It was not however found easy to embody the readily admitted principle that property should make law for property, and persons for persons; since persons and property mixed themselves in every transaction. At last it seemed settled that the rightful distinction was that the proprietors should have more elective franchise than non-proprietors, on the Spartan principle of " calling that which is just, equal; not that which is equal, just."

That principle no longer looks so self-evident as it appeared in former times, partly because doubts have arisen whether too much weight had not been allowed in the laws to property, and such a structure given to our usages as allowed the rich to encroach on the poor, and to keep them poor; but mainly because there is an instinctive sense, however obscure and yet inarticulate, that the whole constitution of property, on its present tenures, is njurious, and its influence on persons deteriorating and degrading; that truly the only interest for the consideration of the State is persons; that property will always follow persons; that the highest end of government is the culture of men ; and that if men can be educated, the institutions will share their improvement and the moral sentiment will write the law of the land.

If it be not easy to settle the equity of this question, the peril is less when we take note of our natural defences. We are kept by better guards than the vigilance of such magistrates as we commonly elect. Society always consists in greatest part of young and foolish persons. The old, who have seen through the hypocrisy of courts and statesmen, die and leave no wisdom to their sons. They believe their own newspaper, as their fathers did at their age. With such an ignorant and deceivable majority, States would soon run to ruin, but that there are limitations beyond which the folly and ambition of governors cannot go. Things have their laws, as well as men ; and things refuse to be trifled with. Property will be protected. Corn will not grow unless it is planted and manured ; but the farmer will not plant or hoe it unless the chances are a hundred to one that he will cut and harvest it. Under any forms, persons and property must and will have their just sway. They exert their power, as steadily as matter its attraction. Cover up a pound of earth never so cunningly, divide and subdivide it ; melt it to liquid, convert it to gas ; it will always weigh a pound ; it will always attract and resist other matter by the full virtue of one pound weight : — and the attributes of a person, his wit and his moral energy, will exercise, under any law or extinguishing tyranny, their proper force, — if not overtly, then covertly ; if not for the law, then against it ; if not wholesomely, then poison- ously ; with right, or by might.

The boundaries of personal influence it is impos sible to fix, as persons are organs of moral or super natural force. Under the dominion of an idea which possesses the minds of multitudes, as civil freedom, or the religious sentiment, the powers of persons are no longer subjects of calculation. A nation of men unanimously bent on freedom or con- quest can easily confound the arithmetic of statists, and achieve extravagant actions, out of all propor- tion to their means ; as the Greeks, the Saracens, the Swiss, the Americans, and the French have done.

In like manner to every particle of property be- longs its own attraction. A cent is the representa- tive of a certain quantity of corn or other commod- ity. Its value is in the necessities of the animal man. It is so much warmth, so much bread, so much water, so much land. The law may do what it will with the owner of property ; its just power will still attach to the cent. The law may in a mad freak say that all shall have power except the owners of property; they shall have no vote. Nevertheless, by a higher law, the property will, year after year, write every statute that respects property. The non-proprietor will be the scribe of the proprietor. What the owners wish to do, the whole power of property will do, either through the law or else in defiance of it. Of course I speak of all the property, not merely of the great estates. When the rich are outvoted, as frequently happens, it is the joint treasury of the poor which exceeds their accumulations. Every man owns something, if it is only a cow, or a wheel-barrow, or his arms, and so has that property to dispose of.

The same necessity which secures the rights of person and property against the malignity or folly of the magistrate, determines the form and methods of governing, which are proper to each nation and to its habit of thought, and nowise transferable to other states of society. In this country we are very vain of our political institutions, which are singular in this, that they sprung, within the memory of living men, from the character and condition of the people, which they still express with sufficient fidelity, — and we ostentatiously prefer them to any other in history. They are not better, but only fitter for us. We may be wise in asserting the advantage in modern times of the democratic form, but to other states of society, in which relig

ion consecrated the monarchical, that and not this
was expedient. Democracy is better for us, because the religious sentiment of the present time
accords better with it. Born democrats, we are nowise qualified to judge of monarchy, which, to our
fathers living in the monarchical idea, was also rel-
atively right. But our institutions, though in coincidence with the spirit of the age, have not any
exemption from the practical defects which have
discredited other forms. Every actual State is
corrupt. Good men must not obey the laws too
well. What satire on government can equal the
severity of censure conveyed in the word *politic*,
which now for ages has signified *cunning*, intimat-
ing that the State is a trick?

The same benign necessity and the same practical abuse appear in the parties, into which each
State divides itself, of opponents and defenders of
the administration of the government. Parties are
also founded on instincts, and have better guides to
their own humble aims than the sagacity of their
leaders. They have nothing perverse in their origin, but rudely mark some real and lasting relation.
We might as wisely reprove the east wind or the
frost, as a political party, whose members, for the
most part, could give no account of their position,
but stand for the defence of those interests in
which they find themselves. Our quarrel with

them begins when they quit this deep natural
ground at the bidding of some leader, and obeying
personal considerations, throw themselves into the
maintenance and defence of points nowise belong-
ing to their system. A party is perpetually cor-
rupted by personality. Whilst we absolve the association from dishonesty, we cannot extend the
same charity to their leaders. They reap the rewards of the docility and zeal of the masses which
they direct. Ordinarily our parties are parties of
circumstance, and not of principle; as the planting
interest in conflict with the commercial; the party
of capitalists and that of operatives: parties which
are identical in their moral character, and which
can easily change ground with each other in the
support of many of their measures. Parties of
principle, as, religious sects, or the party of free-
trade, of universal suffrage, of abolition of slavery,
of abolition of capital punishment, — degenerate
into personalities, or would inspire enthusiasm.
The vice of our leading parties in this country
(which may be cited as a fair specimen of these societies of opinion) is that they do not plant themselves on the deep and necessary grounds to which
they are respectively entitled, but lash themselves
to fury in the carrying of some local and momentary measure, nowise useful to the commonwealth.
Of the two great parties which at this hour almost

share the nation between them, I should say that one has the best cause, and the other contains the best men. The philosopher, the poet, or the religious man will of course wish to cast his vote with the democrat, for free-trade, for wide suffrage, for the abolition of legal cruelties in the penal code, and for facilitating in every manner the access of the young and the poor to the sources of wealth and power. But he can rarely accept the persons whom the so-called popular party propose to him as representatives of these liberalities. They have not at heart the ends which give to the name of democracy what hope and virtue are in it. The spirit of our American radicalism is destructive and aimless: it is not loving; it has no ulterior and divine ends, but is destructive only out of hatred and selfishness. On the other side, the conservative party, composed of the most moderate, able, and cultivated part of the population, is timid, and merely defensive of property. It vindicates no right, it aspires to no real good, it brands no crime, it proposes no generous policy; it does not build, nor write, nor cherish the arts, nor foster religion, nor establish schools, nor encourage science, nor emancipate the slave, nor befriend the poor, or the Indian, or the immigrant. From neither party, when in power, has the world any benefit to expect in science, art, or humanity, at all commensurate with the resources of the nation.

I do not for these defects despair of our republic. We are not at the mercy of any waves of chance. In the strife of ferocious parties, human nature always finds itself cherished; as the children of the convicts at Botany Bay are found to have as healthy a moral sentiment as other children.   Citizens of feudal states are alarmed at our democratic institutions lapsing into anarchy, and the older and more cautious among ourselves are learning from Europeans to look with some terror at our turbulent freedom.   It is said that in our license of construing the Constitution, and in the despotism of public opinion, we have no anchor; and one foreign observer thinks he has found the safeguard in the sanctity of Marriage among us; and another thinks he has found it in our Calvinism.   Fisher Ames expressed the popular security more wisely, when he compared a monarchy and a republic, saying that a monarchy is a merchantman, which sails well, but will sometimes strike on a rock and go to the bottom; whilst a republic is a raft, which would never sink, but then your feet are always in water. No forms can have any dangerous importance whilst we are befriended by the laws of things.   It makes no difference how many tons weight of atmosphere presses on our heads, so long as the same pressure resists it within the lungs.   Augment the mass a thousand fold, it cannot begin to crush us, as long as reaction is equal to action. The fact of two poles, of two forces, centripetal and centrifugal, is universal, and each force by its own activity develops the other. Wild liberty develops iron conscience. Want of liberty, by strengthening law and decorum, stupefies conscience. 'Lynch law' prevails only where there is greater hardihood and self-subsistency in the leaders. A mob cannot be a permanency; everybody's interest requires that it should not exist, and only justice satisfies all.

We must trust infinitely to the beneficent necessity which shines through all laws. Human nature expresses itself in them as characteristically as in statues, or songs, or railroads; and an abstract of the codes of nations would be a transcript of the common conscience. Governments have their origin in the moral identity of men. Reason for one is seen to be reason for another, and for every other. There is a middle measure which satisfies all parties, be they never so many or so resolute for their own. Every man finds a sanction for his simplest claims and deeds, in decisions of his own mind, which he calls Truth and Holiness. In these decisions all the citizens find a perfect agreement, and only in these; not in what is good to eat, good to wear, good use of time, or what amount of land or of public aid each is entitled to claim. This truth and justice men presently endeavor to make appli-

cation of to the measuring of land, the apportion-
ment of service, the protection of life and property.
Their first endeavors, no doubt, are very awkward.
Yet absolute right is the first governor; or, every
government is an impure theocracy. The idea
after which each community is aiming to make and
mend its law, is the will of the wise man. The
wise man it cannot find in nature, and it makes awkward but earnest efforts to secure his government
by contrivance; as by causing the entire people to
give their voices on every measure; or by a double
choice to get the representation of the whole; or
by a selection of the best citizens; or to secure the
advantages of efficiency and internal peace by confiding the government to one, who may himself
select his agents. All forms of government symbolize an immortal government, common to all dy-
nasties and independent of numbers, perfect where
two men exist, perfect where there is only one
man.

Every man's nature is a sufficient advertisement
to him of the character of his fellows. My right
and my wrong is their right and their wrong.
Whilst I do what is fit for me, and abstain from
what is unfit, my neighbor and I shall often agree
in our means, and work together for a time to one
end. But whenever I find my dominion over myself not sufficient for me, and undertake the direc-

tion of him also, I overstep the truth, and come
into false relations to him. I may have so much
more skill or strength than he that he cannot express adequately his sense of wrong, but it is a lie,
and hurts like a lie both him and me. Love and
nature cannot maintain the assumption; it must be
executed by a practical lie, namely by force. This
undertaking for another is the blunder which stands
in colossal ugliness in the governments of the world.
It is the same thing in numbers, as in a pair, only
not quite so intelligible. I can see well enough a
great difference between my setting myself down to
a self-control, and my going to make somebody else
act after my views; but when a quarter of the
human race assume to tell me what I must do, I
may be too much disturbed by the circumstances
to see so clearly the absurdity of their command.
Therefore all public ends look vague and quixotic
beside private ones. For any laws but those which
men make for themselves, are laughable. If I put
myself in the place of my child, and we stand in
one thought and see that things are thus or thus,
that perception is law for him and me. We are
both there, both act. But if, without carrying him
into the thought, I look over into his plot, and, guess-
ing how it is with him, ordain this or that, he will
never obey me. This is the history of governments,
—one man does something which is to bind an

other. A man who cannot be acquainted with me, taxes me; looking from afar at me ordains that a part of my labor shall go to this or that whimsical end, — not as I, but as he happens to fancy. Behold the consequence. Of all debts men are least willing to pay the taxes. What a satire is this on government! Everywhere they think they get their money's worth, except for these.

Hence the less government we have the better, — the fewer laws, and the less confided power. The antidote to this abuse of formal Government is the influence of private character, the growth of the Individual; the appearance of the principal to supersede the proxy; the appearance of the wise man; of whom the existing government is, it must be owned, but a shabby imitation. That which all things tend to educe; which freedom, cultivation, intercourse, revolutions, go to form and deliver, is character; that is the end of Nature, to reach unto this coronation of her king. To educate the wise man the State exists, and with the appearance of the wise man the State expires. The appearance of character makes the State unnecessary. The wise man is the State. He needs no army, fort, or navy, — he loves men too well; no bribe, or feast, or palace, to draw friends to him; no vantage ground, no favorable circumstance. He needs no library, for he has not done thinking; no church, for he is a prophet; no statute book, for he has the lawgiver; no money, for he is value; no road, for he is at home where he is; no experience, for the life of the creator shoots through him, and looks from his eyes. He has no personal friends, for he who has the spell to draw the prayer and piety of all men unto him needs not husband and educate a few to share with him a select and poetic life. His relation to men is angelic; his memory is myrrh to them; his presence, frankincense and flowers.

We think our civilization near its meridian, but we are yet only at the cock-crowing and the morning star. In our barbarous society the influence of character is in its infancy. As a political power, as the rightful lord who is to tumble all rulers from their chairs, its presence is hardly yet suspected. Malthus and Ricardo quite omit it; the Annual Register is silent; in the Conversations' Lexicon it is not set down; the President's Message, the Queen's Speech, have not mentioned it; and yet it is never nothing. Every thought which genius and piety throw into the world, alters the world. The gladiators in the lists of power feel, through all their frocks of force and simulation, the presence of worth. I think the very strife of trade and ambition is confession of this divinity; and successes in those fields are the poor amends, the fig-

leaf with which the shamed soul attempts to hide
its nakedness. I find the like unwilling homage in
all quarters. It is because we know how much is
due from us that we are impatient to show some
petty talent as a substitute for worth. We are
haunted by a conscience of this right to grandeur
of character, and are false to it. But each of us
has some talent, can do somewhat useful, or graceful, or formidable, or amusing, or lucrative. That
we do, as an apology to others and to ourselves for
not reaching the mark of a good and equal life.
But it does not satisfy *us*, whilst we thrust it on
the notice of our companions. It may throw dust
in their eyes, but does not smooth our own brow,
or give us the tranquillity of the strong when we
walk abroad. We do penance as we go. Our talent is a sort of expiation, and we are constrained
to reflect on our splendid moment with a certain
humiliation, as somewhat too fine, and not as one
act of many acts, a fair expression of our permanent energy. Most persons of ability meet in society with a kind of tacit appeal. Each seems to
say, ' I am not all here.' Senators and presidents
have climbed so high with pain enough, not because they think the place specially agreeable, but
as an apology for real worth, and to vindicate their
manhood in our eyes. This conspicuous chair is
their compensation to themselves for being of a

poor, cold, hard nature. They must do what they can. Like one class of forest animals, they have nothing but a prehensile tail; climb they must, or crawl. If a man found himself so rich-natured that he could enter into strict relations with the best persons and make life serene around him by the dignity and sweetness of his behavior, could he afford to circumvent the favor of the caucus and the press, and covet relations so hollow and pompous as those of a politician? Surely nobody would be a charlatan who could afford to be sincere.

The tendencies of the times favor the idea of self-government, and leave the individual, for all code, to the rewards and penalties of his own constitution; which work with more energy than we believe whilst we depend on artificial restraints. The movement in this direction has been very marked in modern history. Much has been blind and discreditable, but the nature of the revolution is not affected by the vices of the revolters; for this is a purely moral force. It was never adopted by any party in history, neither can be. It separates the individual from all party, and unites him at the same time to the race. It promises a recognition of higher rights than those of personal freedom, or the security of property. A man has a right to be employed, to be trusted, to be loved, to be revered. The power of love, as the basis of a State, has never

been tried.   We must not imagine that all things
are lapsing into confusion if every tender protest-
ant be not compelled to bear his part in certain
social conventions; nor doubt that roads can be
built, letters carried, and the fruit of labor secured,
when the government of force is at an end.   Are
our methods now so excellent that all competition is
hopeless? could not a nation of friends even devise
better ways?   On the other hand, let not the most
conservative and timid fear anything from a premature surrender of the bayonet and the system of
force.   For, according to the order of nature, which
is quite superior to our will, it stands thus; there
will always be a government of force where men
are selfish; and when they are pure enough to ab-
jure the code of force they will be wise enough to
see how these public ends of the post-office, of the
highway, of commerce and the exchange of property, of museums and libraries, of institutions of
art and science can be answered.

We live in a very low state of the world, and
pay unwilling tribute to governments founded on
force.   There is not, among the most religious and
instructed men of the most religious and civil nations, a reliance on the moral sentiment and a sufficient belief in the unity of things, to persuade
them that society can be maintained without artificial restraints, as well as the solar system; or that

the private citizen might be reasonable and a good neighbor, without the hint of a jail or a confiscation. What is strange too, there never was in any man sufficient faith in the power of rectitude to inspire him with the broad design of renovating the State on the principle of right and love. All those who have pretended this design have been partial reformers, and have admitted in some manner the supremacy of the bad State. I do not call to mind a single human being who has steadily denied the authority of the laws, on the simple ground of his own moral nature. Such designs, full of genius and full of faith as they are, are not entertained except avowedly as air-pictures. If the individual who exhibits them dare to think them practicable, he disgusts scholars and churchmen; and men of talent and women of superior sentiments cannot hide their contempt. Not the less does nature continue to fill the heart of youth with suggestions of this enthusiasm, and there are now men, — if indeed I can speak in the plural number, — more exactly, I will say, I have just been conversing with one man, to whom no weight of adverse experience will make it for a moment appear impossible that thousands of human beings might exercise towards each other the grandest and simplest sentiments, as well as a knot of friends, or a pair of lovers.

NOMINALIST AND REALIST

———•———

In countless upward-striving waves
The moon-drawn tide-wave strives:
In thousand far-transplanted grafts
The parent fruit survives;
So, in the new-born millions,
The perfect Adam lives.
Not less are summer mornings dear
To every child they wake,
And each with novel life his sphere
Fills for his proper sake.

VIII.

NOMINALIST AND REALIST.

——◆——

I CANNOT often enough say that a man is only a relative and representative nature. Each is a hint of the truth, but far enough from being that truth which yet he quite newly and inevitably suggests to us. If I seek it in him I shall not find it. Could any man conduct into me the pure stream of that which he pretends to be! Long afterwards I find that quality elsewhere which he promised me. The genius of the Platonists is intoxicating to the student, yet how few particulars of it can I detach from all their books. The man momentarily stands for the thought, but will not bear examination; and a society of men will cursorily represent well enough a certain quality and culture, for example, chivalry or beauty of manners; but separate them and there is no gentleman and no lady in the group. The least hint sets us on the pursuit of a character which no man realizes. We have such exorbitant eyes that on seeing the smallest arc we complete the curve, and when the curtain is lifted from the diagram which it seemed to veil, we are vexed to find that no more was drawn than just that fragment of an arc which we first beheld. We are greatly too liberal in our construction of each other's faculty and promise. Exactly what the parties have already done they shall do again; but that which we inferred from their nature and inception, they will not do. That is in nature, but not in them. That happens in the world, which we often witness in a public debate. Each of the speakers expresses himself imperfectly; no one of them hears much that another says, such is the preoccupation of mind of each; and the audience, who have only to hear and not to speak, judge very wisely and superiorly how wrongheaded and unskilful is each of the debaters to his own affair. Great men or men of great gifts you shall easily find, but symmetrical men never. When I meet a pure intellectual force or a generosity of affection, I believe here then is man; and am presently mortified by the discovery that this individual is no more available to his own or to the general ends than his companions; because the power which drew my respect is not supported by the total symphony of his talents. All persons exist to society by some shining trait of beauty or utility which they have. We borrow the proportions of the man from that one fine feature, and finish the portrait symmetrically; which is false, for the rest

of his body is small or deformed. I observe a person who makes a good public appearance, and conclude thence the perfection of his private character,
on which this is based ; but he has no private character. He is a graceful cloak or lay-figure for holi-
days. All our poets, heroes, and saints, fail utterly
in some one or in many parts to satisfy our idea,
fail to draw our spontaneous interest, and so leave
us without any hope of realization but in our own
future. Our exaggeration of all fine characters
arises from the fact that we identify each in turn
with the soul. But there are no such men as we
fable; no Jesus, nor Pericles, nor Cæsar, nor Angelo, nor Washington, such as we have made. We
consecrate a great deal of nonsense because it was
allowed by great men. There is none without his
foible. I believe that if an angel should come to
chant the chorus of the moral law, he would eat too
much gingerbread, or take liberties with private
letters, or do some precious atrocity. It is bad
enough that our geniuses cannot do anything useful, but it is worse that no man is fit for society
who has fine traits. He is admired at a distance,
but he cannot come near without appearing a crip-
ple. The men of fine parts protect themselves by
solitude, or by courtesy, or by satire, or by an acid
worldly manner ; each concealing as he best can
his incapacity for useful association, but they want
either love or self-reliance.

Our native love of reality joins with this experience to teach us a little reserve, and to dissuade a too sudden surrender to the brilliant qualities of persons. Young people admire talents or particular excellences; as we grow older we value total powers and effects, as the impression, the quality, the spirit of men and things. The genius is all. The man, — it is his system : we do not try a solitary word or act, but his habit. The acts which you praise, I praise not, since they are departures from his faith, and are mere compliances. The magnetism which arranges tribes and races in one polarity is alone to be respected ; the men are steel-filings. Yet we unjustly select a particle, and say, ' O steel-filing number one ! what heart-drawings I feel to thee ! what prodigious virtues are these of thine ! how constitutional to thee, and incommunicable !' Whilst we speak the loadstone is withdrawn ; down falls our filing in a heap with the rest, and we continue our mummery to the wretched shaving. Let us go for universals ; for the magnetism, not for the needles. Human life and its persons are poor empirical pretensions. A personal influence is an *ignis fatuus.* If they say it is great, it is great ; if they say it is small, it is small ; you see it, and you see it not, by turns ; it borrows all its size from the momentary estimation of the speakers : the Will-of-the-wisp vanishes if you go too near, vanishes if you go too far, and only blazes at one angle. Who can tell if Washington be a great man or no? Who can tell if Franklin be? Yes, or any but the twelve, or six, or three great gods of fame? And they too loom and fade before the eternal.

We are amphibious creatures, weaponed for two elements, having two sets of faculties, the particular and the catholic. We adjust our instrument for general observation, and sweep the heavens as easily as we pick out a single figure in the terrestrial landscape. We are practically skilful in detecting elements for which we have no place in our theory, and no name. Thus we are very sensible of an atmospheric influence in men and in bodies of men, not accounted for in an arithmetical addition of all their measurable properties. There is a genius of a nation, which is not to be found in the numerical citizens, but which characterizes the society. England, strong, punctual, practical, well-spoken England I should not find if I should go to the island to seek it. In the parliament, in the play-house, at dinner-tables, I might see a great number of rich, ignorant, book-read, conventional, proud men, — many old women, — and not anywhere the Englishman who made the good speeches, combined the accurate engines, and did the bold and nervous deeds. It is even worse in

America, where, from the intellectual quickness of
the race, the genius of the country is more splendid in its promise and more slight in its performance.   Webster cannot do the work of Webster.
We conceive distinctly enough the French, the
Spanish, the German genius, and it is not the less
real that perhaps we should not meet in either of
those nations a single individual who corresponded
with the type.   We infer the spirit of the nation
in great measure from the language, which is a
sort of monument to which each forcible individual
in a course of many hundred years has contributed
a stone.   And, universally, a good example of this
social force is the veracity of language, which cannot be debauched.   In any controversy concerning
morals, an appeal may be made with safety to the
sentiments which the language of the people expresses.   Proverbs, words, and grammar-inflections
convey the public sense with more purity and precision than the wisest individual.

In the famous dispute with the Nominalists, the
Realists had a good deal of reason.   General ideas
are essences.   They are our gods: they round and
ennoble the most partial and sordid way of living.
Our proclivity to details cannot quite degrade our
life and divest it of poetry.   The day-laborer is
reckoned as standing at the foot of the social scale,
yet he is saturated with the laws of the world

His measures are the hours; morning and night, solstice and equinox, geometry, astronomy and all the lovely accidents of nature play through his mind. Money, which represents the prose of life, and which is hardly spoken of in parlors without an apology, is, in its effects and laws, as beautiful as roses. Property keeps the accounts of the world, and is always moral. The property will be found where the labor, the wisdom, and the virtue have been in nations, in classes, and (the whole life-time considered, with the compensations) in the individual also. How wise the world appears, when the laws and usages of nations are largely detailed, and the completeness of the municipal system is considered! Nothing is left out. If you go into the markets and the custom-houses, the insurers' and notaries' offices, the offices of sealers of weights and measures, of inspection of provisions, — it will appear as if one man had made it all. Wherever you go, a wit like your own has been before you, and has realized its thought. The Eleusinian mysteries, the Egyptian architecture, the Indian astronomy, the Greek sculpture, show that there always were seeing and knowing men in the planet. The world is full of masonic ties, of guilds, of secret and public legions of honor; that of scholars, for example; and that of gentlemen, fraternizing with the upper class of every country and every culture.

I am very much struck in literature by the appearance that one person wrote all the books; as if the editor of a journal planted his body of reporters in different parts of the field of action, and relieved some by others from time to time; but there is such equality and identity both of judgment and point of view in the narrative that it is plainly the work of one all-seeing, all-hearing gentleman. I looked into Pope's Odyssey yesterday: it is as correct and elegant after our canon of to-day as if it were newly written. The modernness of all good books seems to give me an existence as wide as man. What is well done I feel as if I did; what is ill done I reck not of. Shakspeare's passages of passion (for example, in Lear and Hamlet) are in the very dialect of the present year. I am faithful again to the whole over the members in my use of books. I find the most pleasure in reading a book in a manner least flattering to the author. I read Proclus, and sometimes Plato, as I might read a dictionary, for a mechanical help to the fancy and the imagination. I read for the lustres, as if one should use a fine picture in a chromatic experiment, for its rich colors. 'T is not Proclus, but a piece of nature and fate that I explore. It is a greater joy to see the author's author, than himself. A higher pleasure of the same kind I found lately at a concert, where I went to hear Handel's Messiah. As the master overpowered the littleness and incapableness of the performers and made them conductors of his electricity, so it was easy to observe what efforts nature was making, through so many hoarse, wooden, and imperfect persons, to produce beautiful voices, fluid and soul-guided men and women. The genius of nature was paramount at the oratorio.

This preference of the genius to the parts is the secret of that deification of art, which is found in all superior minds. Art, in the artist, is proportion, or a habitual respect to the whole by an eye loving beauty in details. And the wonder and charm of it is the sanity in insanity which it de notes. Proportion is almost impossible to human beings. There is no one who does not exaggerate. In conversation, men are encumbered with personality, and talk too much. In modern sculpture, picture, and poetry, the beauty is miscellaneous; the artist works here and there and at all points, adding and adding, instead of unfolding the unit of his thought. Beautiful details we must have, or no artist; but they must be means and never other. The eye must not lose sight for a moment of the purpose. Lively boys write to their ear and eye, and the cool reader finds nothing but sweet jingles in it. When they grow older, they respect the argument. We obey the same intellectual integrity when we

study in exceptions the law of the world. Anomalous facts, as the never quite obsolete rumors of
magic and demonology, and the new allegations of
phrenologists and neurologists, are of ideal use.
They are good indications. Homœopathy is insignificant as an art of healing, but of great value as
criticism on the hygeia or medical practice of the
time. So with Mesmerism, Swedenborgism, Fou-
rierism, and the Millennial Church; they are poor
pretensions enough, but good criticism on the science, philosophy, and preaching of the day. For
these abnormal insights of the adepts ought to be
normal, and things of course.

All things show us that on every side we are very
near to the best. It seems not worth while to execute with too much pains some one intellectual, or
æsthetical, or civil feat, when presently the dream
will scatter, and we shall burst into universal power.
The reason of idleness and of crime is the deferring
of our hopes. Whilst we are waiting we beguile
the time with jokes, with sleep, with eating, and
with crimes.

Thus we settle it in our cool libraries, that all the
agents with which we deal are subalterns, which we
can well afford to let pass, and life will be simpler
when we live at the centre and flout the surfaces.
I wish to speak with all respect of persons, but some-

times I must pinch myself to keep awake and preserve the due decorum. They melt so fast into each
other that they are like grass and trees, and it needs
an effort to treat them as individuals. Though the
uninspired man certainly finds persons a conveniency in household matters, the divine man does not
respect them; he sees them as a rack of clouds, or
a fleet of ripples which the wind drives over the surface of the water. But this is flat rebellion. Nature will not be Buddhist: she resents generalizing,
and insults the philosopher in every moment with a
million of fresh particulars. It is all idle talking:
as much as a man is a whole, so is he also a part;
and it were partial not to see it. What you say in
your pompous distribution only distributes you into
your class and section. You have not got rid of
parts by denying them, but are the more partial.
You are one thing, but Nature is *one thing and the
other thing*, in the same moment. She will not remain orbed in a thought, but rushes into persons;
and when each person, inflamed to a fury of personality, would conquer all things to his poor crotchet,
she raises up against him another person, and by
many persons incarnates again a sort of whole.
She will have all. Nick Bottom cannot play all
the parts, work it how he may; there will be somebody else, and the world will be round. Everything
must have its flower or effort at the beautiful,

coarser or finer according to its stuff. They relieve and recommend each other, and the sanity of
society is a balance of a thousand insanities. She
punishes abstractionists, and will only forgive an in-
duction which is rare and casual. We like to come
to a height of land and see the landscape, just as we
value a general remark in conversation. But it is
not the intention of Nature that we should live by
general views. We fetch fire and water, run about
all day among the shops and markets, and get our
clothes and shoes made and mended, and are the
victims of these details; and once in a fortnight we
arrive perhaps at a rational moment. If we were
not thus infatuated, if we saw the real from hour
to hour, we should not be here to write and to read,
but should have been burned or frozen long ago.
She would never get anything done, if she suffered
admirable Crichtons and universal geniuses. She
loves better a wheelwright who dreams all night of
wheels, and a groom who is part of his horse; for
she is full of work, and these are her hands. As
the frugal farmer takes care that his cattle shall
eat down the rowen, and swine shall eat the waste
of his house, and poultry shall pick the crumbs, —
so our economical mother dispatches a new genius
and habit of mind into every district and condition
of existence, plants an eye wherever a new ray of
light can fall, and gathering up into some man

every property in the universe, establishes thou-
sandfold occult mutual attractions among her offspring, that all this wash and waste of power may
be imparted and exchanged.

Great dangers undoubtedly accrue from this incarnation and distribution of the godhead, and
hence Nature has her maligners, as if she were
Circe; and Alphonso of Castile fancied he could
have given useful advice. But she does not go un-
provided; she has hellebore at the bottom of the
cup. Solitude would ripen a plentiful crop of despots. The recluse thinks of men as having his
manner, or as not having his manner; and as having degrees of it, more and less. But when he
comes into a public assembly he sees that men have
very different manners from his own, and in their
way admirable. In his childhood and youth he has
had many checks and censures, and thinks mod-
estly enough of his own endowment. When afterwards he comes to unfold it in propitious circumstance, it seems the only talent; he is delighted
with his success, and accounts himself already the
fellow of the great. But he goes into a mob, into
a banking house, into a mechanic's shop, into a
mill, into a laboratory, into a ship, into a camp, and
in each new place he is no better than an idiot;
other talents take place, and rule the hour. The
rotation which whirls every leaf and pebble to the

meridian, reaches to every gift of man, and we all take turns at the top.

For Nature, who abhors mannerism, has set her heart on breaking up all styles and tricks, and it is so much easier to do what one has done before than to do a new thing, that there is a perpetual tendency to a set mode. In every conversation, even the highest, there is a certain trick, which may be soon learned by an acute person and then that particular style continued indefinitely. Each man too is a tyrant in tendency, because he would impose his idea on others; and their trick is their natural defence. Jesus would absorb the race; but Tom Paine or the coarsest blasphemer helps humanity by resisting this exuberance of power. Hence the immense benefit of party in politics, as it reveals faults of character in a chief, which the intellectual force of the persons, with ordinary opportunity and not hurled into aphelion by hatred, could not have seen. Since we are all so stupid, what benefit that there should be two stupidities! It is like that brute advantage so essential to astronomy, of having the diameter of the earth's orbit for a base of its triangles. Democracy is morose, and runs to anarchy, but in the State and in the schools it is indispensable to resist the consolidation of all men into a few men. If John was perfect, why are you and I alive? As long as any

man exists, there is some need of him; let him
fight for his own. A new poet has appeared; a
new character approached us; why should we refuse to eat bread until we have found his regiment
and section in our old army-files? Why not a new
man? Here is a new enterprise of Brook Farm,
of Skeneateles, of Northampton: why so impatient
to baptize them Essenes, or Port-Royalists, or
Shakers, or by any known and effete name? Let
it be a new way of living. Why have only two or
three ways of life, and not thousands? Every
man is wanted, and no man is wanted much. We
came this time for condiments, not for corn. We
want the great genius only for joy; for one star
more in our constellation, for one tree more in our
grove. But he thinks we wish to belong to him, as
he wishes to occupy us. He greatly mistakes us.
I think I have done well if I have acquired a new
word from a good author; and my business with
him is to find my own, though it were only to melt
him down into an epithet or an image for daily
use: —

"Into paint will I grind thee, my bride!"

To embroil the confusion, and make it impossible to arrive at any general statement, — when we
have insisted on the imperfection of individuals,
our affections and our experience urge that every

individual is entitled to honor, and a very generous
treatment is sure to be repaid. A recluse sees only
two or three persons, and allows them all their
room ; they spread themselves at large. The statesman looks at many, and compares the few habitually with others, and these look less. Yet are they
not entitled to this generosity of reception ? and is
not munificence the means of insight ? For though
gamesters say that the cards beat all the players,
though they were never so skilful, yet in the contest we are now considering, the players are also
the game, and share the power of the cards. If
you criticise a fine genius, the odds are that you
are out of your reckoning, and instead of the poet,
are censuring your own caricature of him. For
there is somewhat spheral and infinite in every
man, especially in every genius, which, if you can
come very near him, sports with all your limitations. For rightly every man is a channel through
which heaven floweth, and whilst I fancied I was
criticising him, I was censuring or rather terminat-
ing my own soul. After taxing Goethe as a courtier, artificial, unbelieving, worldly, — I took up
this book of Helena, and found him an Indian of
the wilderness, a piece of pure nature like an apple
or an oak, large as morning or night, and virtuous
as a brier-rose.

But care is taken that the whole tune shall be

played. If we were not kept among surfaces,
everything would be large and universal ; now the
excluded attributes burst in on us with the more
brightness that they have been excluded. " Your
turn now, my turn next," is the rule of the game.
The universality being hindered in its primary
form, comes in the secondary form of *all sides ;*
the points come in succession to the meridian, and
by the speed of rotation a new whole is formed.
Nature keeps herself whole and her representation
complete in the experience of each mind. She
suffers no seat to be vacant in her college. It is
the secret of the world that all things subsist and
do not die but only retire a little from sight and
afterwards return again. Whatever does not concern us is concealed from us. As soon as a person
is no longer related to our present well-being, he is
concealed, or *dies*, as we say. Really, all things
and persons are related to us, but according to
our nature they act on us not at once but in succession, and we are made aware of their presence
one at a time. All persons, all things which we
have known, are here present, and many more than
we see ; the world is full. As the ancient said, the
world is a *plenum* or solid ; and if we saw all
things that really surround us we should be imprisoned and unable to move. For though nothing is
impassable to the soul, but all things are pervious

to it and like highways, yet this is only whilst the soul does not see them. As soon as the soul sees any object, it stops before that object. Therefore the divine Providence which keeps the universe open in every direction to the soul, conceals all the furniture and all the persons that do not concern a particular soul, from the senses of that individual. Through solidest eternal things the man finds his road as if they did not subsist, and does not once suspect their being. As soon as he needs a new object, suddenly he beholds it, and no longer attempts to pass through it, but takes another way. When he has exhausted for the time the nourishment to be drawn from any one person or thing, that object is withdrawn from his observation, and though still in his immediate neighborhood, he does not suspect its presence. Nothing is dead: men feign themselves dead, and endure mock funerals and mournful obituaries, and there they stand looking out of the window, sound and well, in some new and strange disguise. Jesus is not dead; he is very well alive: nor John, nor Paul, nor Mahomet, nor Aristotle; at times we believe we have seen them all, and could easily tell the names under which they go.

If we cannot make voluntary and conscious steps in the admirable science of universals, let us see the parts wisely, and infer the genius of nature from the best particulars with a becoming charity. What is best in each kind is an index of what should be the average of that thing. Love shows me the opulence of nature, by disclosing to me in my friend a hidden wealth, and I infer an equal depth of good in every other direction It is commonly said by farmers that a good pear or apple costs no more time or pains to rear than a poor one; so I would have no work of art, no speech, or action, or thought, or friend, but the best.

The end and the means, the gamester and the game, — life is made up of the intermixture and reaction of these two amicable powers, whose marriage appears beforehand monstrous, as each denies and tends to abolish the other. We must reconcile the contradictions as we can, but their discord and their concord introduce wild absurdities into our thinking and speech. No sentence will hold the whole truth, and the only way in which we can be just, is by giving ourselves the lie; Speech is better than silence; silence is better than speech; — All things are in contact; every atom has a sphere of repulsion; — Things are, and are not, at the same time; — and the like. All the universe over, there is but one thing, this old Two-Face, creator-creature, mind-matter, right-wrong, of which any proposition may be affirmed or denied. Very fitly therefore I assert that every man is a partialist, that nature secures him as an instrument by self-conceit, preventing the tendencies to religion and science ; and now further assert, that, each man's genius being nearly and affectionately explored, he is justified in his individuality, as his nature is found to be immense ; and now I add that every man is a universalist also, and, as our earth, whilst it spins on its own axis, spins all the time around the sun through the celestial spaces, so the least of its rational children, the most dedicated to his private affair, works out, though as it were under a disguise, the universal problem. We fancy men are individuals; so are pumpkins; but every pumpkin in the field goes through every point of pumpkin history. The rabid democrat, as soon as he is senator and rich man, has ripened beyond possibility of sincere radicalism, and unless he can resist the sun, he must be conservative the remainder of his days. Lord Eldon said in his old age that " if he were to begin life again, he would be damned but he would begin as agitator."

We hide this universality if we can, but it appears at all points. We are as ungrateful as children. There is nothing we cherish and strive to draw to us but in some hour we turn and rend it. We keep a running fire of sarcasm at ignorance and the life of the senses ; then goes by, perchance, a fair girl, a piece of life, gay and happy, and

making the commonest offices beautiful by the energy and heart with which she does them ; and seeing this we admire and love her and them, and say,
' Lo ! a genuine creature of the fair earth, not dissipated or too early ripened by books, philosophy,
religion, society, or care ! ' insinuating a treachery
and contempt for all we had so long loved and
wrought in ourselves and others.

If we could have any security against moods !
If the profoundest prophet could be holden to his
words, and the hearer who is ready to sell all and
join the crusade could have any certificate that to-
morrow his prophet shall not unsay his testimony !
But the Truth sits veiled there on the Bench, and
never interposes an adamantine syllable ; and the
most sincere and revolutionary doctrine, put as if
the ark of God were carried forward some furlongs,
and planted there for the succor of the world, shall
in a few weeks be coldly set aside by the same
speaker, as morbid ; " I thought I was right, but I
was not,"— and the same immeasurable credulity
demanded for new audacities. If we were not of
all opinions ! if we did not in any moment shift the
platform on which we stand, and look and speak
from another ! if there could be any regulation,
any ' one-hour-rule,' that a man should never leave
his point of view without sound of trumpet. I
am always insincere, as always knowing there are
other moods.

How sincere and confidential we can be, saying all that lies in the mind, and yet go away feeling that all is yet unsaid, from the incapacity of the parties to know each other, although they use the same words! My companion assumes to know my mood and habit of thought, and we go on from explanation to explanation until all is said which words can, and we leave matters just as they were at first, because of that vicious assumption. Is it that every man believes every other to be an incurable partialist, and himself a universalist? I talked yesterday with a pair of philosophers; I endeavored to show my good men that I liked everything by turns and nothing long; that I loved the centre, but doated on the superficies; that I loved man, if men seemed to me mice and rats; that I revered saints, but woke up glad that the old pagan world stood its ground and died hard; that I was glad of men of every gift and nobility, but would not live in their arms. Could they but once understand that I loved to know that they existed, and heartily wished them God-speed, yet, out of my poverty of life and thought, had no word or welcome for them when they came to see me, and could well consent to their living in Oregon for any claim I felt on them, — it would be a great satisfaction.

NEW ENGLAND REFORMERS

In the suburb, in the town,
On the railway, in the square,
Came a beam of goodness down
Doubling daylight everywhere:
Peace now each for malice takes,
Beauty for his sinful weeds,
For the angel Hope aye makes
Him an angel whom she leads.

NEW ENGLAND REFORMERS.

A LECTURE READ BEFORE THE SOCIETY IN AMORY
HALL, ON SUNDAY, MARCH 3, 1844.

WHOEVER has had opportunity of acquaintance
with society in New England during the last twen-
ty-five years, with those middle and with those leading sections that may constitute any just representation of the character and aim of the community,
will have been struck with the great activity of
thought and experimenting. His attention must be
commanded by the signs that the Church, or religious party, is falling from the Church nominal, and
is appearing in temperance and non-resistance societies; in movements of abolitionists and of social-
ists; and in very significant assemblies called Sabbath and Bible Conventions; composed of ultraists,
of seekers, of all the soul of the soldiery of dissent,
and meeting to call in question the authority of the
Sabbath, of the priesthood, and of the Church. In
these movements nothing was more remarkable
than the discontent they begot in the movers. The
spirit of protest and of detachment drove the members of these Conventions to bear testimony against

the Church, and immediately afterwards to declare their discontent with these Conventions, their independence of their colleagues, and their impatience of the methods whereby they were working. They defied each other, like a congress of kings, each of whom had a realm to rule, and a way of his own that made concert unprofitable. What a fertility of projects for the salvation of the world! One apostle thought all men should go to farming, and another that no man should buy or sell, that the use of money was the cardinal evil; another that the mischief was in our diet, that we eat and drink damnation. These made unleavened bread, and were foes to the death to fermentation. It was in vain urged by the housewife that God made yeast, as well as dough, and loves fermentation just as dearly as he loves vegetation; that fermentation develops the saccharine element in the grain, and makes it more palatable and more digestible. No; they wish the pure wheat, and will die but it shall not ferment. Stop, dear nature, these incessant advances of thine; let us scotch these ever-rolling wheels! Others attacked the system of agriculture, the use of animal manures in farming, and the tyranny of man over brute nature; these abuses polluted his food. The ox must be taken from the plough and the horse from the cart, the hundred acres of the farm must be spaded, and the man must

walk, wherever boats and locomotives will not carry
him.   Even the insect world was to be defended, —
that had been too long neglected, and a society for
the protection of ground-worms, slugs, and mosquitos was to be incorporated without delay.   With
these appeared the adepts of homœopathy, of hy-
dropathy, of mesmerism, of phrenology, and their
wonderful theories of the Christian miracles!   Others assailed particular vocations, as that of the lawyer, that of the merchant, of the manufacturer, of
the clergyman, of the scholar.   Others attacked the
institution of marriage as the fountain of social
evils.   Others devoted themselves to the worrying
of churches and meetings for public worship ; and
the fertile forms of antinomianism among the elder
puritans seemed to have their match in the plenty
of the new harvest of reform.

   With this din of opinion and debate there was a
keener scrutiny of institutions and domestic life
than any we had known ; there was sincere protest-
ing against existing evils, and there were changes
of employment dictated by conscience.   No doubt
there was plentiful vaporing, and cases of backslid-
ing might occur.   But in each of these movements
emerged a good result, a tendency to the adoption
of simpler methods, and an assertion of the suffi-
ciency of the private man.   Thus it was directly in
the spirit and genius of the age, what happened in

one instance when a church censured and threatened to excommunicate one of its members on account of the somewhat hostile part to the church which his conscience led him to take in the anti-slavery business ; the threatened individual immediately excommunicated the church, in a public and formal process.   This has been several times repeated : it was excellent when it was done the first time, but of course loses all value when it is copied.   Every project in the history of reform, no matter how violent and surprising, is good when it is the dictate of a man's genius and constitution, but very dull and suspicious when adopted from another.   It is right and beautiful in any man to say, ' I will take this coat, or this book, or this measure of corn of yours,' — in whom we see the act to be original, and to flow from the whole spirit and faith of him ; for then that taking will have a giving as free and divine ; but we are very easily disposed to resist the same generosity of speech when we miss originality and truth to character in it.

There was in all the practical activities of New England for the last quarter of a century, a gradual withdrawal of tender consciences from the social organizations.   There is observable throughout, the contest between mechanical and spiritual methods, but with a steady tendency of the thoughtful and virtuous to a deeper belief and reliance on spiritual facts.

In politics for example it is easy to see the progress of dissent. The country is full of rebellion; the country is full of kings. Hands off! let there be no control and no interference in the administration of the affairs of this kingdom of me. Hence the growth of the doctrine and of the party of Free Trade, and the willingness to try that experiment, in the face of what appear incontestable facts. I confess, the motto of the Globe newspaper is so attractive to me that I can seldom find much appetite to read what is below it in its columns: " The world is governed too much." So the country is frequently affording solitary examples of resistance to the government, solitary nullifiers, who throw themselves on their reserved rights; nay, who have reserved all their rights; who reply to the assessor and to the clerk of court that they do not know the State, and embarrass the courts of law by non-juring and the commander-in-chief of the militia by non-resistance.

The same disposition to scrutiny and dissent appeared in civil, festive, neighborly, and domestic society. A restless, prying, conscientious criticism broke out in unexpected quarters. Who gave me the money with which I bought my coat? Why should professional labor and that of the counting-house be paid so disproportionately to the labor of the porter and woodsawyer? This whole business

of Trade gives me to pause and think, as it constitutes false relations between men ; inasmuch as I
am prone to count myself relieved of any respon-
sibility to behave well and nobly to that person
whom I pay with money; whereas if I had not that
commodity, I should be put on my good behavior
in all companies, and man would be a benefactor to
man, as being himself his only certificate that he
had a right to those aids and services which each
asked of the other.   Am I not too protected a person ? is there not a wide disparity between the lot
of me and the lot of thee, my poor brother, my
poor sister ?   Am I not defrauded of my best culture in the loss of those gymnastics which manual
labor and the emergencies of poverty constitute ?
I find nothing healthful or exalting in the smooth
conventions of society ; I do not like the close air
of saloons.   I begin to suspect myself to be a
prisoner, though treated with all this courtesy and
luxury.   I pay a destructive tax in my conformity.

The same insatiable criticism may be traced in
the efforts for the reform of Education.   The popular education has been taxed with a want of truth
and nature.   It was complained that an education
to things was not given.   We are students of
words : we are shut up in schools, and colleges, and
recitation-rooms, for ten or fifteen years, and come
out at last with a bag of wind, a memory of words,

and do not know a thing. We cannot use our
hands, or our legs, or our eyes, or our arms.
We do not know an edible root in the woods, we
cannot tell our course by the stars, nor the hour of
the day by the sun. It is well if we can swim and
skate. We are afraid of a horse, of a cow, of a
dog, of a snake, of a spider. The Roman rule was
to teach a boy nothing that he could not learn
standing. The old English rule was, ' All summer
in the field, and all winter in the study.' And it
seems as if a man should learn to plant, or to fish,
or to hunt, that he might secure his subsistence at
all events, and not be painful to his friends and
fellow-men. The lessons of science should be ex-
perimental also. The sight of a planet through a
telescope is worth all the course on astronomy ; the
shock of the electric spark in the elbow, outvalues
all the theories ; the taste of the nitrous oxide, the
firing of an artificial volcano, are better than volumes of chemistry.

One of the traits of the new spirit is the in-
quisition it fixed on our scholastic devotion to the
dead languages. The ancient languages, with great
beauty of structure, contain wonderful remains of
genius, which draw, and always will draw, certain
likeminded men,— Greek men, and Roman men,—
in all countries, to their study ; but by a wonderful
drowsiness of usage they had exacted the study of

all men. Once (say two centuries ago), Latin and
Greek had a strict relation to all the science and
culture there was in Europe, and the Mathematics
had a momentary importance at some era of activity in physical science. These things became ste-
reotyped as *education*, as the manner of men is.
But the Good Spirit never cared for the colleges,
and though all men and boys were now drilled in
Latin, Greek, and Mathematics, it had quite left
these shells high and dry on the beach, and was
now creating and feeding other matters at other
ends of the world. But in a hundred high schools
and colleges this warfare against common sense
still goes on. Four, or six, or ten years, the pupil
is parsing Greek and Latin, and as soon as he
leaves the University, as it is ludicrously styled, he
shuts those books for the last time. Some thousands of young men are graduated at our colleges in
this country every year, and the persons who, at
forty years, still read Greek, can all be counted on
your hand. I never met with ten. Four or five
persons I have seen who read Plato.

But is not this absurd, that the whole liberal
talent of this country should be directed in its best
years on studies which lead to nothing? What
was the consequence? Some intelligent persons
said or thought, ‘Is that Greek and Latin some
spell to conjure with, and not words of reason? If

the physician, the lawyer, the divine, never use it to come at their ends, I need never learn it to come at mine. Conjuring is gone out of fashion, and I will omit this conjugating, and go straight to affairs.' So they jumped the Greek and Latin, and read law, medicine, or sermons, without it. To the astonishment of all, the self-made men took even ground at once with the oldest of the regular graduates, and in a few months the most conservative circles of Boston and New York had quite forgotten who of their gownsmen was college-bred, and who was not.

One tendency appears alike in the philosophical speculation and in the rudest democratical movements, through all the petulance and all the puerility, the wish, namely, to cast aside the superfluous and arrive at short methods; urged, as I suppose, by an intuition that the human spirit is equal to all emergencies, alone, and that man is more often injured than helped by the means he uses.

I conceive this gradual casting off of material aids, and the indication of growing trust in the private self-supplied powers of the individual, to be the affirmative principle of the recent philosophy, and that it is feeling its own profound truth and is reaching forward at this very hour to the happiest conclusions. I readily concede that in this, as in every period of intellectual activity,

there has been a noise of denial and protest; much
was to be resisted, much was to be got rid of by
those who were reared in the old, before they could
begin to affirm and to construct.   Many a reformer
perishes in his removal of rubbish; and that makes
the offensiveness of the class.   They are partial;
they are not equal to the work they pretend.   They
lose their way; in the assault on the kingdom of
darkness they expend all their energy on some
accidental evil, and lose their sanity and power of
benefit.   It is of little moment that one or two or
twenty errors of our social system be corrected, but
of much that the man be in his senses.

The criticism and attack on institutions, which
we have witnessed, has made one thing plain, that
society gains nothing whilst a man, not himself
renovated, attempts to renovate things around him:
he has become tediously good in some particular
but negligent or narrow in the rest; and hypocrisy
and vanity are often the disgusting result.

It is handsomer to remain in the establishment
better than the establishment, and conduct that
in the best manner, than to make a sally against
evil by some single improvement, without sup-
porting it by a total regeneration.   Do not be so
vain of your one objection.   Do you think there
is only one?   Alas! my good friend, there is no
part of society or of life better than any other

part. All our things are right and wrong together.
The wave of evil washes all our institutions alike.
Do you complain of our Marriage? Our marriage
is no worse than our education, our diet, our trade,
our social customs. Do you complain of the laws
of Property? It is a pedantry to give such impor
tance to them. Can we not play the game of life
with these counters, as well as with those? in the
institution of property, as well as out of it? Let
into it the new and renewing principle of love, and
property will be universality. No one gives the
impression of superiority to the institution, which
he must give who will reform it. It makes no
difference what you say, you must make me feel
that you are aloof from it; by your natural and
supernatural advantages do easily see to the end
of it,—do see how man can do without it. Now
all men are on one side. No man deserves to be
heard against property. Only Love, only an Idea,
is against property as we hold it.

I cannot afford to be irritable and captious, nor
to waste all my time in attacks. If I should go
out of church whenever I hear a false sentiment
I could never stay there five minutes. But why
come out? the street is as false as the church, and
when I get to my house, or to my manners, or
to my speech, I have not got away from the lie.
When we see an eager assailant of one of these

wrongs, a special reformer, we feel like asking him, What right have you, sir, to your one virtue? Is virtue piecemeal? This is a jewel amidst the rags of a beggar.

In another way the right will be vindicated. In the midst of abuses, in the heart of cities, in the aisles of false churches, alike in one place and in another,—wherever, namely, a just and heroic soul finds itself, there it will do what is next at hand, and by the new quality of character it shall put forth it shall abrogate that old condition, law or school in which it stands, before the law of its own mind.

If partiality was one fault of the movement party, the other defect was their reliance on Association. Doubts such as those I have intimated drove many good persons to agitate the questions of social reform. But the revolt against the spirit of commerce, the spirit of aristocracy, and the inveterate abuses of cities, did not appear possible to individuals; and to do battle against numbers they armed themselves with numbers, and against concert they relied on new concert.

Following or advancing beyond the ideas of St. Simon, of Fourier, and of Owen, three communities have already been formed in Massachusetts on kindred plans, and many more in the country at large. They aim to give every member a share in the manual labor, to give an equal reward to labor and to talent, and to unite a liberal culture with an education to labor. The scheme offers, by the economies of associated labor and expense, to make every member rich, on the same amount of property that, in separate families, would leave every member poor. These new associations are composed of men and women of superior talents and sentiments; yet it may easily be questioned whether such a community will draw, except in its beginnings, the able and the good; whether those who have energy will not prefer their chance of superiority and power in the world, to the humble certainties of the association; whether such a retreat does not promise to become an asylum to those who have tried and failed, rather than a field to the strong; and whether the members will not necessarily be fractions of men, because each finds that he cannot enter it without some compromise. Friendship and association are very fine things, and a grand phalanx of the best of the human race, banded for some catholic object; yes, excellent; but remember that no society can ever be so large as one man. He, in his friendship, in his natural and momentary associations, doubles or multiplies himself; but in the hour in which he mortgages himself to two or ten or twenty, he dwarfs himself below the stature of one.

But the men of less faith could not thus believe, and to such, concert appears the sole specific of strength. I have failed, and you have failed, but perhaps together we shall not fail. Our house-keeping is not satisfactory to us, but perhaps a phalanx, a community, might be. Many of us have differed in opinion, and we could find no man who could make the truth plain, but possibly a college, or an ecclesiastical council, might. I have not been able either to persuade my brother or to prevail on myself to disuse the traffic or the potation of brandy, but perhaps a pledge of total abstinence might effectually restrain us. The candidate my party votes for is not to be trusted with a dollar, but he will be honest in the Senate, for we can bring public opinion to bear on him. Thus concert was the specific in all cases. But concert is neither better nor worse, neither more nor less potent, than individual force. All the men in the world cannot make a statue walk and speak, cannot make a drop of blood, or a blade of grass, any more than one man can. But let there be one man, let there be truth in two men, in ten men, then is concert for the first time possible; because the force which moves the world is a new quality, and can never be furnished by adding whatever quantities of a differ-ent kind. What is the use of the concert of the false and the disunited? There can be no concert

in two, where there is no concert in one. When
the individual is not *individual*, but is dual ; when
his thoughts look one way and his actions another ;
when his faith is traversed by his habits ; when his
will, enlightened by reason, is warped by his sense ;
when with one hand he rows and with the other
backs water, what concert can be ?

I do not wonder at the interest these projects inspire. The world is awaking to the idea of union,
and these experiments show what it is thinking of.
It is and will be magic. Men will live and communicate, and plough, and reap, and govern, as by
added ethereal power, when once they are united ;
as in a celebrated experiment, by expiration and
respiration exactly together, four persons lift a
heavy man from the ground by the little finger
only, and without sense of weight. But this union
must be inward, and not one of covenants, and is
to be reached by a reverse of the methods they
use. The union is only perfect when all the uniters
are isolated. It is the union of friends who live in
different streets or towns. Each man, if he attempts
to join himself to others, is on all sides cramped
and diminished of his proportion ; and the stricter
the union the smaller and the more pitiful he is.
But leave him alone, to recognize in every hour and
place the secret soul ; he will go up and down doing
the works of a true member, and, to the astonish-

ment of all, the work will be done with concert,
though no man spoke. Government will be adamantine without any governor. The union must be
ideal in actual individualism.

I pass to the indication in some particulars of
that faith in man, which the heart is preaching to
us in these days, and which engages the more regard, from the consideration that the speculations
of one generation are the history of the next following.

In alluding just now to our system of education,
I spoke of the deadness of its details. But it is
open to graver criticism than the palsy of its members : it is a system of despair. The disease with
which the human mind now labors is want of faith.
Men do not believe in a power of education. We
do not think we can speak to divine sentiments in
man, and we do not try. We renounce all high
aims. We believe that the defects of so many
perverse and so many frivolous people who make
up society, are organic, and society is a hospital of
incurables. A man of good sense but of little faith,
whose compassion seemed to lead him to church as
often as he went there, said to me that "he liked
to have concerts, and fairs, and churches, and other
public amusements go on." I am afraid the remark is too honest, and comes from the same origin as the maxim of the tyrant, " If you would rule

the world quietly, you must keep it amused." I
notice too that the ground on which eminent public
servants urge the claims of popular education is
fear; 'This country is filling up with thousands
and millions of voters, and you must educate them
to keep them from our throats.' We do not believe that any education, any system of philosophy,
any influence of genius, will ever give depth of insight to a superficial mind. Having settled ourselves into this infidelity, our skill is expended to
procure alleviations, diversion, opiates. We adorn
the victim with manual skill, his tongue with languages, his body with inoffensive and comely manners. So have we cunningly hid the tragedy of
limitation and inner death we cannot avert. Is it
strange that society should be devoured by a secret
melancholy which breaks through all its smiles and
all its gayety and games?

But even one step farther our infidelity has gone.
It appears that some doubt is felt by good and wise
men whether really the happiness and probity of
men is increased by the culture of the mind in those
disciplines to which we give the name of education.
Unhappily too the doubt comes from scholars, from
persons who have tried these methods. In their
experience the scholar was not raised by the sacred thoughts amongst which he dwelt, but used
them to selfish ends. He was a profane person,

and became a showman, turning his gifts to a mar-
ketable use, and not to his own sustenance and
growth. It was found that the intellect could be
independently developed, that is, in separation from
the man, as any single organ can be invigorated,
and the result was monstrous. A canine appetite
for knowledge was generated, which must still be
fed but was never satisfied, and this knowledge, not
being directed on action, never took the character
of substantial, humane truth, blessing those whom
it entered. It gave the scholar certain powers of
expression, the power of speech, the power of poetry, of literary art, but it did not bring him to
peace or to beneficence.

When the literary class betray a destitution of
faith, it is not strange that society should be dis-
heartened and sensualized by unbelief. What remedy? Life must be lived on a higher plane. We
must go up to a higher platform, to which we are
always invited to ascend; there, the whole aspect
of things changes. I resist the skepticism of our
education and of our educated men. I do not believe that the differences of opinion and character
in men are organic. I do not recognize, beside the
class of the good and the wise, a permanent class
of skeptics, or a class of conservatives, or of malig-
nants, or of materialists. I do not believe in two
classes. You remember the story of the poor wo-

man who importuned King Philip of Macedon to
grant her justice, which Philip refused: the woman
exclaimed, " I appeal: " the king, astonished, asked
to whom she appealed: the woman replied, " From
Philip drunk to Philip sober." The text will suit
me very well. I believe not in two classes of men,
but in man in two moods, in Philip drunk and
Philip sober. I think, according to the good-
hearted word of Plato, " Unwillingly the soul is
deprived of truth." Iron conservative, miser, or
thief, no man is but by a supposed necessity which
he tolerates by shortness or torpidity of sight. The
soul lets no man go without some visitations and
holydays of a diviner presence. It would be easy
to show, by a narrow scanning of any man's biography, that we are not so wedded to our paltry performances of every kind but that every man has at
intervals the grace to scorn his performances, in
comparing them with his belief of what he should
do ; — that he puts himself on the side of his ene,
mies, listening gladly to what they say of him, and
accusing himself of the same things.

What is it men love in Genius, but its infinite
hope, which degrades all it has done? Genius
counts all its miracles poor and short. Its own
idea it never executed. The Iliad, the Hamlet, the
Doric column, the Roman arch, the Gothic minster,
the German anthem, when they are ended, the

master casts behind him. How sinks the song in
the waves of melody which the universe pours over
his soul! Before that gracious Infinite out of which
he drew these few strokes, how mean they look,
though the praises of the world attend them. From
the triumphs of his art he turns with desire to this
greater defeat. Let those admire who will. With
silent joy he sees himself to be capable of a beauty
that eclipses all which his hands have done; all
which human hands have ever done.

Well, we are all the children of genius, the children of virtue, — and feel their inspirations in our
happier hours. Is not every man sometimes a radical in politics? Men are conservatives when they
are least vigorous, or when they are most luxurious.
They are conservatives after dinner, or before taking their rest; when they are sick, or aged: in the
morning, or when their intellect or their conscience
has been aroused; when they hear music, or when
they read poetry, they are radicals. In the circle
of the rankest tories that could be collected in England, Old or New, let a powerful and stimulating
intellect, a man of great heart and mind act on
them, and very quickly these frozen conservators
will yield to the friendly influence, these hopeless
will begin to hope, these haters will begin to love,
these immovable statues will begin to spin and revolve. I cannot help recalling the fine anecdote

which Warton relates of Bishop Berkeley, when he was preparing to leave England with his plan of planting the gospel among the American savages. "Lord Bathurst told me that the members of the Scriblerus club being met at his house at dinner, they agreed to rally Berkeley, who was also his guest, on his scheme at Bermudas. Berkeley, having listened to the many lively things they had to say, begged to be heard in his turn, and displayed his plan with such an astonishing and animating force of eloquence and enthusiasm that they were struck dumb, and, after some pause, rose up all together with earnestness, exclaiming, ' Let us set out with him immediately.' " Men in all ways are better than they seem. They like flattery for the moment, but they know the truth for their own. It is a foolish cowardice which keeps us from trusting them and speaking to them rude truth. They resent your honesty for an instant, they will thank you for it always. What is it we heartily wish of each other? Is it to be pleased and flattered? No, but to be convicted and exposed, to be shamed out of our nonsense of all kinds, and made men of, instead of ghosts and phantoms. We are weary of gliding ghostlike through the world, which is itself so slight and unreal. We crave a sense of reality, though it come in strokes of pain. I explain so, — by this manlike love of truth, — those excesses and errors into which souls of great vigor, but not equal insight, often fall. They feel the poverty at the bottom of all the seeming affluence of the world. They know the speed with which they come straight through the thin masquerade, and conceive a dis gust at the indigence of nature : Rousseau, Mira beau, Charles Fox, Napoleon, Byron, — and I could easily add names nearer home, of raging riders, who drive their steeds so hard, in the violence of living to forget its illusion : they would know the worst, and tread the floors of hell. The heroes of ancient and modern fame, Cimon, Themistocles, Alcibiades, Alexander, Cæsar, have treated life and fortune as a game to be well and skilfully played, but the stake not to be so valued but that any time it could be held as a trifle light as air, and thrown up. Cæsar, just before the battle of Pharsalia, dis courses with the Egyptian priest concerning the fountains of the Nile, and offers to quit the army, the empire, and Cleopatra, if he will show him those mysterious sources.

The same magnanimity shows itself in our social relations, in the preference, namely, which each man gives to the society of superiors over that of his equals. All that a man has will he give for right relations witn his mates. All that he has will he give for an erect demeanor in every com pany and on each occasion. He aims at such things as his neighbors prize, and gives his days and nights, his talents and his heart, to strike a good stroke, to acquit himself in all men's sight as a man. The consideration of an eminent citizen, of a noted merchant, of a man of mark in his profession ; a naval and military honor, a general's commission, a marshal's baton, a ducal coronet, the laurel of poets, and, anyhow procured, the acknowledgment of eminent merit, — have this lustre for each candidate that they enable him to walk erect and unashamed in the presence of some persons before whom he felt himself inferior. Having raised himself to this rank, having established his equality with class after class of those with whom he would live well, he still finds certain others before whom he cannot possess himself, because they have somewhat fairer, somewhat grander, somewhat purer, which extorts homage of him. Is his ambition pure ? then will his laurels and his possessions seem worthless : instead of avoiding these men who make his fine gold dim, he will cast all behind him and seek their society only, woo and embrace this his humiliation and mortification, until he shall know why his eye sinks, his voice is husky, and his brilliant talents are paralyzed in this presence. He is sure that the soul which gives the lie to all things will tell none. His constitution will not mislead him. If it cannot carry itself as it ought, high and unmatchable in the presence of any man; if the secret oracles whose whisper makes the sweetness and dignity of his life do here withdraw and accompany him no longer, — it is time to undervalue what he has valued, to dispossess himself of what he has acquired, and with Cæsar to take in his hand the army, the empire, and Cleopatra, and say, " All these will I relinquish, if you will show me the fountains of the Nile." Dear to us are those who love us ; the swift moments we spend with them are a compensation for a great deal of misery ; they enlarge our life ; — but dearer are those who reject us as unworthy, for they add another life : they build a heaven before us whereof we had not dreamed, and thereby supply to us new powers out of the recesses of the spirit, and urge us to new and unattempted performances.

As every man at heart wishes the best and not inferior society, wishes to be convicted of his error and to come to himself,— so he wishes that the same healing should not stop in his thought, but should penetrate his will or active power. The selfish man suffers more from his selfishness than he from whom that selfishness withholds some important benefit. What he most wishes is to be lifted to some higher platform, that he may see beyond his present fear the transalpine good, so that his fear, his coldness, his custom may be broken up like fragments of ice, melted and carried away in the great stream of good will. Do you ask my aid? I also wish to be a benefactor. I wish more to be a benefactor and servant than you wish to be served by me; and surely the greatest good fortune that could befall me is precisely to be so moved by you that I should say, 'Take me and all mine, and use me and mine freely to your ends!' for I could not say it otherwise than because a great enlarge-ment had come to my heart and mind, which made me superior to my fortunes. Here we are para-lyzed with fear; we hold on to our little properties, house and land, office and money, for the bread which they have in our experience yielded us, al-though we confess that our being does not flow through them. We desire to be made great; we desire to be touched with that fire which shall com-mand this ice to stream, and make our existence a benefit. If therefore we start objections to your project, O friend of the slave, or friend of the poor or of the race, understand well that it is because we wish to drive you to drive us into your meas-ures. We wish to hear ourselves confuted. We are haunted with a belief that you have a secret which it would highliest advantage us to learn, and we would force you to impart it to us, though it should bring us to prison or to worse extremity.

Nothing shall warp me from the belief that every

man is a lover of truth. There is no pure lie, no pure malignity in nature. The entertainment of the proposition of depravity is the last profligacy and profanation. There is no skepticism, no atheism but that. Could it be received into common belief, suicide would unpeople the planet. It has had a name to live in some dogmatic theology, but each man's innocence and his real liking of his neighbor have kept it a dead letter. I remember standing at the polls one day when the anger of the political contest gave a certain grimness to the faces of the independent electors, and a good man at my side, looking on the people, remarked, "I am satisfied that the largest part of these men, on either side, mean to vote right." I suppose considerate observers, looking at the masses of men in their blameless and in their equivocal actions, will assent, that in spite of selfishness and frivolity, the general purpose in the great number of persons is fidelity. The reason why any one refuses his assent to your opinion, or his aid to your benevolent design, is in you : he refuses to accept you as a bringer of truth, because though you think you have it, he feels that you have it not. You have not given him the authentic sign.

If it were worth while to run into details this general doctrine of the latent but ever soliciting Spirit, it would be easy to adduce illustration in particulars of a man's equality to the Church, of his equality to the State, and of his equality to every other man. It is yet in all men's memory that, a few years ago, the liberal churches complained that the Calvinistic church denied to them the name of Christian. I think the complaint was confession: a religious church would not complain. A religious man, like Behmen, Fox, or Swedenborg is not irritated by wanting the sanction of the Church, but the Church feels the accusation of his presence and belief.

It only needs that a just man should walk in our streets to make it appear how pitiful and inartificial a contrivance is our legislation. The man whose part is taken and who does not wait for society in anything, has a power which society cannot choose but feel. The familiar experiment called the hydrostatic paradox, in which a capillary column of water balances the ocean, is a symbol of the relation of one man to the whole family of men. The wise Dandamis, on hearing the lives of Socrates, Pythagoras and Diogenes read, " judged them to be great men every way, excepting that they were too much subjected to the reverence of the laws, which to second and authorize, true virtue must abate very much of its original vigor."

And as a man is equal to the Church and equal to the State, so he is equal to every other man.

The disparities of power in men are superficial; and all frank and searching conversation, in which a man lays himself open to his brother, apprises each of their radical unity. When two persons sit and converse in a thoroughly good understanding, the remark is sure to be made, See how we have disputed about words! Let a clear, apprehensive mind, such as every man knows among his friends, converse with the most commanding poetic genius, I think it would appear that there was no inequality such as men fancy, between them; that a perfect understanding, a like receiving, a like perceiving, abolished differences ; and the poet would confess that his creative imagination gave him no deep advantage, but only the superficial one that he could express himself and the other could not; that his advantage was a knack, which might impose on indolent men but could not impose on lovers of truth; for they know the tax of talent, or what a price of greatness the power of expression too often pays. I believe it is the conviction of the purest men that the net amount of man and man does not much vary. Each is incomparably superior to his companion in some faculty. His want of skill in other directions has added to his fitness for his own work. Each seems to have some compensation yielded to him by his infirmity, and every hinderance operates as a concentration of his force.

These and the like experiences intimate that man stands in strict connection with a higher fact never yet manifested. There is power over and behind us, and we are the channels of its communications. We seek to say thus and so, and over our head some spirit sits which contradicts what we say. We would persuade our fellow to this or that; another self within our eyes dissuades him. That which we keep back, this reveals. In vain we compose our faces and our words; it holds uncontrollable communication with the enemy, and he answers civilly to us, but believes the spirit. We exclaim, 'There's a traitor in the house!' but at last it appears that he is the true man, and I am the traitor. This open channel to the highest life is the first and last reality, so subtle, so quiet, yet so tenacious, that although I have never expressed the truth, and although I have never heard the expression of it from any other, I know that the whole truth is here for me. What if I cannot answer your questions? I am not pained that I cannot frame a reply to the question, What is the operation we call Providence? There lies the unspoken thing, present, omnipresent. Every time we converse we seek to translate it into speech, but whether we hit or whether we miss, we have the fact. Every discourse is an approximate answer: but it is of small consequence that we do not get it into verbs and nouns, whilst it abides for contemplation forever.

If the auguries of the prophesying heart shall make themselves good in time, the man who shall be born, whose advent men and events prepare and foreshow, is one who shall enjoy his connection with a higher life, with the man within man; shall destroy distrust by his trust, shall use his native but forgotten methods, shall not take counsel of flesh and blood, but shall rely on the Law alive and beautiful which works over our heads and under our feet. Pitiless, it avails itself of our success when we obey it, and of our ruin when we contravene it. Men are all secret believers in it, else the word justice would have no meaning : they believe that the best is the true ; that right is done at last ; or chaos would come. It rewards actions after their nature, and not after the design of the agent. 'Work,' it saith to man, 'in every hour, paid or unpaid, see only that thou work, and thou canst not escape the reward : whether thy work be fine or coarse, planting corn or writing epics, so only it be honest work, done to thine own approbation, it shall earn a reward to the senses as well as to the thought : no matter how often defeated, you are born to victory. The reward of a thing well done, is to have done it.'

As soon as a man is wonted to look beyond

surfaces, and to see how this high will prevails without an exception or an interval, he settles himself into serenity. He can already rely on the laws of gravity, that every stone will fall where it is due; the good globe is faithful, and carries us securely through the celestial spaces, anxious or resigned, we need not interfere to help it on: and he will learn one day the mild lesson they teach, that our own orbit is all our task, and we need not assist the administration of the universe. Do not be so impatient to set the town right concerning the unfounded pretensions and the false reputation of certain men of standing. They are laboring harder to set the town right concerning themselves, and will certainly succeed. Suppress for a few days your criticism on the insufficiency of this or that teacher or experimenter, and he will have demonstrated his insufficiency to all men's eyes. In like manner, let a man fall into the divine circuits, and he is enlarged. Obedience to his genius is the only liberating influence. We wish to escape from subjection and a sense of inferiority, and we make self-denying ordinances, we drink water, we eat grass, we refuse the laws, we go to jail: it is all in vain; only by obedience to his genius, only by the freest activity in the way constitutional to him, does an angel seem to arise before a man and lead him by the hand out of all the wards of the prison.

That which befits us, embosomed in beauty and wonder as we are, is cheerfulness and courage, and the endeavor to realize our aspirations. The life of man is the true romance, which when it is valiantly conducted will yield the imagination a higher joy than any fiction. All around us what powers are wrapped up under the coarse mattings of custom, and all wonder prevented. It is so wonderful to our neurologists that a man can see without his eyes, that it does not occur to them that it is just as wonderful that he should see with them; and that is ever the difference between the wise and the unwise: the latter wonders at what is unusual, the wise man wonders at the usual. Shall not the heart which has received so much, trust the Power by which it lives? May it not quit other leadings, and listen to the Soul that has guided it so gently and taught it so much, secure that the future will be worthy of the past?